toleration of many reactionary social and political attitudes.

On the other hand, as the author points out, these same denominations contributed to the greater democratization of America by encouraging widespread participation in voluntary and civic organizations and emphasizing egalitarianism, the dignity of the individual, the importance of achievement, and devotion to duty.

Protestants and Pioneers is a temperate but penetrating corrective to overstatements about the role of individualism in settling the North American continent.

T. SCOTT MIYAKAWA is associate professor of sociology at Boston University. For the two academic years 1963–65 he is visiting associate professor of sociology, associate research historian, and director of the Japanese-American research project of the University of California at Los Angeles. A graduate of Cornell and Columbia universities, he has been on the staffs of the universities of Missouri, Michigan, and Doshisha (Japan). He has also taught in Ceylon and served as consultant on Far Eastern economy.

PROTESTANTS AND PIONEERS

PROTESTANTS AND PIONEERS

*Individualism
and Conformity
on the American Frontier*

T. SCOTT MIYAKAWA

THE UNIVERSITY OF CHICAGO PRESS

CHICAGO AND LONDON

Library of Congress Catalog Card Number: 64-22247

THE UNIVERSITY OF CHICAGO PRESS, CHICAGO & LONDON

The University of Toronto Press, Toronto 5, Canada

© *1964 by The University of Chicago. All rights reserved*

Published 1964. Printed in the United States of America

To M.B.S.

Acknowledgments

As an essentially sociological treatment of a historical topic, this study has freely used the personal observations and publications of many scholars and civic and religious leaders. Although it is not possible to acknowledge individually my debt to everyone in the notes, I should like at least to express here my grateful appreciation for their contributions.

For his active encouragement, I wish to thank especially Dr. Robert M. MacIver, and for their suggestions, Professors Reinhold Niebuhr, Robert S. Lynd, Theodore Abel, Elizabeth K. Nottingham, and Jean C. Hendry, Mr. Arthur M. Schlesinger, Jr., and Mrs. Doris O. M. Ginsburg. Deeply appreciated were the thoughtful comments and co-operation of Professors Agnes Moreland, Albert Morris, Walter G. Muelder, Carl E. Purinton, Irwin T. Sanders, Frank L. Sweetser, Jr., Warren S. Tryon, and Alvin D. Zalinger, Mrs. Nicole Meunier Humbert, and Mrs. Ann Staffeld Mendez. I should like also to mention the active concern of the late Professors Edward W. Blakeman and Clyde Kluckhohn. A faculty fellowship from the Ford Foundation Fund for the Advancement of Education enabled me to observe several aspects of the British and Continental background of the popular denominations.

Contents

INTRODUCTION

Introduction

Many accounts of modern American society describe frontier life in the early nineteenth-century West as the prototype of later American individualism, and slight the social, and indeed, conformistic, role of pioneer organizations and communities which made for the unique quality of this frontier heritage. The religious denominations and their discipline and their secular implications receive still less attention. The larger Protestant denominations in the early West attempted to regulate the entire personal, social, and economic life of members and their families in accordance with standards which were essentially uniform for each denomination throughout the country. The first major thesis of the present study is therefore that these frontier church adherents, far from being lone individuals in an atomistic society, were members of disciplined groups and an increasingly organized society.

These Protestant denominations, however, were not remote formal organizations imposed on the people from the outside, but intimate voluntary groups. As essentially lay organizations, their membership as a whole assumed responsibility for their activities. Many laymen consequently acquired experience in conducting religious and organizational affairs. To a considerable extent, the churches were at once centers of religious and social life, advocates of public order, and schools for group and community leadership. In the West, they had a pervasive role which to a degree paralleled that of the New England towns in fostering responsible democracy. Somewhat in contrast to those who emphasized the individualism in American life, other early observers have focused on

3

Americans as "joiners." Even these interpreters, however, did not investigate the major developments in this tradition of belonging. The first thesis has, therefore, a further implication or corollary: These religious denominations helped to create a society in which people resorted to voluntary associations for achieving objectives unattainable by single individuals, a society permeated with organized groups rather than a mere aggregation of isolated individuals.

The present study is essentially a sociological rather than a historical inquiry into western pioneer life, particularly among the members of the popular Protestant denominations. Instead of trying to consider all denominations in the West, it will concentrate on the Methodists and the Baptists as the largest and perhaps the most characteristic. In addition, it includes the Presbyterians and the Friends, as the two extremes in belief and polity. In the early West, Presbyterianism represented the formal church with its strong emphasis on proper doctrines and professional ministry. The Society of Friends, at the other extreme, was perhaps the least formally ecclesiastical of the important western denominations. Essentially, it was a lay organization, and every member was a minister. Herbert W. Schneider aptly summarizes the historic Presbyterian and Quaker contrasts: "The Quakers were the left wing of the Puritan movement — democratic, individualistic, apocalyptic, revolutionary. They were quite different from the right-wing Presbyterians — theocratic, nationalistic, rationalistic, conservative." [1]

In general, except for Presbyterianism, the largest and most influential western denominations originated virtually as dissenting sects in the Old World and in the Atlantic seaboard colonies of America. As defined by Ernst Troeltsch, a sect is characterized by intimate fellowship, rigorous discipline, and absence of universalism and cosmopolitanism. Sect members have strong fraternal ties within the group, and regard themselves as a voluntary company of regenerates set apart from the larger society, "in but not of the world." They feel that the quality of their behavior and fellowship should prove their Christian faith. A sect stresses active lay participation and leadership in its religious life and may be opposed to a professional clergy. In any case, its pastors are essentially lay ministers and do not constitute a separate order even when they are paid. Radical sects may seek to reform society, but most sects prefer to minimize their contacts with the secular world. The attempt to withdraw from the "world" may be expressed in hostility to many cultural interests, such as drama, music, fine arts, and even formal literature, as well as to certain types of recreation and some governmental activities. Unlike the great churches, the sect does not think in terms of incorporating and spiritualizing the entire life of a nation, and does not usually assume responsibility for promoting secular culture.

Several of the sectarian groups with which we are concerned, however, grew rapidly to become, by the 1840's, the largest denominations in the United States. They encouraged their members to follow an active calling and to participate in the economic and political life of the community. In the process, they influenced the secular society and also helped to establish the recognized American religious pattern, the coexistence of many denominations. We shall therefore need to reconsider the Troeltsch typologies of sect and church in the light of the American experience, regardless of their past usefulness for religious research, and shall do so later (especially in chapter vii, together with a brief discussion on the ideal of the calling). For the earlier years of the present study, however, with care we can still use the familiar Troeltsch distinctions fruitfully. During this period, while changing in some ways, these denominations retained many sectarian traits.

These characteristics suggest our second major thesis: The Baptists, Methodists, and other popular denominations helped to infuse secular society in the American West with certain traits now regarded as typically western, if not characteristically American. Among these qualities are familiarity with voluntary organizations, faith in the common man, equalitarianism, "practical idealism," and similar attributes valued highly today by many leaders of democracy. In the early nineteenth century, the popular denominations were usually also indifferent or hostile to scholarship and learning, to the fine arts, and to some forms of recreation. Such deprecation of intellectual and cultural interests may have stimulated the later growth of the alleged materialism that these same denominations deplore today. Rigorous group discipline enforced by the popular denominations during the early years of the nineteenth century, combined with indifference to cultural attainments, may also have encouraged indifference to the culture of other peoples.

In this study, such expressions as Dissent, Dissenting denominations, popular denominations, and free churches refer mainly to the sects which, as we shall see below, were at first despised and often persecuted by the conservatives and the established churches in New England and Virginia. They include the Baptists, Methodists, Quakers, and other present-day American sectarian denominations. The word Dissent perhaps carries a misleading connotation in the present context, since the Dissenting groups became the largest and possibly the most influential Protestant denominations in the country. Far from dissenting in the West, they helped to mold its institutions and cultural outlook. The term is retained partly because various scholars have used it to differentiate these sects from the sacramental Protestant churches and partly because of its convenience.[2]

The denominations stemming from the sacramental state churches of the Old World (aside from Presbyterianism included here for reasons mentioned above) are not classified in the following pages with Dissent or popular denominations, though in America, through cultural isolation or conflict with the secular culture and dependence on voluntary support, some have developed sectarian traits. A church, according to Troeltsch, generally regards itself as an objective organization ordained by God and possessing miraculous powers of sacramental grace. It is inclusive, seeking to draw into its fold all society and the secular culture which it would spiritualize. Its formally ordained professional ministry is distinct from the laity. Of course, in popular usage the word "church" often means a local congregation or meeting house and in this particular sense has been used throughout this essay when it is appropriate (and also, as noted above, in the term "free church" as an alternative to Dissent). Today America has no established church and the larger religious associations are more properly defined as denominations. A denomination may begin to resemble a church in having an increasingly formal organization, professional clergy, and birthright membership, but it coexists in a given territory with other religious groups. It tries neither to control nor to withdraw from secular society. The Baptists, Methodists, and similar denominations were once sects or movements which successfully won substantial memberships and made their peace with the world. Some denominations began as American extensions of the Old World churches which in the United States had to accept voluntary membership and legal equality with other religious organizations.

The present inquiry is essentially limited to the trans-Allegheny settlements in the Ohio River Valley between 1800 and 1836. The term "West" as used here applies primarily to the territory now incorporated in Kentucky, Ohio, Indiana, Illinois, and to a lesser extent, Michigan and Tennessee. The well-known historian of American religion, W. W. Sweet, regards this early frontier as the most significant for the major western denominations, particularly the Methodists, Baptists, and Presbyterians, since during these years and in this region they developed the techniques essential to their rapid expansion on successive later frontiers. In his comparative study of the frontier folkways, Dr. Leyburn suggests further reasons for selecting this area and period. Settlers from the South, East, and Europe met and formed the folkways and attitudes which many Europeans consider typically American. Middletown, Winesburg, and Zenith, he observes, are regarded as representative American towns and are in the Middle West. We might add to his list the more recently publicized Elmtown and Jonesville.[3]

Frederick Jackson Turner and his followers have emphasized the basic importance of this frontier and epoch in the development of American democracy and many current traits and institutions that they regard as peculiarly American, distinct from those of Europe. Turner often considered frontier life in quite individualistic terms: "Society became atomic"; "the unchecked development of the individual was the significant product of this frontier democracy"; and "society itself seemed to have dissolved into its individual atoms." In his opinion, the West as a self-conscious entity began to evolve with the first trans-Allegheny settlements in Kentucky and the Ohio River Valley. This frontier effectively Americanized the settlers and became the "most American" part of the country. Western isolation, Turner believed, accentuated its peculiarly American tendencies and stripped from its institutions many European and Atlantic seaboard influences. "The men of the 'Western World' turned their backs upon the Atlantic Ocean" and upon the seaboard society.[4]

Several historians have criticized the Turner usage of such terms as "the West" and "the frontier" as clichés endowed with varying meanings. Daniel B. Aaron asks whether the Turnerites are referring to the West of a Louisville grocer, a river boatman, a log cabin settler, an editor, a $1.25-a-day mechanic, or a Harvard-trained Cincinnati lawyer engaged in lucrative practice. Many in such urban centers as Cincinnati came directly from eastern cities and were never frontiersmen in the Turner sense at all.[5] Dr. Leyburn, however, would regard the frontier as that region on the edges of settlements where, in order to survive, the pioneers had to adjust to a rough environment. "It is," he says, "a region, it is a process, it is even a state of mind."[6] At any rate, the present inquiry is not primarily concerned with the formal definition of the frontier, but rather with the Dissenting denominational life and activities in the West, whether on the fringes of the settlements or in the rising cities, and their implications for present-day America.

An examination of Dissenting religious life will reveal group or collectivistic as well as individualistic features of western secular life not often appreciated by some frontier theorists. Popular legends may portray the backwoodsmen as individualists, without explaining the possible ambiguity, and may then discuss pioneer sociability and "joining" habits. A view which considers frontier society as essentially an aggregation of discrete individuals cannot readily assume that it is the prototype of the later complex American society. On the other hand, as suggested above by the first thesis and its corollary, a modern society distinguished by many voluntary groups and perhaps even "togetherness" and conformity could more readily develop from a frontier society permeated with Dissenting and other voluntary organizations. Several schools of thought, as noted before, have long emphasized the importance of voluntary groups in American life, but they generally have not given as much attention to the specific forces and processes which helped to foster both the system of voluntarism and also its particular forms and quality. The present study will attempt to trace some of the ways the popular denominations significantly influenced the tradition of voluntary associations and their outlook.

The Dissenters played a large part in settling and "civilizing the turbulent frontier" of the American West, a role not entirely new to sectarian groups. Similar sects in the Old World had encouraged their members to raise themselves economically and socially. Western popular denominations, however, had unusual freedom to realize their potentialities. They were not inhibited by a powerful established church or by an entrenched upper class. The Methodist role in the West, asserts Dr. Sweet, paralleled that of Puritanism in New England. While many scholars have studied the Puritan impact, he notes further, the western Methodist influence has received comparatively little attention.[7] Subsequent research would perhaps suggest that his assertion be expanded to include the contributions of all the major popular denominations to the West and to America. They have left a permanent impress on the West, and their achievements are an integral part of twentieth-century American life, secular as well as religious.

CHAPTER II

The Background of Western Popular Denominations

IN THE EASTERN STATES

In order to understand western developments better, let us look briefly at the time of the earlier Dissent (roughly between 1740 and 1790) in the seaboard colonies. Many scholarly works have dealt with this period in detail and indicate that the popular denominations, influenced by the Great Awakening, appreciably modified the character of even such established societies as that in Virginia. The Great Awakening was among the first, if not the first, major "national" religious revival; it swept nearly all the English colonies destined to form the United States. This popular movement helped to link the hitherto separate settlements and everywhere promoted democratic principles and practices.

Prior to the Great Awakening, in Virginia the upper classes enjoyed special privileges in society, church, and politics. The local vestry rather than the governor, the commissary, or the distant Bishop of London controlled the parish churches of the Anglican Establishment. Many vestries had become self-perpetuating oligarchies, though originally they had been elective bodies. The vestrymen were also members of the county courts, the House of Burgesses, or the Governor's Council; in short, they were the repositories of power in the colony. Although the Presbyterians in Tidewater Virginia played a less active part in the struggle for religious freedom than did the humble Baptists, they, too, helped to break the Anglican Establishment and its whole social framework. At first the gentry looked askance at them. Gentlemen never became Presbyterians or attended Presbyterian meetings, it was once said. Indeed, such an interest would have been "a scandalous thing." However, the personality and ability of such leading Presbyterians as Samuel Davies, then one of the foremost pastors in British North America and later president of Princeton, began to win upper-class converts.

Of the three Baptist groups then in Virginia, the most aggressive in winning new converts was the latest arrival, the so-called Separate Baptists. They were mostly humble and plain everyday people, usually ignorant and often illiterate. Others described them as disturbers of peace, callers of unlawful assembly, perverters of good order, and an ignorant and illiterate set. The upper-class culture of the Enlightenment had not filtered down to the less privileged Baptists who denounced the Anglican clergy for preaching supposedly irreligious sermons which, the Baptists insisted, were more like pagan philosophical discourses than Christian homilies. Anglican sermons, of course, reflected the contemporary rationalistic temper.

The authorities at first ignored the Baptists, but popular opposition was aroused early. The Baptists were often abused, and wild and unfounded tales about them spread far and wide. Eventually, the officials began to accuse the Baptists of disturbing the peace, thus shifting the charges from a legally dubious religious basis to an enforceable civil one. Several writers have considered this persecution as negligible, but the Baptists suffered severely and many were physically assaulted as well as imprisoned.

The old order opposed the Baptists for various reasons. Some regarded them as law breakers because the Baptists insisted upon complete religious freedom and consequently scorned any resort to the Toleration Act which was designed to permit certain recognized Dissenters to preach. Many looked on the Baptist ministers as false leaders who deluded poor people, and others were shocked by the early Baptist custom of ordaining a laborer, a mechanic, or a simple small farmer without formal theological training almost entirely on his own assurance of being called by God. Again, the Baptists received into membership women, regardless of the objections by their husbands, and slaves, despite the views of their masters. To some of the gentry such practices seemed to undermine the social order. In preaching and practicing democratic principles, the Baptists obviously appealed to the hitherto underprivileged classes. Indeed, the elite at times resented the assertion by the Baptists of their rights as an "impertinence" contrary to the established order. The more tolerant among the plantation owners were often disturbed by the bitter Baptist attacks on the Anglican Church and by the Baptist demands for the separation of church and state. The emotionalism at many Baptist meetings in itself seemed outrageous to the educated classes accustomed to the orderly Anglican services.

The issue, of course, was individual freedom, here expressed as religious liberty. The Baptists believed that each person had an inalienable right to worship God in accordance with the dictates of his conscience so long as he did not infringe upon the rights of others. Religion had to be voluntary, and no earthly power, civil or ecclesiastical, could compel anyone to support or conform to any church.[1] The Baptists fought persistently and vigorously over the years for religious freedom — successfully organizing support in many sections of Virginia and capitalizing on the need for their collaboration in the struggle for national independence. In the legislature they found powerful allies in Thomas Jefferson and James Madison. Finally, in 1786, the religious freedom bill became law, and under relentless Baptist pressure, the legislature in 1802 passed an act to dispose of the remaining public land which the former establishment still had.

The social situation in Virginia partly explained the eventual Baptist triumph. The Baptist preachers appealed to the commoners hitherto neglected by the Anglicans. These untrained, unpaid ministers understood the poorest elements and associated with them as social equals. For the first time the least privileged had an organization of their own, democratic in operation and flexible in structure. They could think for themselves and provide their own leadership. The long and bitter struggle for recognition had, however, aroused Baptist resentment against the pretensions of the more privileged classes and perhaps accentuated the Baptist hostility to formal learning. Most early Baptist preachers were only semiliterate. John Leland, their outstanding leader, records that, as far as he knew, not one Baptist minister participating in the campaign for religious liberty was a college man. The Baptists' success in converting people hardened their conviction that learning was non-essential, perhaps even harmful, and that the educated Anglican clergy were largely arrogant persecutors and pagans. Education made men proud and made them trust human learning instead of the Holy Spirit, some Baptists said, and many Baptists equated revivalistic excitement with spiritual quickening.

In the meantime, the Methodists were also growing rapidly in Virginia, thanks partly to the Reverend Mr. Jarratt, their Anglican supporter and friend. The Methodist organization combined flexibility at the local levels with centralized direction, and democratic resort to local lay talents with guidance by experienced circuit riders. In the early struggle for religious freedom the Methodists had not participated. Indeed, the Methodist petition to the first Republican legislature of 1776 supported the Anglican Establishment, of which Methodists were then considered members. Nevertheless, from the first the Methodists and the traditional Anglicans differed sharply. American Methodist moralism frowned upon music, drama, and popular upper-class amusements. The Anglican clergy enjoyed many of these interests, but the Methodists regarded them as sinful even for laymen. Upon his conversion a former dancing master gave up his occupation. He "found the guilt and load of his sin removed from his conscience, and the pardoning love of God shed abroad in his heart," declared an early Methodist historian. Again, unlike the rationalistic Anglican addresses, the Methodist sermons appealed directly to the emotions. Robert Williams, perhaps the first Virginia Methodist, astonished a Norfolk audience by his frequent use of such terms as "hell," "devil," and "damnation." Though they liked parts of his discourse, they thought him a "wicked, swearing preacher," for they had never heard an "evangelical" sermon before. The nature of the sermon suggests another difference between some Methodists and the Anglicans.

Devereux Jarratt has described the impact of the Dissenting movement. This Anglican friend of the Methodists frequently conducted prayer meetings in private homes. The "poorer sort, who at first may be shy in speaking," he reported, "soon wore off their shyness, and spoke as freely as others."[2] Dissenting denominations, adhering to the democratic principle of equality, attempted to reach everyone, thereby recognizing the value of each person. At the same time they expected all to participate in their activities. That the "poorer sort" should dare to speak in public, to lead services, to handle organizational business, and to exercise public leadership was unprecedented. In brief, Dissent not only preached democracy but also helped to train the people to assume public responsibilities.

The Dissenters appreciably changed the cultural outlook in Virginia. They were opposed to many pleasures and recreations of the Anglican gentry. An item in the Minutes of the Broad Run Church which records the expulsion and excommunication of a member "for Playing the Violin and Associating in the company of wicked men" is typical.[3] During their struggle for freedom, the Baptists replied to the conservative criticisms that much time was lost at Baptist meetings by charging that

days could be spent in card playing, horse racing, cock fighting, fish frying, barbecueing, and other fashionable vices without magisterial interference, and the perpetrators go off with impunity — and often those who bore the civil sword, were shamefully guilty of these enormities, and in some instances ringleaders.[4]

In his study on the rise of Dissent, John M. Mecklin questions whether the substitution of sectarianism which looked on card playing, fish frying, and shooting matches as shameful enormities for the urbane and on the whole tolerant spirit of the plantation gentry was an unmixed blessing.

The hostility to "wanton tunes" suggests the culturally adverse impact of Dissent on its membership. The greatest secular and often religious music — the compositions of Bach, Handel, Haydn, Mozart, and later, Beethoven — could readily come under the Baptist and Methodist ban as wanton tunes. Ignorant piety could regard Bach's *B Minor Mass* or the *Passion of the Lord According to St. Matthew* as enormities. Yet, music was once important in upper-class education in Tidewater Virginia, and thoughtful leadership might have popularized it to benefit culturally the state and the West. The music master was a frequent visitor at such great plantation homes as that of Robert Carter. Councilor Carter owned fine instruments, including an organ, and, despite his many responsibilities, regularly practiced his music.

Dissenters rejected also the more scholarly intellectual interests of the gentry. A number among the elite were not only widely read but were also personally acquainted with various Old World thinkers. In contrast, at this stage Dissenters were often only semiliterate and, regardless of their native abilities, had no background for the appreciation of academic subjects, even if their religion had been more permissive. It should be noted, however, that many people, including Dissenters, were familiar with the political and pragmatic concepts of such writers as Locke. These ideas were frequently utilized in the public discussion of the Revolutionary War and the subsequent political and constitutional issues and in the appeals and writing of the Dissenting leaders.

The Dissenters faced hostility not only in Virginia but also, with the exception of Rhode Island, in New England. Their Connecticut experience is illustrative. President Ezra Stiles of Yale denounced them as coarse and turbulent, while his successor (in 1795), Timothy Dwight, was outraged by the Baptist custom of ordaining simple, uneducated workmen and farmers as preachers. Their very shortcomings, however, endeared the Baptist ministers to the lower classes. The ministers boasted of being democratic and, in contrast to the established elite, the "Standing Order," associated as equals with the less privileged elements. Even the seating in the Baptist churches was open, whereas in the Congregational churches it depended upon age and wealth (a certain amount of wealth counting as a year).[5]

In the Baptist fight for religious freedom in Connecticut, Isaac Backus and later John Leland became the best-known leaders. Leland had been outstanding in the Baptist struggle for liberty in Virginia and was consequently an experienced crusader. Since the Federalists and the Establishment were allied, he realized that the opponents would have to join the Jeffersonians whom he had known as friends from his Virginia days. The alleged "ungodliness" of the democratic party did not disturb this admirer of Jefferson. At least on this particular issue, the so-called infidels had acted on right reasons and were closer to the true Christian revelation than was the state church. In common with many Baptists, Leland believed that religion had to renounce state aid and show the world religion could stand alone in order to prevent the spread of deism and infidelity.

In contrast to the Baptists, the Methodist leadership was again relatively slow to awaken to the situation. Bishop Asbury, the "Father of American Methodism," deplored what he regarded as the evils of the Establishment. Yet in the beginning, he apparently failed to understand this common struggle for religious freedom, as indicated by his hostile reaction to the Baptist request for Methodist help, partly because he was annoyed by the Baptist criticism of the episcopal system. The local Methodists, however, understood the issue and by 1800 were active Jeffersonians. The Standing Order came to look on the Methodists as a wilder, more revolutionary party than the Baptists, a menace to both religion and the state. To the Yale-educated Congregational minister, the untutored Methodist lay preachers from the fields and the shops sounded, if anything, worse than the Baptists. Their very enthusiasm at revivals and camp meetings seemed highly improper.

By the turn of the century, the Baptists had become more respectable in some districts and at least the more settled churches ceased having noisy sessions. Some revivals were no longer wildly exuberant but were attended "with solemnity and reverence."[6] The Methodists, however, continued to appeal to the poorest elements, and for years their meetings, especially revivals, were as enthusiastic as ever.

IN THE WEST

Although the majority of the first migrants to the West were law-abiding citizens, early frontier conditions inhibited the development of various traditional institutions for maintaining order and exercising restraint. Law enforcement agencies were often weak or non-existent. Violence and rowdyism reached dangerous proportions in some localities. At times the citizens had pitched battles with the lawless elements, as pioneer records eloquently testify. Yet, it is necessary to scrutinize carefully the contemporary eastern comments on the so-called western disorderliness, since many observers categorized as lawless the simple non-observance of strict Sabbath, social visiting, playing games, dancing, hunting, and popular Sunday recreations in general, as well as brutal fighting, gouging, and armed raids.

The mere superiority in gunpower of the law-abiding elements, however, did not bring law and order permanently. Rather, the positive forces for order, notably the frontier religious societies, began to exercise social discipline and influence for decency and peace. Any comment today on the role of the churches would seem exaggerated. Frontier religious life was inextricably involved in the neighborhood gatherings, quilting bees, clubs, and other semisecular activities. Far from being aloof and formal ecclesiastical institutions, the churches were usually the first organizations in a community (aside from families) and formed, one might say, a matrix for satisfying widely different social and religious needs. This mixture of the religious and the social was to characterize the thoughts and practices of all the early nineteenth-century frontier denominations.[7]

The following four chapters will stress the social discipline in the leading western denominations. Typical American denominationalism — the co-existence of many sects and churches — found full expression in the Ohio River Valley and farther West, where the Dissenters did not have to contend with a firmly rooted Establishment. "The popular symbol of social stability . . . was not, as in our day, the Constitution of the United States or the Supreme Court, but was rather the village church whose spire pointed significantly heavenward," observes Ralph Henry Gabriel in his history of American democratic thought.[8] We should perhaps modify his summary, for the middle western village usually had at least a few churches and the early Methodist churches probably had no spires, since many pioneer Methodists were opposed to spires!

In the Dissenting tradition, as already mentioned, the church was a voluntary association of regenerates, a company of true believers seeking inward perfection and Christian fellowship. Applicants for membership usually had to have conversion experience and were placed on probation for some months before being accepted. The church demanded that the members comply with its discipline. Unlike the present, the number of people who went regularly to the meetings but were not members was apparently several times the membership. Thus, for the 1837–38 conference year, Allen Wiley, a pioneer Indiana Methodist presiding elder, gave roughly three thousand as the membership of the Crawfordsville District and twelve thousand as the total for those present at the services. A Baptist historian, J. Newton Brown, estimated the Baptist national membership at approximately six hundred thousand in 1840 and their "population" at three million. The figures on the proportion of non-members attending seem exaggerated, but a British Congregational delegate to America, Dr. Andrew Reed, reported in 1835 that the two Presbyterian churches in Lexington, Kentucky had twelve hundred at the services and three hundred members, the two Baptist meetings about one thousand attendants and two hundred communicants, and the two Methodist societies about eleven hundred regular visitors and four hundred members. In any case, the denominational influence was far wider than the stated membership.[9]

PART I

THE DISCIPLINE AND ORGANIZATION
OF THE POPULAR DENOMINATIONS
IN THE WEST

CHAPTER III

The Presbyterians

Toward the close of the eighteenth century, with their sturdy Scotch-Irish members already occupying the western fringes of the frontier, which then extended from New England to South Carolina, the Presbyterians were in a favorable position for rapid expansion to the West. It is this old frontier area, especially in Pennsylvania and its ethnic "peninsula" stretching southward into western Virginia and the Carolinas and, roughly, between the falls of the Atlantic rivers and the Alleghenies, which Turner regards as the breeding ground for the first settlers who pushed their way into the valley of the Ohio. None had more ardently supported independence than the Presbyterians, and the church emerged from the Revolution with increased prestige. Shortly after the war, recognizing the new scope of their responsibilities, the Presbyterians reorganized their denomination on a national basis and also made some fundamental alterations in their Confession and regulations. They had able leaders, including John Witherspoon, the only clergyman to sign the Declaration of Independence. Their ministers on the whole were still relatively well educated.

From its organization in 1789, the General Assembly sent ministers on western preaching tours, some on a full-time basis and others for limited periods. The various presbyteries and synods also participated; several had been active from the colonial days. The Redstone Presbytery, constituted in May, 1781, was the first in the West. In setting up a new church, the traveling minister would generally visit the assembled Presbyterians and examine their church papers. After the service, he would call the meeting to order. The family heads then elected their elders and other necessary officers. In October, 1790, the United Congregation of Cincinnati and Columbia was formed in this manner. This church began with eight members and grew slowly because only a few people in the community had adequate doctrinal knowledge.

On the frontier, the Presbyterian church was a force for public order and education. It was concerned with the whole life of members and their families, making little distinction between private and public life or between religious and secular life. The denomination sought to extend its influence over the wider society as well. Church discipline began with and was symbolized by the communion service which in those days was held only once or twice a year and, in good weather, outdoors. Services were held regularly over the entire weekend and continued until Monday. Members of the other congregation served by the minister and of neighboring churches and also the people at large came for the whole period and stayed with friends and relatives in the vicinity. Obviously, these occasions provided opportunities for pleasant social gatherings and for many romances to begin among the younger people. To emphasize the distinction between members who conformed to its discipline and the rest, the Presbyterians admitted to the communion only those who were properly prepared. Publicly separating those qualified from the others appeared to be effective in promoting discipline, partly because of the intimate social relationships among the members. In any case, deviations became known throughout the community. At the same time, Presbyterianism itself pre-eminently symbolized an orderly system of government, and participation in its life would help to inculcate respect for law and order.

Frontier Presbyterian church sessions devoted considerable time to administering the discipline. Officially, the ministers and the ruling elders in the congregation constituted the session and were responsible for the spiritual government of the congregation. The pastor served as the moderator of the session. It had the power to investigate the Christian conduct of the church members and could summon and examine witnesses, and where called for, could admonish, suspend, or exclude the offenders from the sacraments. The session also admitted members into the church, initiated action to promote its spiritual welfare, and appointed the delegates to the higher judicatories of the church. In addition, the session was required to keep accurate records of its own proceedings as well as of the baptisms, marriages, new members, deaths, persons admitted to the communion, and those dismissed or dropped.

The formal session meetings followed the church laws and regulations as prescribed in *The Form of Government and Forms of Process, of the Presbyterian Church.* Two ways were provided for bringing cases of assumed misconduct to trial. Either various individuals brought charges or the matter came to the attention of the session through "common fame." The session then summoned the necessary witnesses as well as the member concerned to its next meeting when it questioned the witnesses before the accused. The latter had the right to examine and to refute their testimony. Unlike the secular courts, the sessions banned professional counsel. Cases tried before the church sessions typically involved such diverse charges as consenting to illegal marriage, excessive drinking, questionable business practices, refusing to commune because of difficulties with another person, publicly accusing others before taking steps as prescribed by the church, attending or allowing one's children to attend places of "vain amusement," imprudent and unchristian conduct, and obstinate refusal to honor the church.

The proceedings of a session in an actual case will best illustrate the nature of these trials. In April, 1829, Dr. J. R. Wilson of Murfreesboro, Tennessee, was charged by common fame with dubious business practices. The following session records of the First Presbyterian Church are self-explanatory:

April 11th. . . .

Resolved that the following communication be transmitted to Doc. J. R. Wilson.

DEAR BROTHER.

Being appointed as the guardians of the spiritual interests of the Presbyterian Church in this place, of which you are a member, we have thought it advisable for your sake and for the sake of this Church to apprize you, that certain charges are rumored abroad concerning you, deeply injurious to you as a member of the Church and prejudicial to its interests: These are 1st that you have been guilty of intoxicating a Mr. Johns and when he was in that condition defrauding him out of a valuable tract of land.

2nly. That you have been guilty of oppressing Mrs Massy a woman whose husband had forsaken her.

3rdly. That you had disceived and attempted to defraud Mr. Robert McLin in a monied transaction. We specify these charges of public rumor to give you an opportunity of vindicating yourself and thereby wiping away the present reproach cast upon your character. And it is desirable this should be done at as early a period as possible. We therefore cite you, to meet the Church Session on tuesdy the 21st of this month at our Church at Nine Oclock A.M. We have delayed acting on these charges with a hope, they would die away, until public rumor has become so clamerous, that justice to you, to ourselves and to the Church loudly calls upon us, to adopt this course. Signed by order of Session. April 11th, 1829   Wм D Baird S.C.

Dr. Wilson heeded the summons:

April 21st. . . .

Docr. John R. Wilson appeared according to citation and being call'd upon to answer to the charge, specified in the citation — Replied not guilty, and for his justification presented as to the first charge, the following certificate.

"I certify that the report of Doctor Wilson having made me drunk and defrauding me out of my land in the trade we made by exchanging the land for his house and lot, is false, malicious and unfounded, I also certify that the trade was made, honestly and farely [sic] and without any misrepresentations on the part of Docr. Wilson, He acted a fare, open, and liberal part and we traded after having examined both pieces of property satisfactoraly — That it was a trade of my own proposing and an agreement to a proposition made by myself" —

Given under my hand the day and date above written.

In presence of

    his   Signed on 6th Sept. 1828. John H. Johns

Wм Rullege

    X

    mark

The session then heard and questioned the witnesses:

Ruben Bowls being duly sworn, deponeth and saith, I have reason to believe that persons unfriendly to Docr. Wilson have made impressions on Mr. Johns mind disrespectful of Doc. Wilson relative to the land transaction between them, and the same I told Doc. Wilson long ago.

Question by Session. Did you ever have any conversation with Mr Johns himself on this subject?

Answer. I did, he stated to me about the first of December 1828 that people had made themselves very busy about the trade, between him and Doc. Wilson and he wished they would mind their own business — That he made his own trades and intended to do so, and if it didnot please other people he didnot care — and further your witness saith not.

To the 2nd Charge Doc. Wilson presented the following certificate

"I certify that the report of Doc. Wilson have oppressed me when my husband left me, last winter is false and malicious, for his treatment to me was directly the reverse, he did every thing I could have asked of a humane man and friend.

He bought a bed and furnature among many other things and gave them to my sons — He gave me the pork — the cotton as much as I wanted to spin — the loom and many other articles, and took only such things as I didnot want or thought I could do without — he did this at a time when others had attachments and would have taken every thing I had on earth — I feel grateful for his kindness and shall always do so.

Given under my hand this 13th April 1829.

Attest

J. B. HENDERSON   Signed SARAH MASSY.

In answer to charge 3rd Mr. S. P. Black being duly sworn saith, that of the monied trasaction alluded to in the charge, he new [sic] nothing until the time he was called on by C. T. Bowen to go his Security upon an appeal, from the Magistrates decission upon a Note on Robert McLin which had been transferred to him by Doctor Wilson, I agreed to stand his security, but finding the trivial amount I undertook of my own accord to act as an agent in bringing about a compromise between them. I saw Mr. McLin and bore a proposition from him to Doctr. Wilson which was acceded to on the part of Doctr Wilson. The proposition I bore from Mr. McLin was that he would give up the officers receipt to Doctr. Wilson; And provided the amount stil due Docr. Wilson which I understood to be about fourteen Dollars was not made out of the receipt by Christmas, that he would pay four Dollars, which was nearly one third — I having stated to him before such a trifling matter should go to Court and that by family connections that I would rather loan one third myself; And in this way I understood the matter settled between the parties and the appeal withdrawn — and further he saith not. —

adjourned to meet on the 24th Inst. . . .

WM. D. BAIRD S.C.

Often the trial continued over several days or sessions, as in this case:

April 24th. . . .

Resolved that the case of common rumor against Doctr. Wilson, in the 3rd. Charge be laid over until the 1st Tuesdy in May next; and that Jonathan Currin, be cited to give evidence in the case, and that Wm. Ward, Enoch Jones, and Eli Allan, be requested to attend and give evidence on that occasion. . . .   WM D BAIRD S.C.

1st Tuesdy in May. Session met

Constituted with prayer

Present Rev. John W. Hall Moderator and Messrs. B. McCulloch, Wm D. Baird, and James C Mitchell. Mr. J. Currin attended according to citation and was duly sworn.

Question? Did you hear a conversation between Doc. Wilson and William Ward, respecting some money, which said Ward had to collect for Doc. Wilson.

Answer. I did. Doctor Wilson asked him if he had collected that money; Ward said he had not, but would have collected it, if he had not been stoped.

Question. Do you know whether the money here spoken of was that alluded to in the transaction between R. McLin and Doctor Wilson.

Answer — I do not — but it was money to be collected from Eli Allan.

Question by Doctor Wilson. Do you know whether this conversation between Mr. Ward and myself took place before or after I had obtained McLins note for the money, he had borrow'd of me.

Answer — I do not.

Having heard the evidence, the session came to a decision:

The Session having heard all the testimony, appointed Messrs. McCulloch and Mitchell a committee to prepare a report on the above charges of rumor against Doctor Wilson.

The committee appointed to prepare a report in the case of common fame against J. R. Wilson a member of this Church, after patient and laborious examination of all the testimony procured, submit the following as their report.

1st. That the charge of said Wilson having intoxicated Mr J. H Johns and while in that situation defrauding him out of his tract of land, as appears from a certificate from under the said Johns own hand, to the contrary, and other credible testimony.

2nly. That the charge against him for having oppressed Mrs Massy is also entirely untrue, as appears from the certificate of Mrs Massy taken by a disinterested person, in which she states, that so far from Doctor Wilson's having oppressed her, that he had acted in such away towards her, as would ever excite her gratitude.

3rly. That as to the charge against him of having deceived and attempted to defraud R. McLin in a monied transaction — altho Mr McLin came before the Session and stated he could substanciate the charge by certain Witnesses and citations were issued and placed in the hands of Mr. McLin ten days previous to the day set apart for the investigation of the case, yet on the day of trial, no testimony came before the Session that was calculated to impress a belief on their minds that the charge was true. Wherefore the committee recommend the Session to withdraw each of these charges: The 1st & 2nd being proven to be entirely unfounded and the 3rd not being supported by any testimony that has come before them.

This report was adopted and ordered to be spread on the Minutes. Concluded with prayer.

WM. D. BAIRD SC

April [May?] 26th, 1829. . . .
Doctor John R. Wilson's name at his own request was erased from the list of members of this Church.[1]

Except for the defendant's withdrawal from the church after first clearing himself, this case illustrates unusually well the comprehensiveness of the Presbyterian trials. The various session records reveal a common pattern, as we would expect from a church with such a definite polity.

Chronic drunkenness was a frequent disciplinary problem on the frontier. The Presbyterians did not object to drinking as such, and neither did most Dissenters early in the nineteenth century. Members often contributed whisky toward ministerial salaries.

The issue was intemperance, not drinking per se. The Duck Creek (Ohio) Church session followed a typical procedure in dealing with a certain member charged by a common fame with intemperance.[2] The case was continued for two years, from August 27, 1821, to August 23, 1823. During that time, several committees called on the member who readily admitted his weakness. He expressed hopes for improvement and begged for patience by the session, while he consented to virtual suspension. His efforts to improve failed, and he did not attend the August 23, 1823, meeting to which he had been called. After appointing another member to defend him, the session examined the evidence and unanimously agreed to his suspension. Not only laymen but also some pastors drank to excess. Presbytery minutes record trials of ministers for chronic intoxication.

Drs. Reed and Matheson, the British Congregational delegates to American Congregational and Presbyterian churches, commented in 1835 on the disciplinary practices of a town church in Granville, Ohio. Its overseers entered "all points of conduct, under separate heads, during the year" and furnished a complete report to the minister at its end. "This report, and the names of the parties, he reads from the pulpit, with rebuke or commendation, and the year begins afresh. Every one knows, therefore, that he is subject to report."[3] In addition, the entire church prayed for each person once by name. This custom, of course, did not eliminate the usual disciplinary responsibilities of its session. These random cases make clear the comprehensive nature of the discipline.

The inclusiveness of the Presbyterian discipline to an extent reflected the structure and the polity of the Presbyterian church. The Presbyterian organization of that period may be regarded as a series of assemblies: congregational, presbyterial, provincial or synodical, national, and ecumenical, with each larger unit containing the smaller. An extremely tenuous parallel may perhaps be drawn between the relations of the American local, state, and national governments and of the various Presbyterian groupings, but in Presbyterianism each higher body is superior to the lower one. Presbyterian polity and procedure were partly derived from

Scottish law, which in turn was based on Roman civil law rather than on British common law.

Probably the most important unit in their system at this time was the presbytery. It met more frequently than the larger councils, chose the representatives to the synods and assemblies, and had considerable control over the church constitution. Its jurisdiction generally extended over a manageable area, granted that later in the nineteenth century in some presbyteries with great many congregations the supervision was more difficult. The sole power of ordination and licensure and the primary jurisdiction over the ministry were in the hands of the presbytery, while the discussions on the sermons at its sessions made it a center for theological education. The ministers who resided within the bounds of the presbytery belonged to the presbyterial church but not to the congregational church. Their ordination by the presbytery was transferable from one congregation to another.

Originally, the eldership was another outstanding factor in Presbyterianism. The elders had life tenure and equal voting rights with the ministers. They were said to be not markedly inferior to the pastors in their knowledge of the Scriptures and doctrine; at least they made serious efforts to study theological subjects and in addition had extensive practical experience. Their competence to pass judgment on most questions before the presbytery and higher judicatories was thought to be essentially equal to that of the pastor. This and similar aristocratic practices had definite consequences for the Presbyterians in the American West.

The records indicate that their missionaries and ministers went to the frontier looking primarily for Presbyterians and only in a few instances attempting to form new churches with previously non-Presbyterian members. This procedure and the high religious standards expected of the applicants were among the reasons for the small size and slow growth of many frontier Presbyterian churches. The United Congregation of Cincinnati and Columbia began, as mentioned above, with eight members. In Indiana, the Corydon Church had seven members; one church in Greene County had only five; and the New Albany Church which called Isaac Reed as its pastor had fifteen, although the Indianapolis and Rushville congregations totaled twenty-five each.[4] On rare occasions, however, the missionary not only examined the papers of the Presbyterians but also questioned other candidates for membership about their doctrinal knowledge and moral condition. Those with proper qualifications were then accepted. In contrast, the Methodist tried to convert the non-Methodists and to organize Methodist societies everywhere.

The Presbyterian emphasis on a doctrinally informed membership also implied a relatively rigid creedal statement and polity. Many disputes consequently rose from this inelasticity in the face of the changing conditions on the frontier and hindered the denominational expansion. Since the Presbyterians had repudiated the spectacular forms of revivalism, for all their early leadership in initiating the western camp meetings, they could not resort to this method for attracting new members at a time when revival conversion was popularly regarded as a necessary prerequisite for joining a church. On the contrary, numerous Presbyterian groups interested in using revivalism withdrew from the church after heated controversies with the anti-revivalist orthodoxy.

Although western Presbyterianism was far from the historic Calvinistic state churches in its cultural level, the denomination still had high standards for its clergy compared with those of the Dissenting sects. Western Presbyterian growth was consequently delayed by the shortage of qualified ministers and of parishioners to whom they would appeal. The rising frontier generation found in the Presbyterian services an intellectualism remote from their everyday life. "The stiff, technical theology, or dry, speculative orthodoxy" of the Presbyterian ministers did not appeal to most frontiersmen, who found the Baptist and Methodist simplicity and emotionalism more to their liking.[5]

Nonetheless, the denomination exerted a far greater influence in the West than mere numbers would indicate. The well-knit Presbyterian organization in itself gave the church greater power to act as a group than was usually possible for the more decentralized Baptists. The relatively better educational background of the Presbyterian clergy and membership was another reason for their influence. The bitter controversy over Transylvania University in Kentucky, notably between 1823 and 1827, revealed that many leaders prominent in the public life of the state were Presbyterian. The university was a state institution, but the Presbyterians sought to keep it as their denominational school. Their pretensions to prerogatives that as a rule only established churches would assume, despite the rationalistic secular culture prevailing among the non-Presbyterian majority of the Kentucky aristocracy, displayed more than a trace of the Presbyterian theocratic heritage. They seemed reluctant to permit religious liberty in practice, while verbally professing loyalty to democracy. Furthermore, those Kentucky leaders opposed to the War of 1812 were Presbyterians who were hostile to French democracy. The Reverend Mr. James Blythe of Kentucky clearly expressed the older Presbyterian outlook when in his 1815 National Fast Day address he denounced the separation of church and state as originating in anti-Christian philosophy "rocked in the cradle of French atheism." [6] The religious people in America, he continued, have said that it matters not whether their legislators are atheists, gamblers, deists, debauchees, or spendthrifts, and "thus we are impiously dissevering what God has joined together." Consequently, in several western states, Presbyterianism was accused of seeking to become the new establishment or assuming its prerogatives regardless of the legal separation of church and state. [7]

These examples from its disciplinary proceedings and the social nature of its organization and activities suggest to some extent the scope and unity of western Presbyterianism. Its discipline covered almost the entire life of its members and their families. The church was also definitely concerned with advancing the moral and educational standards of the community at large. These efforts helped to bring order to the frontier, to awaken the people to their responsibilities, and to lay the foundations of modern American society. The Presbyterians were in a position to exert individual and collective influence. Since the non-members regularly attending the Presbyterian services during this period in many places outnumbered the members several-fold, the church was able to propagate its ideals and standards of conduct and leadership among appreciably more people than its membership figures would suggest. Far from being the isolated rugged individualists depicted in popular legend, the pioneer Presbyterians accepted responsibilities and fostered social regulations which now would seem unbearably rigorous to many Americans, even to many Presbyterians. The discipline and the group unity in turn facilitated the growth of fellowship and friendly ties among the members.

CHAPTER IV

The Baptists

The migrating Virginia Baptists became the most influential element among the early western Baptists. The West apparently attracted a large proportion of those Baptists who were most hostile to the Virginia gentry and to the Anglican clergy and most interested in religious and social freedom. They were among the first settlers in Kentucky and they, with their Kentucky-born children, also pioneered in many parts of Ohio, Indiana, and Illinois. Everywhere these Baptists went, their Virginia experience was evident. Regardless of their social and economic rise in the West, the long struggle in Virginia had left bitter memories. Furthermore, the early West had but few schools and the majority of the new Baptist generation may have had less schooling and less appreciation for formal education than their parents. At any rate, the quaint spelling and charming indifference to grammar in the various frontier Baptist records reveal the educational limitations characteristic of even the ministers and clerks of the meetings.

The frontier Baptist ministers were generally unpaid and as a rule earned their living as farmers. They were of two classes, the licensed and the ordained. When a member felt called to the ministry, he might inform his church, or fellow members might suggest that he preach. If they approved of his "gifts" after hearing his trial sermon, they would grant him a license to preach, usually within the boundaries of the church. If he continued to improve, in time he could perhaps serve within the limits of his association (an organization of local churches). That the Baptists regarded this disciplinary control over their ministers seriously is illustrated by Isaac McCoy's confession before the Silver Creek Church, to preaching several times outside his assigned area. The members forgave him. When a church called a licensed minister to serve as its pastor, it usually ordained him.[1]

The early experience of John Mason Peck, who became perhaps the outstanding Baptist missionary in the West, was typical. After moving into a new settlement in New York State in 1811, he joined a Baptist church. Soon afterward its members began to ask him if he should not preach. He agreed, and later, when the members became better acquainted with his qualifications, the church voted to have him "improve his gifts" by preaching "wherever Divine Providence might open the door."[2] A real minister, Peck characteristically said, will not wait until called by a church, but will go to some "destitute field, sustain himself and family by his own industry, *and proceed to call a church.*" Another pioneer western minister, Jacob Bower, began by announcing at a meeting that there would be preaching at a given place, and then speaking himself.[3] As a rule, capable preachers were hard to find in the West. The revival system had no regular procedure for selecting and educating able men for the ministry. Actually, the best leaders were often ordained late in life, and after receiving their call, they still had to spend nearly all their time earning a living with little or no time left for study and preparation. Short pastorates were common in western Baptist churches. The Bethel (Indiana) Church had forty-three different ministers during its first century and had none at all during one-fifth of that period.

Some prosperous Baptist congregations had practices quite different from those of earlier or of the less wealthy societies. Nevertheless, opposition to regularly salaried clergy persisted. Timothy Flint attended a Baptist service in Franklin, Kentucky, at which the preacher was a judge and former member of Congress. "I had never yet seen a man, discharging the duties of a christian minister, so splendidly dressed," observed Flint, who also regarded the opposition to adequate support for the ministry as a western characteristic: "The people think in general, that attendance upon preaching, sufficiently compensates the minister."[4] Although this custom had advantages, it also deprived the congregations of the energy and time that their pastors had to devote to earning a living.

To organize a new Baptist church, a licensed or ordained minister would frequently bring together a group of his neighbors, including a number not previously Baptist. Some settlements had several preachers who would co-operate to establish the meeting. John Taylor, a leading Baptist minister in early Kentucky, described in his autobiography the founding of the Clear Creek Church in this manner.[5]

Taylor also recorded many documents, among them the Covenant, the Articles of Faith, and the Rules of Decorum of the Buck Run Church.[6] These statements were based on earlier texts, but they may be regarded as typical, since the new western churches copied or adapted their formal documents from older models. With the Covenant, the Articles or the Constitution, and the Rules at hand, the members of the prospective church were ready to invite at least three or four neighboring Baptist meetings to send their elders to act as a special council or presbytery to complete their formalities. If pressed for time, they occasionally asked the elders to participate as individuals. Older meetings helped the new churches to organize themselves. The Delphi (Indiana) Church participated about once a year in establishing new Baptist congregations. Elder Jesse Vawter of Madison, Indiana, assisted in founding twelve churches and three associations. At times, if no ministers were available in a settlement, holders of church letters met together and drew up the Articles of Faith and the Rules of Decorum which they usually copied from older statements. In the case of Harbert's Creek (Indiana) Church, the prospective members who held church letters convened and organized without any outside aid. Such action was permissible under Baptist polity but not recommended. When a query was addressed to the Silver Creek Association in Indiana in 1819 — "Can an orderly set of brethren constitute themselves into a church state?" — the Association answered yes — "yet, for the sake of church union we think it commendable to obtain the advice of neighboring churches."[7]

The rapid growth of Baptist societies in the areas near the

Silver Creek Association which nursed new churches and associations demonstrates the importance of competent leadership to the Baptist cause. The Vawter and the McCoy families, the Stotts, Jesse Holman, and other devoted men provided the needed strength and experience. Baptist meetings had a high mortality rate; many rose and then disappeared. Whether a church survived or not depended greatly on its leadership, especially since the membership was always on the move. Furthermore, Baptist organization seemed more adapted to rural than to urban communities. At any rate, general missionary agencies had to do almost all the pioneer work in the Indiana towns. Baptist societies were also peculiarly liable to disruption by disputes. Arguments over predestination, closed communion, and revival methods split many churches. Perhaps a more important reason for this tendency to separate was that any dissatisfied person able to command a following could form a new church. John Mason Peck suggests as another source of Baptist difficulties the "mischievous" rule of unanimity on all questions involving fellowship. Some members also interpreted the customary question asked at the outset of the meeting, "if all were in peace," to mean "think over your grievances and 'hurts'" and see if any complaint against another member was possible. "It is astonishing to notice what trifling things made these 'hurts,'" Peck adds. Many quarrels arose merely because the members, even preachers, often refused to use a dictionary to check the meaning of the words over which they were disputing.[8]

A moderator and a clerk, elected annually, assumed the responsibility for conducting the regular church business. The minister and deacons directed the religious work. Frequently the pastor was the moderator. In the usual business meeting, the inquiries concerning the church peace came first (this question was often the excuse for troublesome complaints) followed by the admission of new members, the unfinished business, the questions referred to committees, and finally the new business. The Rules of Decorum controlled the proceedings. Although the moderator could not vote except in the case of a tie, he and the visiting brethren participated in the discussion. Business sessions generally met at

11:00 A.M. on a designated Saturday each month, with the quorum being as low as three male members for Sharon, Wirt, Bethel, Morgantown, and several other Indiana churches. Disciplinary action by the meeting involved three types of offenses; first, the maintenance of order, attendance at the business meetings, and compliance with the church doctrines and rules; second, the violations of public statutes and ethical standards of the church; and third, the private offenses by one individual against another, especially those apt to destroy the church fellowship. The moderator and the deacons usually enforced the questions of order. All were required to recognize the authority of the church. The scriptural basis for the court was the eighteenth chapter of Matthew, verses 15 to 17.

No complaint was possible until the "gospel steps" had been taken, except in instances involving public trespasses, which did not require rigid adherence to this procedure. In such situations, a member was allowed to bring direct charges against the accused who could demand a hearing. Usually the offended and the offending members first met each other. If this effort did not bring reconciliation, two or three witnesses went to aid the disputants. Should this step also fail, the matter came before the church. The refusal by a member to submit to an examination of his alleged misconduct made him liable to immediate expulsion. For notorious misconduct not publicly acknowledged before the church, the meeting might exclude the guilty person without formally dealing with him. Some cases involving gross scandal were dismissed to avoid publicity. Often, in more difficult situations, "helps" were invited from neighboring churches. Where the majority agreed and the accused did not appear, a committee was appointed to cite him to answer the charges at the next meeting, which would hold a fair hearing. He had the right to bring witnesses to support his views, but if he did not attend this and several successive sessions, the church expelled him. Exclusion usually required the unanimous vote of all not involved, but some meetings, including the Forks of Elkhorn (Kentucky) Church, acted on two-thirds majority.

Despite the tendency to promote tattletaling and controversy, such discipline seemed to be the only means the churches had to maintain their group standards and unity in the rough frontier society. Furthermore, the Baptists long retained their original suspicion of public authority and most Baptist churches had a strict rule against members suing each other at law before "the ungodly." It is claimed that the very contrast between their ideals of Christian conduct toward each other and the lower standards in the community at large gave their fellowship a meaning and a measure of vitality. Intoxication, unseemly language, and sexual irregularities appear to have been the most common public offenses, followed by such charges as "fighting, betting on shooting matches, Sabbath violations, lying, defrauding, dancing," and participating in lotteries. Individual heresy charges, as distinguished from group disputes, seemed rare. Perhaps it was too easy for the suspects to move elsewhere or for them and their friends to form new churches. Among the private complaints, the commonest were wife-beating, neglecting children, and laxity in their discipline. Civil issues included repudiating contracts, refusal to pay for land, wrongfully occupying houses or land, abusing another's livestock, discounting notes, and departing from the community without paying creditors. These accusations, it should be noted, cover nearly the entire personal, social, and business life of the frontier communities.

The terse business meeting records do not reveal the full extent of this church discipline. For example, the Wood River (Illinois) Church record for February, 1813, reads, "The first Sattarday in febuary the Church met and nohing don." Again, in March, 1815, after it had "pitcht" the last Saturday of the following month for fasting and praying, it did "nothing mor."[9] These statements do not mention the detailed inquiry by the pastor and by the congregation as a whole into the personal life and spiritual experiences of each member and the encouragement or reprimand he received as warranted by his case. Only when his behavior deviated enough to require a trial and official disciplinary proceedings did the action appear on the records.

The discipline began in a real sense with the probationary period imposed on the applicants for membership. After some months, during which they attended the meetings regularly, the church would consider their requests. The pastor and all interested members questioned the candidates on doctrine and experience. Churches were thorough in evaluating the applicants, who were often advised to wait a month or two longer. As described by John Mason Peck, church unity and discipline were based on the regular renewal of the covenant:

The pastor then introduced the old custom of "renewing covenant" by all the members, male and female, giving an expression of their feelings, and their trials, their hopes, aspirations, and joys, during the past month. All spoke with frankness and apparent sincerity. The "door was opened" to hear "experiences of grace" from others.[10]

On his American tour, Dr. Cox of the British Baptist delegation met many Baptist ministers. One read to him the covenant of his church, which was similar to those of nearly all other churches and was renewed monthly. It consisted of the mutual agreement of "members in christian fellowship, to fulfil the obligations which their relationship to each other and to God involves."[11] At times the discipline extended even to publications by individuals. Thus, in January, 1811, Isaac McCoy wrote a "piece" on "absolute perseverance of the saints" which his church asked him to publish.

The Baptist discipline maintained in nearly all their churches and associations was based on common experience and practice and the renewal of the covenant. The willingness to expel recalcitrant members when necessary and the caution in accepting new members suggest that the frontier Baptist churches were not interested in numbers as such. Instead, they wanted organized fellowship. Nevertheless, precipitate acts could lead to injustices, all the more when only a few voted while the rest refrained. John Taylor notes the unfairness of dropping a member by a majority vote under such circumstances. In one church, charges involving land claims were brought against an influential member. Only three voted, two for expulsion and one in his favor. One of the two insisted that the accused was expelled according to the church rules. The meeting, however, would not let this vote stand, but "by a great majority, in a second vote cleared the accused man."[12]

We have seen that the church as a whole heard the Baptist disciplinary trials, as distinct from the Presbyterian session trials, but the Baptist cases were similar in their variety, range, and purpose. The following random extracts from the Records of the Forks of Elkhorn Baptist Church will illustrate the hearings (only excerpts of the minutes for any single day are given):

2nd Saturday in Sepr. [1801] the Church met and after Divine Worship proceeded to business

Charges brought against Bro, Shackleford for various reports circulating respecting his Immoral conduct Gaming etc & Brethn, J Price & Haydon is appointed to Cite him to Meeting to Morrow morning

A Charge Brought against Sister Wooldriges Sanders for putting away his wife & taking another Was taken up after conversing upon the Matter it was agreed to refer it to our next Meeting. . . .

Thos. Hickman came forward confess,d his fault & was restored. . . .

2nd. Saturday in January 1804 the Church met & after Divine worship proceeded to business.

Bro. Zacheriah Ross is Excluded from this Church for drinking too an Excess & for disobeying the call of the Church.

Bren. Edmund Ware & Daniel Peak is appointed to cite Bro, Baker Ewing to our next Monthly Meeting to answer some complaints.

Br. Thomas Hickman is Excluded from this Church for drinking to an Excess & for fighting

WILLIAM HICKMAN M.

The church discipline extended even to family quarrels.

The 2nd, Saturday in March 1805 the Church met and after Divine Worship proceeded to business

A Charge was brought against Sister Polly Edrington for frequently giving her Mother the lie, & calling her a fool and for Indeavouring by tattleing to set several of the Neighbours at strife with each other — She was Excluded for the same. . . .

The 2nd. Saturday in April 1812 after divine worship proceeded to business

A Charge brought against Sister Sally Brown a member of this Church for improperly talking. Continued untill our next meeting in course — Charges brought by Brother Me. Daniel against Brother Jesse Cole Charge 1st. for making unrighteous landmarks on brother John Graves land — Not supported
Charge 2nd. for accusing Brother Me.Daniels sons of destroying corner trees and trying to enforce a belief on the neighbours it was true — Not Supported.
Charge 3rd. for making Illnatured expressions (that is to say) he had no more fellowship for me, than he had for the Devil — The 3rd. Charge Acknowledged to by Brother Cole and the expressions reprobated the Church feel satisfied with Brother Cole. . . .

The 2nd. Saturday in June 1812 after divine worship proceeded to business

Took up the referrence from our last meeting to this, respecting the Charges of Bro. McDaniel against Bro. Cole — Bro. McDaniel having obtained leave from the Church to explain his first charge against Bro. Cole — placed it in the following words — viz. 1st. For runing an Incorrect line between himself and Bro. Graves without giving notice to Bro. Graves — Bro. Cole acknowledged the above charge, — But when Bro. Graves mentioned to Bro. Cole that he thought the line Incorrect. Bro. Cole stated he thought it was right or nearly so but proposed to get Bro. Price and run the line, which was consented to by Bro. Graves, and Bro. Cole Immediately sent for Bro. Price, and Bro. Price came and run the line, and both parties agreed they were satisfied.

The 2nd. Charge was taken up, and it was agreed to let it stand as on the record.

The 3rd.Charge was taken up, and it was agreed to let it stand as on the record. . . .[13]

The tradition of transferring memberships by church letters helped to maintain the denominational unity. These letters soon became standardized and as a rule differed only in the details of the little doctrinal summary serving as a preamble. The preamble enabled the receiving churches to determine if the applicant had come from a congregation which held the same doctrines as they did. As indicated by their records, the churches honored not only the letter but also the disciplinary action by the church which had issued the letter.

In Baptist polity, the local church was the only center of authority. The various churches generally formed associations and wider organizations for mutual aid and fellowship or to conduct certain activities, but, regardless of their importance, the associations were not representative governing bodies comparable to the Presbyterian assembly, synods, and presbyteries. The delegates to the associations were technically "messengers" and the correct name was significant, John Mason Peck emphasizes. They "acted solely upon their own responsibility as a body of Christian men" and were not official delegates of the congregations, since under Baptist polity an individual cannot represent a church. In theory, the local meetings still remained the highest authority, and indeed associations sometimes refused to supply preachers for churches without pastors. To take another instance, the La Motte (Illinois) Church asked a church in an Indiana association to send a committee to see if it was fit to belong to that association. The request was refused in conformity with Baptist polity. "One Baptist church cannot sit in judgment upon another," the La Motte Church was informed.[14]

The western Baptists followed one of the several alternative procedures in organizing new associations. Frequently, several churches would form an association. Some — for example, the Little Pigeon Association of Indiana — were begun with the permission and often with the aid of older associations. Churches could join established associations by unanimous vote, but unless they had letters of dismissal from a recognized association they had to prove the propriety of their organization and Articles of Faith. No church was obligated to join or remain in an association. As long as the church was a member, however, it had to meet the association standards and when its messengers were absent from the meetings, it had to give an explanation. The association could exclude the recalcitrants. Technically, the association withdrew from the church, but in any case it meant nonrecognition.

Associations usually held their annual meetings in the dry season. The sessions continued several days, generally from Friday until Monday. Often large crowds assembled; at times these events resembled camp meetings and were scenes of revivals. Continuous preaching went on in the groves, while the business meeting was simultaneously held inside the church. Member churches, though not individuals, could initiate and address queries to the association which could demur if the questions were too controversial and threatened to involve all in a dispute. In reality, associations undermined the complete independence of the individual church, particularly in the East where the associations tended to increase their authority. They represented a compromise between congregational independence and the necessity for wider fellowship, common council, and mutual aid for sheer survival. The frontier Baptists perhaps could never have overcome the great difficulties confronting them in the new country without organized intercongregational co-operation. Especially in the beginning, the local meetings were apt to be weak and small and their leadership often inexperienced, narrow in outlook, and constantly changing. Only by marshaling the abilities of the outstanding leaders and by uniting the limited strength of the local churches were they able to expand and meet the religious needs of their members.

In the West, church councils composed of several neighboring societies became increasingly important. They were subgroups within the associations and assumed three duties: organizing new churches, judging disputes within a church or between churches, and ordaining ministers and deacons. In their second role, the councils saved the associations from many embarrassing controversies; their rulings were usually final. In common with many other frontier Baptist institutions, councils developed naturally from accepted practice. This is a significant social development, for these institutional patterns were then incorporated into the Baptist polity.

The preceding examples of disciplinary measures and established polity scarcely added up to irresponsible individualism either in practice or in theory. Isolated individualists do not enter into solemn covenants to assemble regularly, to quote from the Covenant of the Buck Run (Kentucky) Church, to "watch over each other in brotherly tenderness," to endeavor to edify each other, to strive for the benefit of the weak, to "bear each other's burdens, and so fulfill the law of Christ," and to give each other in agreement, their "hands, and hearts."[15] The constant renewal of the covenant and the Baptists' concern for their fellowship testify to their sense of community. The seemingly flexible ministerial ordination itself followed definitely institutionalized procedures. This Baptist heritage assumed the orderly democratic association of free persons but not the irresponsible individualism of the twentieth-century economic myth. Both individually and collectively, the Baptists promoted behavior conducive to the general social order and well-being. Their local meetings and discipline fostered understanding fellowship among members who had lost their personal ties when they had moved from their old homes, and church letters of dismissal helped those migrating once more to re-establish friendly contacts in a new settlement.

CHAPTER V

The Methodists

The Methodists became a separate American denomination at the historic Christmas Conference of 1784 in Baltimore. At that time, they had scarcely 15,000 members, 43 circuits, and 83 itinerants. Less than 2,600 members lived north of Maryland, their main following being in Virginia and Maryland. Nevertheless, they soon became the largest denomination in the United States. By 1844 Methodism had 3,988 circuit riders, 7,730 local preachers, and 1,069,000 members. The second largest American denomination, the Baptists, had 632,000 members that year.

Early American Methodism adopted with relatively few modifications the organization created by John Wesley for England. The Americans made an overt change in formally establishing an episcopal system of administration, a system personified by Wesley. Below the episcopacy came the presiding eldership, an office exemplified by Wesley's personal assistants who planned the work of the circuits and supervised the activities of the preachers. In America the presiding elder was responsible for a district with several circuits, each of which in turn was in charge of one or more itinerants. A number of local societies and classes with their local preachers, exhorters, class leaders, and other lay leaders composed a circuit. Wesley in England had also found it helpful to bring together his assistants and lay workers at various conferences. In the United States without Wesley, the Annual Conference, composed of all the circuit riders (itinerants), presiding elders, and bishops, became the supreme denominational ruling agency. As Methodism grew, the Annual Conference evolved into the delegated quadrennial General Conference, below which came the present regional annual conferences and the district quarterly conferences.

By far the outstanding leader of early American Methodism was Francis Asbury. Although he had only an elementary schooling, he had become a lay worker under Wesley in England and in 1771, when twenty-six years old, volunteered for service in the New World to help the struggling Methodist movement in the colonies. By sheer will and exemplary self-sacrifice he, with other British lay workers, brought order and discipline to the American organization and made the preachers itinerants rather than occupants of town churches. He had no home and was on the road constantly, for the whole United States was his diocese. "The king's business requires haste," he declared and hence he could wait for no man. To the time of his death in 1816, more Americans, it was said, had seen and heard Asbury personally than any other individual.[1]

Asbury's contribution to American Methodism and American society was far-reaching, although his attitude was often sectarian. "Come out from among them, and be ye separate" seems to have been a favorite theme. Or again, he wrote, "My mind was troubled by turning on political subjects, which are out of my province. Alas! what a small matter may interrupt our communion with God; and even draw away our affections from him." His *Journal* reflected his intense seriousness: "A cloud rested on my mind, which was occasioned by talking and jesting," and "when amongst my friends, my mind inclines to a degree of cheerfulness bordering on levity. O for more watchfulness!" Again, "I lamented the gayety of the children of Methodists; but yet they do not appear to be so full of enmity against God and his people as other children."[2] Readers may encounter almost morbid passages in his *Journal* which followed his crushing self-imposed burdens. Not all Methodist bishops were like Asbury, however. Bishop Roberts, for one, was noted for his cheerfulness and amiability.

Nathan Bangs, a leading Methodist historian and contemporary of Asbury, found two major weaknesses in the bishop's outstanding leadership, weaknesses that were virtually incorporated into the American Methodism of his day. First, Dr. Bangs asserted,

Asbury did not sufficiently value learning and education. In reality, the bishop was greatly concerned with elementary education. It was higher education and formal scholarship which he did not adequately appreciate, notwithstanding his habit of reading daily about one hundred pages of serious material. The Methodist neglect of broader learning, Dr. Bangs observed in the 1840's, "was a fault which will require years of bitter repentence and assiduous amendment to atone." His criticism emphasizes an important distinction between early American and British Methodism.[3] The religious enthusiasm of the American Methodists was not tempered by sound education and real interest in learning among their leaders, whereas the British society had educated leaders like John and Charles Wesley and John Fletcher.

The second weakness that Dr. Bangs saw in Bishop Asbury's churchmanship was the usual Dissenting tendency to overlook the necessity for providing the ministers, especially family men, with material support.[4] The meager allowance forced many outstanding circuit riders to "locate" when they married. In contrast and partly in reaction, Asbury commended the Shakers for their celibacy. They were "as the angels of heaven," he remarked, although he reluctantly admitted that marriage is "honourable in all." Yet to him "it is a ceremony awful as death. Well may it be so, when I calculate we have lost the travelling labours of two hundred of the best men in America, or the world, by marriage and consequent location." It would have been more practical to have accepted married itinerants and to have planned accordingly, Dr. Bangs believed.

Among Asbury's many positive insights was his early appreciation of the future significance of the West for America and the enormous task confronting the Methodists and other denominations in that region.[5] The crudity of western life and indeed its perils, plus the tendency of some frontiersmen living under harsh conditions to violence, cruelty, and ever lower cultural standards, Asbury experienced directly. This intimate knowledge explains his insistence on confronting the settlers with order and morality.

Everywhere the Methodists were identified with the common people, and Bishop Asbury himself set the example. He drove his itinerants hard, but he drove himself harder. Whatever hospitality the poorest pioneer cabins had to offer, he accepted, no matter how crowded, smelly, filthy, and insect- and disease-ridden they were. His immediate successors followed the same course, and consequently the frontier bishops were regarded as essentially "shirt-sleeved" workingmen. In short, power and authority did not exempt them from the hardships of the common man.

Authority the bishops had. The episcopal message to the 1840 General Conference, for example, frankly noted the difference between civil and church government. As their primary duty the bishops had to preserve the itinerant ministry and common administrative standards in every department of the church. The clear authority and the constant travel by the bishops and itinerants gave the Methodists a substantially national outlook at a time when, as we shall see shortly, provincialism virtually paralyzed Baptist denominational efforts in sections of the West. During the years covered in this study, however, a number of Methodist groups separated from the denomination, at least partly in protest against this centralized control, which they considered undemocratic.[6]

The average laymen may not have been too acutely aware of the centralized authority, since they participated mainly in their classes and local societies and their own neighbors and relatives served as local preachers, exhorters, and class leaders. At the same time, the personal democracy of the presiding elders and of the itinerants who were changed each year to a degree bridged the gap between the formal organization and its local members. The relative ease with which lay workers could become local deacons or elders or indeed circuit riders further blurred, psychologically, the distinction between the rank and file and the official staff. All met at the quarterly conferences. Nevertheless, Dr. Sweet doubts if the frontiersmen would have accepted the highly autocratic Methodist polity had not the bishops and the itinerants as individuals completely identified themselves with the common people. To explain the Methodist success we need to modify the more individualistic interpretations of western life and give greater weight to democratic organizations under leadership vested with authority but identified with the common people, responsive to the popular will, and outwardly free from aristocratic pretensions — a feature later associated with Jacksonianism.

In their rapid growth, the Methodists had many major assets. Among them were the itinerancy, the Arminian theology of free grace, the democratic approach, the publishing house and its inexpensive books, and even their enthusiastic hymn singing. The most valuable asset, some scholars suggest, was the first. It was the circuit rider who penetrated the wilderness. Hardly any individual was more closely associated with the frontier than the Methodist itinerant, identified in later years by the "grave, earnest countenance, the straight-breasted coat, the oil-skin covering of the hat, the leather saddle-bags, and the staid gait of the horse." A familiar expression in the West on bitterly cold days was said to be, "There is nothing out today but crows and Methodist preachers."[7]

By the time Methodism began expanding westward, the circuit riders were ordained deacons or elders who had generally started as lay leaders. It was a hard life, and many itinerants were forced to settle down, to "locate" — some, perhaps the majority, for financial reasons, but many because of the hardships and health hazards involved. Dr. Stevens, a leading Methodist historian, states: "Nearly half of those [circuit riders] whose death are recorded [by the end of the eighteenth century] died before they were thirty years old; about two thirds died before they had spent twelve years in the laborious service."[8] We can better understand this grim situation when we realize that it often took five or six weeks for an itinerant to tour his wilderness circuit. William Burke began working on a six-week circuit and refers to an eleven-week one. In 1803, Benjamin Young was assigned nearly all Illinois as a virtual circuit, while John Stewart once had a rugged mountain circuit covering almost all of present West Virginia. Many circuits had more than thirty preaching stations, but the average was from fifteen to twenty-five.

The itinerant had to ride constantly except perhaps Mondays, when he supposedly wrote his reports, completed unfinished business, and washed and mended his meager wardrobe. He slept in frequently uncomfortable and filthy cabins. A pioneer circuit rider, Jacob Young, told his people that whenever possible he intended to "avoid sleeping among fleas and bed-bugs." The careless housekeepers felt insulted. The cleanliness of Boston, as compared with most western towns, impressed Young. The Boston horse stables were cleaner than some homes he knew in the West. The discomfort and lack of privacy made rest difficult during the few hours the itinerant had free.

The book of regulations (known as the *Discipline*) called on the circuit rider to rise at four in the morning when his pastoral duties and discussions with his parishioners often kept him busy until midnight or later. The itinerant preached wherever he went and also co-ordinated the activities of the class leaders, the exhorters, and the local preachers. They reported to him on the condition of their society or class and every member. He regularly met each class on his visits and called on the ill and others needing personal attention. Once a quarter he reviewed the work of the class leaders and other local officials to see how effective they had been.

In principle, the Methodists compensated their circuit riders. The salary was very meager, however, and what made it harder for the distressed itinerants was that they often received only a fraction of the stated amount. Beginning in 1816, the pay was officially raised from $80 to $100 per year, but in reality the western circuit riders were given a small percentage of this sum and were at the same time constantly called upon to contribute to various causes. As a consequence, some found it impossible to replace their tattered clothing. James Finley, an outstanding frontier presiding elder, once had to sell his boots to purchase food for his family before starting on a circuit. Henry Bascom, destined to become a bishop, traveled the rugged Guyandotte circuit in the West Virginia mountains one year for the Ohio Conference, covering 3,000 miles as well as preaching to over 400 congregations and tending to the pastoral duties. He received only $12.10! One year in Indiana, Joseph Tarkington received $14.00, James Garner, the preacher in charge, $28.00, and F. C. Holliday, the presiding elder, almost nothing. No wonder Peter Cartwright, perhaps the most famous itinerant, declared that in nine cases out of ten the circuit rider could not get half of the $80.00, and indeed, many did not get a quarter of it. As for the family allowances, he noted, such was their poverty that this specification in "the Discipline was a perfectly dead letter."[9]

Among the earliest western settlers were some local preachers and class leaders. No sooner did they build their cabins and clear a few acres than they invited their neighbors to their cabins for religious services. The first itinerants pushing their way through the wilderness found classes already organized and Methodism established. In 1783 when James Haw arrived in Kentucky, he discovered that Francis Clark, a local preacher from Virginia, had a class under way. Crossing the river in 1798 into the Ohio Territory, John Kobler met with classes formed by Francis McCormick, who had settled near Cincinnati three years previously. Ordinary laymen themselves often took the initiative. Methodist settlers on the lower Whitewater petitioned John Sale, the presiding elder of the Ohio District, for regular preaching. He sent Joseph Oglesby in the spring of 1806. By the September Conference time, Oglesby had organized a four-week circuit along both banks of the Whitewater, formed classes, appointed their leaders, and reported a membership of sixty-seven, with, of course, a list of the local preachers, exhorters, and class leaders.

The 1796 General Conference permitted the lay preachers who were responsible for the local societies, if suitably "improved," to become local deacons after serving four years. Local deacons became eligible to local eldership by a decision of the 1812 General Conference. The deacons could marry, bury, baptize, and help the elders at communion; the elders could perform all these duties and also administer communion. These laymen with the exhorters, class leaders, and others provided the grass-roots leadership.

In the early nineteenth century the Methodists were often poor, at least "land poor," and some virtually penniless, but from the first some members were well-to-do and many others were ambitious. In a few years, the denomination was to occupy a far higher social and economic status, as was foreshadowed in Ohio from the very first by the public leadership of such pioneer Methodists as Thomas Scott, a preacher and Chief Justice of the Ohio Supreme Court; Edward Tiffin, lay preacher, outstanding Jeffersonian, first governor of Ohio, United States senator, and holder of many other public offices; Allen Trimble, Speaker of the Ohio House, later governor, and a leading promoter of Ohio agriculture; Thomas Worthington, governor, United States senator, advocate of public education, and reformer; and John McLean, at various times Justice of the Ohio Supreme Court and the United States Supreme Court and active in the cabinets of Presidents Monroe and J. Q. Adams. The denomination similarly provided much of the political, economic, social, and cultural and intellectual leadership in the other states carved from the Old Northwest. In February, 1805, Asbury could think of only two Methodists in Congress, and they had come in with the Jeffersonian triumph; he doubted if the Methodists in all state legislatures together totaled more than twenty. On the other hand, writing in the middle of the century, James Finley was able to refer his readers to the numerous Methodist senators and representatives in Congress as well as to the many outstanding Methodists in all other fields.

In writing nostalgically of their youthful days when their discipline distinguished the Methodists from others, Peter Cartwright, Henry Boehm, James Finley, and other pioneers did not quite realize that in rapidly becoming more prominent Methodism was repeating and strengthening a familiar Dissenting pattern, all the more quickly since the denomination had "middle-class orientation" from the first. Wealth accumulates and educational and cultural standards rise, or the more wealthy and cultured join, the discipline weakens, and the sect increasingly resembles the society at large. Wesley was troubled by this trend, and the *Discipline* warned against this movement toward "worldliness."

Yet, in reminiscing on his younger days, Cartwright was not merely recalling naïve Methodism before it had numerous political, business, and professional leaders as members. He was describing a stage in the Methodist development when, he felt, the faithful attended meetings regularly and refrained from many activities enjoyed by others. They did not permit their children to attend dances or plays, and, added Cartwright, many avoided alcoholic beverages long before temperance movements rose because the *Discipline* "interdicted" drinking. The Methodists dressed plainly without ruffles and jewelry. When someone was converted, he often indicated his decision by changing his clothing. One man at a revival meeting, the fiery itinerant reported, "deliberately opened his shirt bosom, took hold of his ruffles, tore them off, and threw them down into the straw; and in less than two minutes God blessed his soul, and he sprang to his feet, loudly praising God." Henry Boehm commented similarly on early nineteenth-century Methodism: "The people and preachers . . . were patterns of plainess; we [in the 1860's] conform more to the world, and have lost much of the spirit of self-denial they possessed. Our fathers paid great attention to Church discipline." James B. Finley also observed that "the first Methodists were a peculiar people in their personal appearance and manners, and could be distinguished from the world at a single glance." [10]

The most intimate center of disciplinary control and fellowship was the class. Applicants for membership had to give evidence of their desire, as stated in the *Discipline, "to flee from the wrath to come, and to be saved from their sins."* [11] As a rule, each local society was divided into classes grouped geographically according to the residences of the members, that they might watch over each other more effectively and observe whether or not each member was striving for his "salvation." Each class met once a week in members' homes and had no more than twelve persons, including the class leader. It was his duty to see each person at least once a week and to inquire how "every soul in his class prospers," not merely questioning the member's outward behavior but "how he grows in the knowledge and love of God." The leader, indeed the class as a group, probed into and discussed the state of each member's spiritual life, and was expected to "advise, reprove, comfort or exhort, as occasion may require." Naturally, the leader consulted "frequently and freely" with the itinerant and the elders about the individual members.

In describing his first visit to a frontier Methodist class before he became a member, James B. Finley gives us a picture of an actual class session:

It was opened by singing and prayer. . . . After several prayers, the leader — Mr. Sullivan — rose and said, "We are now going to hold our class meeting, and all who have enjoyed this privilege twice or thrice will please retire [visitors were generally allowed to remain only two or three times unless they expected to become members], while those who have not and are desirous of being benefited by the exercises may remain." . . . The leader, as is customary on such occasions, opened the speaking exercises by relating a portion of his own experience, in which he spoke feelingly of the goodness of God to his soul. After this he spoke to the rest in order, inquiring into their spiritual prosperity; addressing to them such language of instruction, encouragement, or reproof, as their spiritual states seemed to require. It was a time of profound and powerful feeling; every soul seemed to be engaged in the work of salvation. I was astonished beyond all expression. Instead of the ranting, incoherent declarations which I had been told they made on such occasions, I never heard more plain, simple, Scriptural, common-sense, yet eloquent views of Christian experience in my life. After all the members had been spoken to the leader came to me, and, in a courteous, Christian manner, inquired into my religious condition.[12]

If some critics have found aspects of the *Discipline* pettily moralistic, it was also rigorous and comprehensive and ranged from songs to self-indulgence, from reading to fighting, and from business to gossiping. Early editions also forbade "unlawful" marriages to "*unawakened* persons" (non-Methodists), since members united with non-members would be handicapped, if not lost. Before taking as serious a step as marriage, the Methodists were expected to consult with their brethren. The *Discipline* called on the preachers to enforce the aspostolic caution and expel members who marry "unbelievers." After 1804, however, Methodists marrying non-members who were seeking the "power of godliness" were merely placed on a six-month probation, but the itinerants and class leaders were still expected to preach against such unions and to bring strong pressure against marrying outside the denomination.[13]

According to the *Discipline*, each deacon was to investigate all disputes between two or more members. If they could not reach an agreement, he was to urge arbitration by a committee consisting of a representative of the plaintiff, a representative of the defendant, and a third person chosen by the two, all to be Methodists. The majority decision was final. If either party refused to accept the judgment, he was excluded. The *Discipline* would expel any member who began a lawsuit against another Methodist before taking these steps. The itinerants were also to warn the members against treats and bribes by political candidates.

The *Discipline* included economic responsibilities. The Methodists were not to use *"many words* in buying and selling"* (that is, they were not to haggle and bargain, but to have a set price for the goods), not to charge usurious interest, and to prevent scandal whenever a member failed in business or contracted a debt which he could not pay: "Let the elder or deacon desire two or three judicious members of the society to inspect the accounts of the supposed delinquents; and if they have behaved dishonestly, or borrowed money without a probability of paying, let them be suspended until their credit is restored." The circuit riders were to enforce the rules "against all frauds, and particularly against dishonest insolvencies; suffering none to remain" a member who was guilty of any fraud. The 1812 General Conference strengthened the section in the *Discipline* on disputes over debts. Whenever a conflict arose and the amount of the debt was determined, the preacher "should call the debtor before a committee of at least three, to say why he does not make payment." The committee then was to determine how valid his appeals for more time and how substantial his security, if any, were. In the event that the debtor refused to accept the committee's decision, he was expelled. He, as well as the creditor, however, could appeal to the quarterly conference. In any case, the quarterly conference decision was final.

The circuit riders were expected to "recommend decency and cleanliness" everywhere. This emphasis continued John Wesley's injunction against filth and slovenliness:

Be cleanly. In this let the Methodists take pattern by the Quakers. Avoid all nastiness, dirt, slovenliness, both in your person, clothes, house and

all about you. Do not stink above ground. This is bad fruit of laziness.
. . . Whatever clothes you have, let them be whole; no rags, no tatters,
no rents. These are a scandal to either man or woman, being another
fruit of vile laziness. Mend your clothes, or I shall never expect you to
mend your lives. Let none ever see a ragged Methodist.[14]

According to Henry Boehm, who for a time accompanied Asbury
on his travels, the bishop indeed regarded cleanliness as second
only to godliness. He bitterly protested against the dirty and
smelly western cabins and inns and the slovenly western families
whom he often encountered. It was a relief for him to return to
the cleaner and more settled Pennsylvania communities.

The personal cleanliness and good order among the circuit
riders and members should not be exaggerated. At home on the
roughest frontier far from the refinements of settled communities,
many knew but little about social amenities. They often resented
anyone careful enough to make them appear untidy in comparison, as young Henry B. Bascom, later a bishop, soon discovered.
Bascom came from a very poor family, but he was immaculate.
The pioneer preachers resented his neatness and thought he was
proud and ambitious. Many felt that he would not long remain
a Methodist preacher. Consequently, he was sent, as we have seen,
to the tough Guyandotte circuit to break him or to drive him
out, and he received a salary of $12.10 for that whole year.

Once the Presbyterian Church of Columbus, Ohio, invited the
Methodists to use its facilities for a conference. The delegates
stained the woodwork and the carpet with pools of "tobacco
juice." The appreciative itinerants obviously did not mean to
be destructive; many were simply unaccustomed to rugs and clean
floors. Cartwright tells an amusing story about James Axley.
These two colorful itinerants were guests of Governor and Mrs.
Tiffin of Ohio at dinner, during which Axley whistled for a dog
and threw some bones on the floor. The amused governor had
difficulty in repressing his laughter. Later when Cartwright told
Axley that he had committed an error in etiquette, Axley was
chagrined. No one had better intentions than this heroic frontiersman, who had been looking forward to sleeping for the first
time in a plastered house.

Not all circuit riders enforced the *Discipline* as effectively as the more enthusiastic ones. In 1817 Peter Cartwright came to the Red River Circuit and threw himself into the task of applying the *Discipline* (the situation seems to contradict his previous comments). Many members dealt in slaves, dressed extravagantly, and lived fashionably until Cartwright through strenuous efforts brought order into the circuit. Similarly, William Burke and James Finley expelled violators without hesitation.

Methodism was not content merely to preach against what it regarded as sins. It assumed realistically that many members and some in the ministry would transgress, and consequently it had definite procedures for discouraging deviations and for punishment.[15] The composition of the committees trying ministers and laymen differed. In cases involving the clergy, a bishop, or, in his absence, the presiding elder summoned the elder or deacon charged with an offense to appear before a committee of ministers. If found guilty, the accused was suspended from all official work for the church until the next annual conference, which would reconsider his case. For minor transgressions, such as "improper tempers, words, or actions," his superior reprimanded him. Should he once more commit similar misdeeds, the superior then rebuked him in the presence of one or more ministers as witnesses. If again charged with misbehavior, he was tried before the annual conference and, if found guilty, expelled from the church. When complaints involved local preachers, deacons, and elders, the circuit rider in charge summoned three or more local preachers, or if they were unavailable, local exhorters and class leaders, to hear the charges. Defendants declared guilty of certain serious violations were suspended until the next quarterly meeting which would try them. Those found guilty were permitted to appeal to the next annual conference.

The society to which he belonged or several of its members tried the ordinary layman in the presence of a bishop, elder, deacon, or preacher. Non-members could testify in lay cases. Those found guilty of transgressions "sufficient to exclude a person from the kingdom of grace and glory" were expelled. The preacher or leader privately reprimanded minor offenders. The third violation even of a minor nature called for a hearing before the society or committee. Those found guilty and impenitent were excluded from the church. Members could, however, appeal for a new hearing before the quarterly meeting unless they had stayed away from the original trial. Absence from the trial was regarded as evidence of guilt.

As far as possible, both the accuser and the accused were present at the trial. Minutes of the proceedings were kept. First came the arraignment at which the complaints were presented against the accused who replied to the charge. The plaintiff then examined his witnesses, who were subsequently cross-examined by the defendant. The latter next presented his evidence. The accuser and the accused were allowed to submit rebutting testimony, followed by the closing arguments from both sides. Finally, the presiding official would announce the committee decision. While more formal than many Baptist hearings, the trials were not unlike those by the Presbyterian church sessions. Officers, titles, and the composition of the various boards and committees differed among the denominations, but the procedures were sufficiently alike not to require individual illustrations.

Records of early western Methodists and independent observers reveal the Methodist concern for group unity, discipline, and fraternity. The Methodists sought to organize and maintain a closely knit and well-disciplined organization, and not unbridled individualism. James Finley was referring at least to their ideals and objectives when he wrote on the "Origin and Progress of Methodism in Cincinnati" (in *Sketches of Western Methodism*):

With Christian charity they bore each other's burdens, and with Christian zeal and fidelity they watched over each other for good. Each one seemed to be the insurer of the other's reputation, and felt himself as responsible for his upright character as though he was his special guardian: hence, every thing that indicated, in the slightest degree, a departure from the path of holy rectitude, would at once awaken the liveliest apprehensions and interest on the part of the rest. If any one of the members was absent from class meetings, they were immediately inquired after, and as much care and solicitude manifested as if it had been the unexpected absence of some member of a family.[16]

CHAPTER VI

The Friends

Although the first Monthly Meeting west of the Alleghenies was formed at Westland, Pennsylvania, in 1785, the great Southern Quaker migration to the Old Northwest did not assume substantial proportions until the turn of the century. The first Monthly Meetings in the Northwest Territory were organized in December, 1801, at Concord and at Waynesville (known later as the Miami Monthly Meeting). Centers of Quaker population and influence included Mount Pleasant, Salem, Damascus, Waynesville, and New Vienna in Ohio, and Richmond, Fountain City, Salem, Bloomingdale, and Spiceland in Indiana. Mount Pleasant became known not only as an industrial center but even more as a literary and educational center. The *Philanthropist,* the first abolitionist paper, was founded there in 1817. Salem, Ohio, and Fountain City, Indiana, became prominent antislavery centers.[1]

In 1839 the Indiana Yearly Meeting first published its own book of *Discipline* (edited in 1838). It was almost identical with the 1819 Ohio *Discipline* which the Indiana Friends had previously used. Typically, the Indiana *Discipline* covered not merely the personal, religious, and devotional practices but also the public, social, and economic life of the members.[2] It outlined the procedures for settling disputes, including the right of arbitrators to secure legal counsel in more complicated cases. Law suits were permitted only when delays were dangerous or possibly disastrous. Moreover, continued the *Discipline,* Friends had a duty to help maintain the liberty of conscience as the common right of all men, particularly religious societies. No public office inconsistent with Quaker principles could be held. Friends were not to be active in electing fellow members or anyone else to offices which involved obligations contrary to their "Christian testimony." As pacifists, they could not join forces with persons who opposed or "reviled" those in authority, the *Discipline* insisted.

Friends were to shun worldly vanities. The *Discipline* emphasized that even funerals and burials were to be simple — no mourning garb and no monuments of distinction. Extravagance and ostentation expressed vanity and tempted people to sharp business practices or unmanageable speculation. Under all circumstances, the *Discipline* cautioned, members were to deal humanely in their business relations and never to impose on anyone. They could not venture into business they did not understand or extend themselves at the risk of others but were always to be in a position to meet their obligations. Speculative habits, especially those endangering others, were to be avoided. If their liquid assets just equaled their debts, Friends were required by the *Discipline* to inform their creditors and to consult with judicious members about their financial condition. They were to place all creditors on equal basis. The use of paper credits and other dubious practices were "inconsistent with the truth."

The *Discipline* called on the members to draw up wills while they enjoyed good health and sound mind. It was preferable to use competent legal aid to avoid any misunderstanding which might arise should unexpected death occur. Friends were not to serve uncritically as co-security when such action could leave their widows and children destitute. Parents were to give first consideration to their children's future and to follow the *Discipline*'s suggestions for child care and training. For instance, moving from established communities was often found to be detrimental to the "growth in the truth" of both the parents and the children, particularly when "worldly motives" determined the move.[3] To protect their children's welfare and property widowed parents were advised against marriage to persons with designs on their property, which their children were to inherit. In any case, no one was to marry less than a year after the death of his previous spouse. To reduce the number of marriages with non-members, parents were to encourage their children to associate with other Friends.

Before members could marry, they had to notify the Monthly Meeting in writing. Then, accompanied by their parents — and in some places by two additional men and women — the couple entered the women's meeting and "declared their intentions." If the parents were not present, their consent was read. The same group next entered the men's meeting where the pair repeated their intentions. The two sessions then appointed a committee to investigate the couple to see if there were any obstacles to their marriage. Only after a favorable report could the young people marry. The Monthly Meeting arranged for a proper ceremony, often at a mid-week worship meeting. Any wedding other than the one planned by the Meeting was disapproved. During this period, marriages to non-members invariably led to disciplinary action, usually expulsion, even for parents who sanctioned such unions. Rufus Jones, an outstanding Quaker leader and scholar, regards this rule as unreasonable, especially on the frontier where it was difficult to find satisfactory mates.

In the eighteen years from 1793 to 1811, the Redstone Monthly Meeting alone had 146 cases of marriage "contrary" to *Discipline* — most of them being marriage with a non-member and therefore requiring the services of a minister, that is, a "priest" or a "hireling Teacher" as the Friends called him. The Meeting disowned 104 of these 146 for the "offense" and forgave the rest, who had "humbly expressed their sorrow and regret." It is doubtful, Rufus Jones concludes, whether any religious society could flourish for long under such drastic discipline, particularly since the Friends were no longer seeking converts.

These brief references to several rules in the *Discipline* suggest the parallels between Quaker discipline and that of the Methodists, Baptists, and Presbyterians. As in the trials held by these denominations, charges of drunkenness, illicit sex relations, using bad language, bearing false witness, and failing to settle contracts were involved in cases tried before Quaker meetings. The Quakers may have been more inclusive and more rigorous in enforcing their rules than other denominations, but otherwise their disciplinary practices did not differ fundamentally. Instead of further discussion of trials, therefore, it will perhaps be more fruitful for this inquiry to consider the relations between the discipline and the humanitarian and ethical activities of the Friends. Such a survey will not only illustrate the range of their discipline but also introduce features of Dissenting ethics and attitudes which several following chapters will discuss at greater length.

From the first the Quakers were concerned with the welfare of the Indians, and the denomination has had an outstanding history of befriending them.[4] The Indiana Yearly Meeting co-operated with the Baltimore and the Ohio Yearly Meetings in their work at Wapaughkonnetta (or Wapakoneta) originally begun in 1811. The following summaries from the minutes of the Indiana Yearly Meeting referring to its committee on Indian affairs will perhaps best show this Quaker concern in operation. The Indian Affairs Committee, the 1822 minutes record, purchased suitable land, erected several buildings, and employed two couples to conduct a school for the Shawnee Indians at Wapaughkonnetta. Two years later they closed the school but continued the general work. The school reopened the following year. The Shawnees were confused and restless because of the government decision to move them west of the Mississippi, and consequently the school was shut again. Some Indians had already gone to the new tract and the rest were momentarily expecting their turn. The Friends reopened the school once more, however, at the request of the chiefs still at Wapaughkonnetta and in addition placed a number of the children in various outside schools.

Other denominations had proposed missionary activities among the Indians, but the Shawnees preferred the Friends because the Quakers had always "given them good advice, and told them things which made them glad." By 1832 the Shawnees were in a desperate condition. They had disposed of their holdings in good faith since the federal government had told them to be prepared to move on short notice. The government then did nothing further and ignored the resultant hardships. Quaker representatives accompanied the Shawnee delegation to Washington to intercede for them, and Congress was finally persuaded to appropriate $30,000 in fifteen annual installments to meet the situation. Eventually all the Shawnees had to leave their old homes. Weeping, they bade farewell to the Friends and asked for their help in the new home across the Mississippi.

The Friends did not forget them. Three from the Indiana Meeting visited the Shawnees in 1833 on the west bank of the Missouri near where Kansas City now is. The Indians welcomed them and asked them to continue their work. The Baltimore, Indiana, and Ohio Yearly Meetings agreed to carry out a joint program. Meanwhile, the Indian Committee had received £300 from the London Meeting, which was pleased to hear about the Indian interest in agriculture and mechanical arts. Where a sufficient number of Friends lived, the Committee thought it feasible to have joint schools with the Indian children to help them at least to learn the language. The Quakers could also begin a meeting for worship, to which the Indians would be invited but not required to attend. The mission work combined education; practical training in agriculture, black-smithing, mill-work, and home-making; and religious instruction. It served not only the Shawnees but also other tribes.

The 1838 Meeting approved the Indian Committee petition to Congress opposing the use of the Shawnee Indians in the war against the Seminoles. They forwarded the appeal to the Baltimore Meeting for direct transmittal, but meanwhile Joseph John Gurney with two others had seen the President and the Secretary of War, who promised to withdraw the Shawnees as soon as possible and in the future to avoid such practices. The Meeting also printed for national circulation 25,000 copies of a sixteen-page address on Indian rights, based on the Quaker Memorial to Congress on behalf of the Indians.[5] The address asked the American people and Congress to acquit themselves of the debt they owed the Indians by extending Christianity and civilization to them. It referred to the record of William Penn and asserted that the Indians judged the Americans by their acts rather than by their words. Unlike John Elliott (Eliot), who preached to the Indians, the Puritans and other settlers had ruthlessly slaughtered the Indians. Commenting on how the Indians exiled to Deer Island behaved with dignity and Christian forebearance, the address observed: "What a contrast to the conduct of their highly professing

[Puritan] masters!" Christian Americans were rapidly exterminating the Indians and were depriving them of their land, notwithstanding the obvious progress Indians had made in agriculture and settled life wherever they had a fair opportunity. "Our
conduct towards them has become a matter of history," the address reminded the American Christians who possessed the land
that had once belonged to the Indians.

To prevent the complete ruin of the Indians, the address insisted, Americans had to allow the Indians to retain adequate
land secured to "them and their posterity forever, for possession
beyond the power of alienation." Indians needed assistance in
organizing a government in which they were to participate. It
was vital to grant them congressional representation as soon as
possible. Friends asked for the Indian right to keep their still remaining land in the East, a mere fragment of their former holdings. American Christians had to realize, the address continued,
that God made of one blood all nations of men, that He was the
"refuge of the poor" and the "avenger of the wrongs" inflicted
on the oppressed, and that with "what measure ye mete, it shall
be measured to you again." This brief account shows that contrary to the strong frontier hatred against the Indians, western
Friends had some concern from the first for their welfare and
made it one of their individual and official responsibilities.
The Quaker attitude in itself revealed their strong group spirit.

The Friends also became concerned with abolishing slavery
and establishing the Negroes as free citizens.[6] The earliest appeals
for abolition came from some German and Dutch Quakers, but it
was John Woolman and his associates who in the mid-eighteenth
century initiated the main impetus to eradicate slavery from their
Society. Woolman pleaded with Friends not only on social but on
religious grounds and told the Quaker slaveowners that they
would have to justify their conduct to God.

After some years of prayers and sustained appeals to the slaveholders, under the "guidance of the Inner Light" the Quakers
eliminated the institution of slavery from their ranks. By the
1780's the few remaining slaveholders, except those entrusted with

the infirm, aged, or orphaned slaves needing protection, were dropped, and the positive testimony for freedom became a disciplinary requirement. The Society not only sought to free the slaves but also insisted that they needed education, employment, and legal protection to live as free men. We can better appreciate the Quaker achievement when we consider their large Southern membership at that time.

With the opening of the Old Northwest, the Southern Quakers began migrating on a large scale. Indeed, some historic Virginia and North Carolina meetings lost so many members that they were "laid down." Several groups moved as organized meetings to Ohio and Indiana, among them the Trent River (North Carolina) Monthly Meeting which had early interested others in going to Ohio and the Bush River (South Carolina) Monthly Meeting. Eastern Quakers, however, migrated to the West not because of slavery but to find new land and perhaps to seek greater freedom and opportunities.

The *Discipline* demanded that the Quakers have no slaves, that they avoid becoming executors of estates with slaves, and that they consider how they could most effectively work to abolish slavery and to aid the Negroes around them. Periodically, most monthly, quarterly, and yearly meetings petitioned the state legislatures and Congress to end slavery and helped Negroes in some practical manner. Minutes of the Indiana Yearly Meeting typically included queries and answers on bearing testimony against slavery and its evils.

In addition, the Indiana Meeting had an active committee on "People of Color," which in 1824 reported recovering a boy kidnapped in Brown County and taken to Kentucky. An investigation was also under way on other kidnappings. The Indiana Friends were assisting the North Carolina Negroes who had settled in Brown County in virtual wilderness. Slavery left its victims not only impoverished but also in ignorance. Fortunately, against great difficulties, continued the report, these Negro immigrants had "established a character for honesty, and industry," and through diligence had generally become self-sustaining. Nevertheless, they, and above all their children, needed education. The committee appealed for more active Quaker support and additional funds for schools.

In 1826, the committee assisted the Negroes in the Blue River area and commented on the schools opened for Negroes in Brown County. The North Carolina Friends asked the Indiana Meeting for aid to free Negroes who wished to move to the North. The report reminded the Indiana Quakers that they must not let worldly prejudices deter them from helping these migrants to go where they wanted. The attention of the members was called to the discriminatory Ohio laws under which Negroes had to post bond for maintenance and good behavior and under which white employers of Negroes who did not comply were liable to fines. The act was disastrous for the over two thousand Cincinnati Negroes; in desperation many plunged into the wilderness bound for Canada. The Quakers protested to the Ohio legislature and asked it to repeal the law, while the Committee on "People of Color" appealed to the public for relief funds. The Indiana Yearly Meeting was affected by Ohio legislation, since its jurisdiction extended to the western Ohio Meetings.

Each year the minutes of the Meeting reported on similar activities. The committee reminded the 1831 Meeting that the Indiana law also required Negroes to post bond as security for good behavior and maintenance. Otherwise, they were forcibly "hired out," auctioned for six months at the "best price," or expelled from the state. As in Ohio, whites employing unbonded Negroes were subject to fine. The Meeting on Sufferings was asked to petition the Indiana legislature to repeal this law and to invite the Ohio Yearly Meeting jointly to request the Ohio legislature to revoke the Ohio act. It also appealed to the federal government to abolish slavery.

The Indiana Meeting published an Epistle on slavery in 1836 and with it a message from the London Yearly Meeting supporting abolition. Friends had a positive duty to strive actively to end slavery and to give the slaves equal citizenship. The Quakers were not to participate in allegedly emancipationist organizations which in reality were attempting to expatriate the former slaves.

This warning against the so-called colonization societies revealed an early Quaker insight into the problem. Within several years the abolitionists in general came to consider these agencies, among them the American Colonization Society, designed to free and settle the slaves in Africa, as actually obstructing abolition. The emancipationists and such foreign observers as Harriet Martineau felt that slaveholders supported the Colonization Society primarily to eliminate the free Negroes from their midst.

The Indiana committee again reminded its members in 1837 to stand up firmly and quietly for abolition and not let persecution deter them from their testimony. Each had to find the best way to use his own talents to secure universal emancipation. The committee issued 20,000 copies of an address on slavery for national circulation among those "who profess the Christian religion." [7] The address began by stating that as pacifists, Friends could not condone violence for any ends however good, but for some years they, "as a religious society, have, both by example and precept, borne testimony against slavery."

They bore this testimony on "religious grounds" and on this principle continued to bear it. It was impossible to avoid having dire forebodings over slavery, the address asserted, when the very nation founded on the premise that all men "are created equal" upheld such cruelty as slavery. Some Americans wanted to suppress even the appeals for the slaves and to bar any discussion on slavery which was a "violation of the laws of God, and an outrage on the most sacred rights of man." The churches had a direct responsibility to face this issue, the address declared. It then turned to the slaveowners to express solicitude for their "present and everlasting" welfare. The Friends were concerned lest the slaveholders confer with the "flesh" and lose the "heavenly vision" and come under the "condemnation of that servant who knew his master's will but did it not."

The 1837 Meeting also petitioned Congress not to admit Texas to the Union since the step was intended to spread and perpetuate slavery and was therefore contrary to all Christian doctrines of good will. The 1838 committee report deplored as erroneous the widespread belief that Negroes were incapable of enjoying natural liberties or that they required long periods of training to live in society or that they had to be expatriated. As members of a Christian community, Friends were to reject discrimination against any people for all were equally God's creations and equally the objects of His redeeming love. The significance of the religious basis for the Quaker appeals for the slaves and the Indians will become clearer in the later chapters. Some popular denominations which openly claimed that they were morally superior to other churches ignored these problems by considering them as secular issues of little or no concern to "pure" religion.

This summary has not referred to the work of many individual Friends or by Quaker antislavery organizations not officially a part of the Indiana Yearly Meeting. Benjamin Lundy and Benjamin Hanna, grandfather of Mark Hanna, were among the outstanding agents of the abolitionist cause. Levi Coffin of Fountain City, a former North Carolinian often known as the "President of the Underground Railroad," is estimated to have saved between 3,000 and 3,500 slaves fleeing from the South via its routes and stations. Behind every notable leader stood tens or more of unknown but dedicated individuals who made the Underground Railroad possible and supported the various movements. Yet even this interest did not imply Quaker unanimity on any specific plan or program. Many conservatives were reluctant to associate with actual abolitionist societies, some organizations being regarded as too violent and hence not consistent with Quaker ideals. Though persistently promoting abolition, the Friends felt it was important to refrain from hating the slaveowners and instead to consider their spiritual welfare. The Indiana Yearly Meeting on the whole was extremely conservative, and for a time a group advocating more vigorous measures separated from the Yearly Meeting.

The attitudes of the Quakers toward the Indian and the Negro have been stressed here primarily to illustrate their disciplinary requirements of an ethical nature. The Friends had many other characteristic ethical and disciplinary practices, such as their traditional testimony against militarism and war and hence also their refusal to serve in the militia or to pay muster fines in Indiana, their equal treatment of both sexes, and their attempt to provide universal education for their children. The various Quaker concerns reveal their unique heritage, while their organization made possible their strong discipline. At this point, a brief review of their background will help us to understand the Society and its role in America more clearly.[8]

The founder of Quakerism, George Fox (1624–91), and the seventeenth-century Friends belonged to the "most protestant phase of Protestantism" and essentially believed in the priesthood of each believer. God ministers directly to every person willing to wait in humble and patient expectancy. His Spirit, like an infinite ocean of life and love, can overflow and swallow the sea of human sinfulness and despair. Even in this life, many may be delivered by the Spirit from the power of sin and may enter the state of Adam before the Fall. Each person is responsible directly to God and through His Spirit receives light. At the same time, however, he must check his message with the insights of his meeting. The Quakers were unique, not in their theory of the Inner Light, but in trusting it in all men as a sufficient basis for reconstructing all life. To them the Scriptures were not a substitute for the personal knowledge of God but a guide to that knowledge.

For all their apparent individualism, declares Elbert Russell, a Quaker historian, the Friends conceived of their mysticism as social both in worship and in work. To some extent Friends intuitively realized that knowing was a social process, that truth was not a fixed datum but grew through experience and insight. To a more limited extent, it was understood that the quality of a society and the nature of its people mutually influenced each other. Their denominational growth reflected the Quaker belief that the deepest knowledge of the divine was based at least partly on social experience. The Friends felt that in group worship they perceived the Inner Light most clearly and that group experience more fully revealed the will of God. The common judgment served as a standard for the individual views. Furthermore, the Quakers were concerned not only with an individual's own spiritual state but also with the welfare and salvation of others. On the frontier, Friends emphasized corporate worship and maintained mid-week as well as Sunday meetings.

George Fox and his Quaker generation set for themselves the revolutionary task of completely reshaping the "half-pagan" seventeenth-century society. Not the least of their objectives was to eliminate all discrimination based on sex, race, and other invidious distinctions. As a consequence, from the first at least in theory and to a high degree in practice Quaker women enjoyed equality of rights and duties and also suffering. Beginning with Margaret Fell Fox, the wife of George Fox, women have taken a leading part in the movement and all its manifestations, in contrast to their subordinate role in other denominations.

The Friends had lost their great crusading spirit long before they began their western migration. The late eighteenth-century custom of printing their *Discipline* apparently strengthened their rigid discipline, certain peculiarities of language and dress mistakenly regarded as Quaker from the first, and formal membership which in turn led to expulsion of members for marrying non-Quakers. Another sign of this increasing emphasis on discipline and the marked decline in missionary zeal was the greater absorption with philanthropy and specific reforms rather than with evangelization and propagation of basic beliefs.

Most Friends regarded the Yearly Meeting as their unit of authority. Its jurisdiction generally extended over a large enough geographical area to incorporate a substantial membership. During the years covered by this study, the Indiana and Ohio Yearly Meetings included most of the Old Northwest. Every member belonged to a Yearly Meeting, which was not a delegated assembly. Delegates came to it from its constituent Quarterly Meetings mainly to assure adequate representation from each Quarterly Meeting, although the nomination of the officers and similar organizational business fell primarily on the representatives.

The Friends had no president. The clerk combined to a limited extent the role of the chairman and secretary whenever necessary, but actually he was not a presiding officer. The Quakers did not conduct their meetings according to parliamentary rules but on a more inclusive principle of integration. They sought the guidance of the Inner Light even in their business meetings. As far as possible they took new steps only with virtual unanimity or a

consensus, since thoughtful minority opinions merited consideration. This procedure tended to be time-consuming and to make
the meetings conservative, but it also enabled them to incorporate
the creative ideas of those individuals who were more perceptive
than the majority. The Quaker way, it was felt, implied self-
control and sensitivity to the Inner Light, not vain assertion of
the ego. On the other hand, if an individual had a valid concern,
though he was alone at first, he could with patience and humility
win over the whole Society as John Woolman did in his crusade
against slavery.

Each Yearly Meeting was essentially independent of the others
in faith and practice and had its own *Discipline*, which could
differ in some details from others. Yet on the whole, all Friends
maintained a remarkable unity without having an official creed
or established dogmas. It was to the itinerant ministers, those exceptional men and women, that Rufus Jones gave credit for this
unity. In recent years, of course, the Yearly Meetings grouped under the Five Years' Meeting have uniform practices and common
discipline. The various Yearly Meetings have developed increasing contacts through welfare and missionary organizations, delegated advisory conferences, formal letters, and visits of ministers
and members from one Yearly Meeting to others.

The Yearly Meeting had supervision over the Quarterly Meetings within its bounds. Every member within the Quarterly
Meeting jurisdiction could participate in its business, and delegates were sent by the Monthly Meetings primarily to assure full
representation. The activities at the Quarterly Meeting approxi-
mated those at the Yearly Meetings. For the individual members
the Monthly Meeting was usually the chief executive authority
subject to the appeals to the Quarterly and Yearly Meetings. In
reality the superior meetings seldom intervened in the actions of
a Monthly Meeting conducted in conformity with the accepted
procedures. It exercised direct overseeing of the membership
through its officers and committees. In many places, subordinate
to the Monthly Meetings were one or more Preparative Meetings,
but even for those belonging to a Preparative Meeting the
Monthly Meeting was the executive authority.

The regular officers were the elders and overseers. The elders were responsible for encouraging and counseling the ministers and for a "Christian care" over the membership. The overseers served as a committee to receive applicants for membership before they were presented to the Monthly Meeting and were to be on the alert to the needs of any member for spiritual or temporal aid. In addition, they admonished offenders and endeavored to restore them, and if unsuccessful in this effort, they referred the deviants to the Monthly Meeting for subsequent action. In some localities, the overseers held the meeting house property. They also prepared at stated times during the year the answers to certain questions — "Queries" — as required by the *Discipline*. It is essential to note that these officers were laymen and in no sense did they constitute separate religious orders.

The official organization was complete without ministers, notwithstanding their great importance to the denomination. No formal provision existed for training ministers in seminaries and colleges. In theory, the Friends recognized any man or woman who displayed suitable gifts as a recommended, recorded, or acknowledged minister. These ministers were not ordained and they continued their regular occupations. When ministerial duties took them away from home or required excessive time, however, their needs were generally supplied although no salaries were paid. If the minister could be regarded as an officer, he was the only officer (except in the Philadelphia Yearly Meeting) whose position was not affected by changes in residence beyond the bounds of the Monthly Meetings.

The arrangements for ministerial travel were unique to the Society. When a minister felt a call to go to a more or less distant place to do some religious work, he asked his Monthly Meeting for permission. If he expected to be engaged more extensively, he had to secure the consent of the Quarterly Meeting. For overseas activities, his certificate had to include the sanction of the Yearly Meeting of Ministry and Oversight and in later years the approval of the Yearly Meeting as a whole. The *Discipline* provided for a committee to meet the travelers' pecuniary needs while they were engaged in their duties. According to Rufus Jones, these itinerant ministers were the makers and builders of the denomination during the late eighteenth and the early nineteenth centuries. The minutes of the western frontier meetings frequently mention the visits by various Friends from other parts of the country and from overseas. The comments thus far on the Society and its discipline explain why Rufus Jones regarded Quakerism in many ways as "a unique form of democratic organization" which gave the widest latitude for individual freedom and yet was made "peculiarly safe and conservative by the restraints of corporate action, group custom and accumulated habit."

Many western Friends were not only frontiersmen but children and grandchildren of pioneers and had been influenced by their rough environment and the prevailing interest in land and more land. Nevertheless, the western Quaker discipline and concerns emphasize their strong unity. The denomination was not a mere aggregation of discrete individuals. Isolated individuals do not develop consistent group policies at variance with the beliefs of the society at large and cannot build disciplined purposeful group action, such as the Quaker aid to the Indians and Negroes — views and activities bound to incur unpopularity, if not actual persecution. In their testimony and continuous work for the Indians and Negroes, the western Friends had the encouragement and the official support of their fellow Quakers in England, Ireland, and the eastern seaboard. These links and the ceaseless movements by their members and ministers traveling and preaching in other Yearly and local Meetings helped the western Friends to be more aware of the world than were the more isolated sects. Their fraternal ties as well as their discipline revealed their community-mindedness and embodied the opening statement in their *Discipline* that the Friends were agreed to meet together not only for the "worship of God, but also for the exercise of a Christian care over each other, for the preservation of all in unity of faith and practice." Their organization and early leadership in many significant social issues help to explain why the Quakers were able to exert far greater influence on society than their numbers might imply.

PART II

POPULAR DENOMINATIONS AND EDUCATION
IN THE WEST

CHAPTER VII

The Historical Background

Many studies of American history have considered early Calvinism and Dissent together, but churchly Calvinism differed fundamentally from sectarian Dissent. For historic Calvinism, as Troeltsch observes, the basis of the religious system and the agency for mediating salvation was the Church, which was founded on the Bible and identified with the Primitive Church. The Calvinists stressed the catholicity of this Church wherever the sacraments, regarded as the objective divine means of grace, and the divine Word have been maintained, even under the "veil of error and false ceremonies." The ministry was the instrument bearing the churchly power, which was independent of the personal quality of the individual ministers. Calvin himself remarked, "I know full well, thank God, that the true efficacy of the Sacraments does not depend upon the worthiness of him who dispenses it." These views on the objective reality of the Church, the sacraments, and the ministry were churchly, not sectarian. Indeed, as befits its essentially aristocratic outlook and its doubts about the masses, early Calvinism had almost no place for the laity as such in its church leadership, aside from the elders, who after their election were formally set apart from others with life tenure. It did not consider laymen as such suitable for office. Such a churchly view was obviously removed from the Virginia Baptist charges that the Anglican communion was worthless because of the alleged moral defects of its ministry and membership, and far from the Baptist emphasis on lay leadership and hostility to a professional clergy.[1]

Calvinism and early Dissent also disagreed sharply in their concepts of the "world" and the state. The systematic asceticism which medieval Catholicism had reserved for the monastery Calvinism brought into secular life. The fundamental other-worldly orientation of the monastery remained, but now the faithful were to fulfil their religious duties not by withdrawing from the world but by living a disciplined, almost monastic life in the secular society, by conquering the world and shaping it to divine ends. Everyone, saved or damned, was to glorify God by devoting his whole life to a this-worldly calling in systematic, rational, and sanctified work. Labor, long regarded by Christans as both a result of sin and a valuable moral discipline, became as well the supreme means of service to God. While good works and unceasing industry did not at all assure salvation, which was predestined since the beginning of time, the predestined saint would obviously show zeal, uncomplaining fortitude, and faith. A good tree bore good fruit.[2]

Various scholars have traced in Calvinism the emergence of a dynamic approach to this secular calling, a momentous change indeed from the traditional insistence on humbly accepting the lot in which one found oneself. Calvinists began to demand as a moral imperative not merely faithful devotion to duty but also a continuing search for greater service to God. All had responsibility for improving their skills, for excelling, and for overcoming obstacles, since meek resignation to adverse circumstances could indicate sinful sloth or spiritual weakness. Faith and will were everything, circumstances nothing. Every spontaneous impulse, every fleshly desire, was subordinated to effectiveness in the calling. Any concession to the body as such could be spiritually perilous, though austerity was rationally restricted by the necessity for maintaining health and efficiency. The rising small entrepreneurs, the master craftsmen, and the skilled artisans were motivated to face hardships, to work more effectively, to enlarge their opportunities, and to reinvest a substantial share of their income by curtailing personal expenditures to the minimum. The danger of prosperity did not ultimately lie in prosperity itself, but in the temptations associated with it to indulge in sensuous living and to be distracted from the calling. The emphasis was not on greed, which was always sinful, but on rational conduct and devoted labor in the calling. Prosperity per se, however, came to be regarded later in the seventeenth century almost as a sign of divine grace.

Unlike the later capitalistic theory, earlier Calvinism did not intend all this labor and profit only for personal benefit, but also for community welfare. Calvin insisted that all financial transactions must be consistent with the well-being of the commonwealth as a whole. Surplus wealth was to be used for publicly useful work and philanthropy. Perhaps the clearest illustration of this sixteenth-century view was that Geneva, a little city of 13,000, generously received and supported some 6,000 refugees.[3] In the seventeenth century came an increasing stress on the individualistic aspects of Calvinism, while its corporate emphasis began to recede into the background. Troeltsch regards this individualistic outlook as a significant distinction between the earlier Genevan Calvinism and the later English Puritanism. One may observe Calvinistic social ideals changing into that "self-righteous" piety which looked on material prosperity as the "Divine reward of Orthodoxy."

Early Calvinism, then, was communal in outlook and sought to regulate the entire society according to supernatural revelation. Theocracy was naturally its ideal polity. The state had a duty to maintain true religion and to promote peace and prosperity, while the independent church worked in its own domain and cooperated with the state in common obedience to the Word of God. Calvinism, as well as Lutheranism, attempted to suppress the Anabaptists and other sectarian groups, often with violence and cruelty, precisely because early Calvinists and Lutherans were opposed to the sectarian withdrawal into small pietistic groups which held aloof from the world and objected to compulsion in religion. Believing in conformity, Calvinism could not tolerate heresies, and even in the seventeenth and eighteenth centuries the Calvinistic Puritan colonies in New England upheld the idea that the state had a duty to support religion. The efforts of Kentucky Presbyterians to extend their influence over the entire state and to assume prerogatives of an establishment reflected, however faintly, this theocratic heritage.

Calvinism never entirely lost its aristocratic sense, but it became more democratic. One influence was the Calvinists' own concept of equality before God, notwithstanding Calvinist insistence that people differ in their spiritual natures. This equality was not merely a spiritual consolation temporarily lifting individuals out of their misery while leaving society unchanged. It was associated with the living spirit of the church fellowship and Calvinistic individualism, as well as with the Calvinistic emphasis on conquering and reforming the world. Momentous, too, were the appeals by Calvin and his generation of leaders to the public to influence the social aims of the Genevan government when the officials seemed slow to follow their suggestions, although at first these appeals went not to the ordinary people but to those supposedly in position to represent their interests — the lower magistrates and the professional groups.[4]

Culturally, Calvin was a classical humanist. His seeming artistic insensitivity did not necessarily denote hostility to the arts. He strove tirelessly to make Geneva an outstanding intellectual center of Europe and presented to the Council the leading scholars he was able to attract to the city. Even when hostile forces were actually besieging Geneva, Calvin still devoted thought and energy to improving the university. As a consequence, the Genevan schools attracted almost as many people as were driven there by persecution. In short, Calvinism did not place cultural interests in opposition to asceticism and devotion to a calling. It objected to distractions from its main spiritual aims, but assumed the continuation of the European intellectual and artistic life. Scholarly and intellectual pursuits were esteemed callings. To illustrate another aspect of Calvinism, we might note that one day John Knox found "Calvin playing bowls with a quiet conscience." Perhaps Knox should have pondered further over this encounter before returning to Scotland. Good Calvinists enjoyed many forms of recreation and sports, those which "served to refresh both body and mind," and were scarcely the joyless people of modern popular imagination.[5]

It was not the Old World state churches, however, but Ulster Presbyterianism which had the most direct influence on early nineteenth-century American Presbyterianism, especially in the West. Far from being a state church, Presbyterianism in Ulster had been under proscription and had to compete with the Anglican Establishment and the Roman Catholic Church. These historical factors, along with the initial migration of its members from the Scottish cultural centers to Ulster and the resultant cultural isolation, hardships, and voluntary membership, had accentuated the sectarian tendencies in the Ulster church. Compared with the earlier Huguenot settlers in America, frontier Presbyterians were deficient in humanistic and aesthetic culture. The French Calvinists often had artistic and musical backgrounds which helped to enrich the cultural life in the American colonies. The further migration of the Ulsterites to America and again on the moving frontier, the primitive conditions, and the prolonged cultural deprivation strengthened the sectarian traits in American Presbyterianism, which became far less a tradition for the mystics, poets, and artists than a vigorous faith for the rising frontier elite and the later captains of industry.[6]

Calvinism and sectarianism influenced each other and helped to create that ascetic Protestantism which Troeltsch considers one of the two main types of Protestantism. Nevertheless, in the Old World, the two traditions at first differed markedly. The spiritual ancestors of the Dissenters came closer than the great state churches to the extreme position implied but not carried out by Luther. Many advocated the priesthood of all believers; they were the radicals of the Reformation and the English Revolution who ranged from socio-economic radicals such as the Diggers and the Levellers to the essentially pietistic or mystical sects. In contrast to some earlier accounts which neglected the later influence of the sects, several recent studies have stressed the subsequent impact of sectarian organization and discipline. To Dissenting groups the church was a purely voluntary association of true believers seeking inward perfection and Christian fellowship, not an objective institution endowed with sacramental power.[7]

In this tradition, personal experience and inner light under biblical guidance were the ultimate judges of religion and morals. Historic continuity, patristic tradition, and churchly heritage meant little to Dissent, which at first refused to celebrate Christian holidays, even Christmas. Some Dissenters carried their opposition to the established church to the point of secularizing marriage and burial. No special building was necessary for their worship; any convenient place served. The Dissenters were indifferent or hostile to formal liturgy and ceremonialism. To them the sacraments were mere symbols. Baptism was the "symbol and seal of faith" to the faithful and communion merely a memorial ordinance renewing the believer's covenant. As intimate lay fellowships, Dissent had no truly professional priesthood. In Rhode Island the seventeenth-century Baptists paid little attention to whether or not their leaders administering the ordinances were ordained. Instead, lay activities had free rein. The Methodists had ordained itinerants, but dedicated laymen without any professional training could readily become circuit riders. The Quakers had only lay ministers.[8]

Far from seeking to dominate society as the Calvinists did, the Old World sectarians often attempted to withdraw from the "sinful world" (aside from radicals like the English Diggers who wanted to found a new divine kingdom on earth.) Seventeenth-century Rhode Island boldly separated church and state and barred magistrates from asking the citizens about their religious views. For the Calvinistic Puritan in the Massachusetts Bay Colony, his own pure church represented the state's highest obligation, and suppression of deviation was a necessity. Roger Williams and the Rhode Island Baptists believed that the interests of the state and the church could not overlap. The nineteenth-century Baptists admired and supported Jefferson and Madison for placing Christianity, in common with all other religions, outside state responsibility.[9]

In America most sects retained only the principle of voluntary disciplined membership and accepted the system of secular calling from Calvinism. By the late eighteenth century, except among some Friends, the Dissenting concept of the calling included participation in civic and political life, but the Dissenters remained indifferent or hostile to many intellectual and artistic interests until well past the mid-nineteenth century. The Dissenting denominations, as we have seen, also succeeded in maintaining their discipline, fellowship, and essentially lay ministry at least through the 1840's. Even if at first they defined the calling more narrowly than had the Old World Calvinists, the Methodists, Baptists, and many Quakers had become, through their calling, active participants in the economic and civic life of the western society, while retaining these sectarian practices and attitudes. The popular denominations (other than the Friends) also sought converts and grew rapidly. In short, they had rejected to a marked extent the sectarian concept of withdrawing from the world and increasingly, like the Calvinists, helped to shape the secular society and its cultural outlook.

To take into account these developments, a number of social scientists have attempted to modify the Troeltsch typologies of sect and church or to formulate others which would be more broadly applicable, at least to both American and European situations. Some of these newer definitions in turn are limited. For example, the concept of sects as essentially unstable, one-generation organizations which evolve into denominations as they begin to admit the children of members may be applicable to most of the Dissenting groups in their early years, but does not fit the sects which have remained sects over several generations. For the present study thus far, the Troeltsch concepts have proved useful in distinguishing between sectarian and churchly traits. It should be noted, however, that for some purposes the typologies have serious limitations, particularly when applied to the American scene, since this country has no church in the historic Old World meaning used by Troeltsch, and many of its once Dissenting sects accepted the ideal of the calling. Benton Johnson has suggested that a useful criterion for distinguishing sects and churches is the degree to which they accept their social environment. Essentially, churches accept and sects reject the larger society. It would be difficult, however, to evaluate the variables to determine the degree of the popular denominational acceptance of their secular environment, since they continued to be suspicious of the arts and some intellectual interests and maintained discipline and lay leadership, even while they encouraged their members in their calling and participation in civic life. Research has also shown that members of some denominations and churches may have beliefs and practices which vary from churchly to almost sectarian and which are substantially correlated with the levels of education and the social and economic statuses of the members. Church members as a whole, of course, have more churchly beliefs than sect members. In short, for examining denominational traits, we shall need care to use concepts helpful for analysis.[10]

CHAPTER VIII

Attitudes toward Ministerial Education

THE PRESBYTERIANS

One clue to the attitude of a denomination toward learning may be found in its educational requirements for ministerial candidates. The Presbyterians were perhaps the leading religious exponents of education in the early American West. They attempted to maintain high educational qualifications for their clergy in spite of the shortage of ministers in the West. This lack was one reason for slow denominational growth. The church, it was said with some exaggeration, insisted on the same standards for its prospective pastors on the frontier as in the eastern cities — that the candidates first be "gentlemen." Of the 250 ministers ordained between 1758 and 1789, Princeton had trained 120, Yale 20, and the remainder were graduated by other colleges. The first four Presbyterian clergymen west of the Alleghenies, John McMillan, Thaddeus Dod, James Power, and Joseph Smith, were Princeton graduates; they all founded schools, some of which later became colleges. One-fourth of the Kentucky ministers and probationers as late as 1824 came from Princeton.[1]

Actually, many western ministerial candidates did not have college degrees but had studied at school and also under a well-trained clergyman. The Presbyteries examined the candidates to see if they had qualifications roughly equivalent to a college degree. The following extracts from the minutes of the Transylvania Presbytery illustrate the course of an examination:

[PAINT LICK CHURCH, April 2, 1824]

Pby. proceeded to the examination of Mr Holeman as to his acquaint-
ance with experimental religion & his views to the gospel ministry which
was unanimously sustained. . . . Pby. then proceeded to examine Mr
Holeman on the Greek & Latin languages, which was unanimously sustained. . . .

Dr. Reid's, Saturday morning, 8 o'clock. . . . Pby. further proceeded
to the examination of Mr Holeman as to his knowledge of Rhetoric,
Logic, Natural Philosophy, Philosophy of Mind, Geography & Astron-
omy, all which were sustained unanimously as parts of trial. Pby. then
assigned Mr Holeman as further subject of trial a Latin exegesis on the
following words. An sit Christus vere Deus & a critical exercise on Heb.
VI. 4–8, inclusive, to be read at the next stated sessions of pby.[2]

These trials often continued several years. In the meantime, the
candidate carried on his studies, usually guided by the better-
trained ministers.

Connecticut Missionary Society and other New England organizations helped to support Presbyterian ministers in parts of
the West. According to one report to the Society, the Presbyterian
ministers in the Western Reserve whom the Society had assisted
were often less well-educated than the New England Congregational clergy, but still, were qualified for western service.[3] In the
eastern seaboard colonies before the Revolution, their Scottish
common-sense heritage, as well as their Calvinism, encouraged
the Presbyterian clergy to accept the cultural principles of the Enlightenment. While the Scottish common sense philosophy was
not widespread even on the seaboard until John Witherspoon
arrived at Princeton in 1768, Lord Kames and Hutcheson had been
known for at least a decade. According to Ralph Barton Perry,
in his inquiry into Puritanism and democracy, Thomas Jefferson's interest in Lord Kames and his acceptance of Dugald Stewart's ethical teachings suggest the relative ease of assimilating
both Scottish realism and the philosophy of the Enlightenment.[4]

A look at two extreme cases may help to make clear the importance of the orthodox Presbyterian educational requirements
for the ministry. The first example illustrates the impact of the
Enlightenment on an able New York Presbyterian minister, Sam-

uel Miller. In 1803 this young minister, one of the three associated in the collegiate pastorate of Wall Street, Brick, and Rutgers Street Presbyterian Churches, published a two-volume study rather inappropriately entitled *Brief Retrospect of the Eighteenth Century*. In it he reflected on the previous century and agreed with Voltaire and Gibbon in calling it the Age of Enlightenment. As Ralph Gabriel notes, hardly anything written by Thomas Jefferson or Benjamin Franklin surpassed the eloquence of Samuel Miller as he reviewed that Age:

At the close of the seventeenth century, the stupendous mind of Newton, and the penetrating genius of Locke, had laid their systems of *matter* and of *mind* before the world. . . . With cautious, but firm and dauntless steps, they made their way to the entrenchments of fortified error; they scaled her walls; forced her confident and blustering champions to retreat; and planted the standard of truth, where the banner of ignorance and falsehood had so long waved.[5]

The second instance is not of a Presbyterian but of an outsider, the Reverend Mr. George Willits, a "mountain boy" of zeal and ability, who was ordained by the Cumberland Presbyterians despite his lack of formal education. During one of his rare free hours, James Finley (the Methodist presiding elder mentioned earlier) was collecting some botanical specimens in the woods when Willits chanced to see him. Finley had studied at a secondary school taught by his own father, a Princeton-trained Presbyterian minister who later became a Methodist. Since his activities obviously puzzled Willits, Finley tried to tell him what he was doing. Willits then asked Finley if such labor served to glorify God. When Finley told him that many prominent ministers regarded the study of nature as the "study of the first revelation of God," Willits was impressed, "hackneyed" as the explanation was, added Finley.[6]

Samuel Miller and George Willits both contributed greatly to their denominations and country, but their intellectual outlooks could hardly have differed more. This contrast partly explains why the orthodox Presbyterians tenaciously retained their educational qualifications for the ministry. Once the Cumberland Presbyterians (after separating from the regular Presbyterians) had modified the traditional educational requirements, western needs and Dissenting attitudes soon led them to ordain men without formal schooling. On the other hand, later in the nineteenth century, the Presbyterian insistence on trained clergy encouraged the popular denominations in the West to raise their ministerial standards, a major Presbyterian contribution to the development of western culture. One reason for the relatively high Presbyterian standards was, as noted before, the historic churchly concept of the clergy as a professional group set apart from the laity, in contrast to the Dissenting emphasis on lay ministry. In addition, Presbyterian membership as a whole was better educated.[7]

THE BAPTISTS

The great anti-education and anti-mission movement within the western Baptist ranks disrupted the denomination for more than two decades during the first half of the nineteenth century (see chap. xi). The 1853 *Baptist Almanac* estimated that in 1823 only about 100 (and hardly any in the West) of the 2,000 Baptist ministers had been "liberally educated," but by 1853 between 1,000 and 2,000 among the 7,000 had enjoyed liberal education. In the 1830's, Drs. Cox and Hoby, the British Baptist delegates to America, found a growing interest in ministerial education in several regions, including Virginia, where some Baptist leaders were developing an educational program for preachers without previous training.[8] The Virginia Baptist migrants to the West had left the Old Dominion some years before the denominational outlook in the state had begun to change and had carried with them the old hostility at its emotional peak. The Virginia and Kentucky Baptists moving to Ohio, Indiana, and Illinois spread this prejudice against learning to the Old Northwest. The western Baptist preachers had but limited education, and aside from the Bible and hymnbooks, usually had no access to books, much less to libraries. Only the most fortunate saw religious journals now and then.[9]

Brief quotations from two noted Baptist leaders opposed to formal ministerial education will summarize their views. As spokesman for the anti-education and anti-mission movements, they obviously represented the more extreme views. The following comment by Daniel Parker of Illinois is typical:

> Christ, when he was about to send out preachers, he called them, whether they had learning or not, and gives us no account that a Seminary of learning was essential to the ministry.[10]

Alexander Campbell was another anti-mission leader. While still a Baptist, he characteristically criticized an American Education Society statement designed to show the need of education:

> The scheme of a learned priesthood chiefly composed of beneficiaries, has long since proved itself to be a grand device to keep men in ignorance and bondage; a scheme by means of which the people have been shrewdly taught to put out their own eyes, to fetter their own feet, and to bind the yoke upon their own necks.[11]

Campbell never hesitated to appeal directly to western Baptist prejudices. Would knowing stories of ancient revels and debaucheries, fables, and wars, included in college classics courses, help gospel preaching he asked. All who proposed to teach religion for "hire" and their "contemptible artifices" for raising money among westerners were denounced. Professional training could only produce in a man "a sanctimonious air, a holy gloom . . . a pious sedateness . . . a kind of angelic demeanor in his gait, and a seraphic sweetness in all his movements." This suggestion of collegiate effeminacy was effective with the rough westerners. Later in his career, Campbell withdrew from the Baptists, favored missions, lectured at a Bible college, and raised money for schools, for after all he was a university graduate![12]

The ignorance of most western Baptist ministers shocked such Baptist missionaries to the West as John Mason Peck. Although not a college man himself, this Connecticut Yankee did have common schooling and had made considerable sacrifice to study for a time under a noted Philadelphia pastor. To give the western Baptist ministerial candidates "practical English education," he proposed an academy at Rock Spring, Illinois, only to be met with violent hostility and declarations of "non-fellowship" by churches and associations. This was also the period in which numerous

Baptist ministers were engaged in bitter controversies, many, according to Peck, arising from their illiteracy and inability to distinguish between literal and figurative meaning of words. A good dictionary, a little background in the meaning of words and of figures of speech, and some elementary training in rhetoric, logic, and "mental philosophy" would have greatly benefitted these preachers, concluded Peck, "but some of them were as much afraid of a dictionary as they were of a missionary." He also discovered that the very preachers most aggressive in denouncing educated ministry as an abomination and theological seminaries as devices of the devil did not hesitate to plagiarize the sermons of educated ministers whenever they could do so without detection.[13]

In brief, many western Baptists argued that it was sinful to try to educate a man called by God since He never called an unprepared person. The emotional intensity of their opposition to ministerial education arose partly from the revivalistic insistence on conversion as the only road to grace and from the traditional sectarian emphasis on lay ministry. The Baptists feared a professional priesthood. The local churches wished to retain their right freely to call and ordain men congenial to their tastes from their own ranks, a reflection of their original sectarian heritage. This opposition to theological training in itself became a virtual prerequisite among many western Baptists, as seen in the action of the Sugar Creek Association in Indiana. Its constitution provided for punishment of any church that tolerated members supporting or united with colleges, missions, and Bible and tract societies. The pro-education elements had to promote seminaries and colleges as individuals and private groups to combat the opposition. It required courage to found schools against the bitter hostility within the denomination.

THE METHODISTS

Many frontier Methodists shared Bishop Asbury's conviction about the "evil" of including philosophy and "human learning" in ministerial training. Some may think educated men have a special call to the ministry, Asbury said, "but I presume a simple man can speak and write for simple, plain people, upon simple truths." In contrast to Wesley, who appointed un-schooled persons only because he was unable to find sufficient numbers of educated men to fill the various positions, Asbury apparently preferred unlettered itinerants.[14]

The *Discipline* called for five hours daily of reading and study-ing, and in Section XVIII, gave further advice on ministerial studies. Notwithstanding these references to studies, in reality the itinerants seldom had the opportunity to read on the long arduous western circuits. They were either attending to the pastoral duties or traveling to their next appointments. The partial escape from the demand for regular reading was in Section XXV of the *Dis-cipline*. Preachers were to reprimand all evil even if some feared that in enforcing this disciplinary rule, they would lose much time and thus be deprived of the reading period. While studying was good, saving souls was better, for in this very process the cir-cuit rider would gain "the most excellent knowledge, that of God and eternity." The itinerant should have time for his studies if he limited his sleep and never was "idle or triflingly employed." Still, he was to forego all the libraries in the world rather than be responsible for the loss of a single soul. Yet each preacher was to realize that without "exactness in redeeming time," he could not retain the grace received in justification. Nevertheless, as Cartwright observed, where the itinerants were fully occupied all the time, they actually had no period for study.[15]

Brief extracts from the 1804 minutes of the historic Western Conference, which then covered all the trans-Allegheny West and was the nursery of western Methodism, will illustrate the actual situation:

The Conference proceeded to admit on trial the following persons: . . . 3rd. Cumberland Destrict: . . . 2nd, Peter Cartwright, a native of Virginia, born September the 1st, 1785, has provesed religion about 4 years, has travilled a Circuit 9 months, was well received, and came recommended from the Quarterly Meeting Conference of Wayne Cir-cuit. . . . Ohio District: . . . 2nd, Benjamin Edge, born February 27th, 1774, ... has been in the profession of religion about 3 years, is esteemed for his undoubted piety, but of contracted abilities, accom-pinied with some peculiarities, and came recommended by the Quarterly Conference of Muskingum Circuit.[16]

Peter Cartwright commented at length on his own efforts to study and on the educational background of the pioneer western itinerants. Many had little or no education, indeed, had no books and no time to study if they had had books. There was not even a "respectable common school," let alone a college, within several hundred miles. "Old *Dyke* or *Dilworth*" was their spelling book and what little they learned, Cartwright felt, they had to unlearn, and "this was the hardest work of all." Their library consisted of the pocket Bible, hymnbook, and *Discipline*. "It is true we could not, many of us, conjugate a verb or parse a sentence, and murdered the king's English almost every lick." [17]

The experience of Thomas A. Goodwin, a graduate of the Methodist Indiana Asbury University (now DePauw University) in 1848, and the first college man to join the Indiana conference, shows how long the strong prejudice against college-trained ministers persisted. By 1848, Indiana was not on the frontier, although it was still mainly rural or wooded. Methodism was already a well-established and respectable denomination to which many political, business, and social leaders belonged. Yet the presiding elders were afraid of appearing to favor a college man, so Goodwin was demoted even though his training had been at a Methodist college. Eventually he was driven from the active ministry into the editorship of an antisaloon and antislavery publication, so bitter was the hostility to college men in itineracy.[18]

Years later James Finley wrote about "strange things" heard in Zanesville:

It was rumored that two students from the Ohio University, one of whom was a son of the then Governor of Ohio, had arrived, and would preach in the Methodist Church. What was remarkable in that day was, that they were Methodist preachers. Who had heard, since the days of Wesley, of Methodist preachers coming out fresh from a college to preach the Gospel?[19]

Bishop Asbury's testament read at the 1816 General Conference re-emphasized his opposition to "man-made" ministers and his insistence on the "true call." The Conference Ways and Means Committee, however, asked the bishops or a committee appointed by them in each annual conference to set up a course of reading for the candidates. This was the first practical step taken to implement the *Discipline* on study. Although the program was limited and the examinations superficial in some conferences, it helped appreciably to improve the background of the ministerial applicants, and, moreover, it encouraged the studiously inclined to read despite the hostile opposition. Allen Wiley mentions one circuit rider who could not justify studying even grammar. Once, after this itinerant had finished exhorting, someone told him he had made fourteen grammatical errors. Since his mistakes distracted the people from his message, the itinerant decided he had better study.

In preparing this report on the reading program, the Conference Committee had in mind the increasingly serious losses of the better-educated members, including some potentially able apologists for Methodism, who were unhappy about the low value placed on education by the Methodists. Because several other denominations were vigorously criticizing the Methodists, the Conference was confronted with the need for leaders able to present the Methodist views more adequately. Besides, many members were now prominent in the state and the professions and were demanding better-trained ministers. Finally, in 1844, the General Conference authorized the bishops to prepare a uniform four-year study program applicable to the ministerial candidates in all the conferences.[20]

In the West, the most active promoters of colleges and schools were often the most vigorously opposed to theological seminaries as such. Here again Peter Cartwright is representative. He had helped to found McKendree and MacMurray Colleges, and, while a member of the Illinois Legislature, he had introduced the first bill to establish a state university; but theological training was anathema to him. As Thomas Goodwin's experience has shown, this opposition to formal theological education at times included hostility to college education for the ministry. Again typically, Cartwright expressed his antagonism to theological training in no uncertain terms. If Wesley and Asbury had waited until they had educated ministers, Methodism would have been nothing and infidelity would have swept the United States. While Calvinist churches had sought an educated, salaried ministry and sanctioned instrumental music, Cartwright continued, the Methodists had resolutely opposed these ideas and the "illiterate Methodist preachers actually set the world on fire." Of the thousands of preachers who saved souls and built up the Methodist church, not one had been "trained in a theological seminary or biblical institute" and perhaps less than fifty had anything more than the barest elementary schooling. Yet hundreds were more successful in their ministry than "all the sapient, downy D.D.'s." College education and theological training for the ministry "have proved a perfect failure." Though intellectual pride has ruined many trained ministers, some Methodists still wanted to educate the ministry, Cartwright said in alarm as he concluded:

... I would rather have the gift of a devil-dislodging power than all the college lore or Biblical institute knowledge that can be obtained from mortal man. When God wants great and learned men in the ministry, how easy it is for him to overtake a learned sinner, and, as Saul of Tarsus, shake him a while over hell, then knock the scales from his eyes, and, without any previous theological training, send him out straightway to preach Jesus and the resurrection.[21]

This opposition to a professionally trained ministry as a principle is seen in the Indiana Conference committee report endorsing the establishment of the Indiana Asbury University. The committee explicitly rejected any possibility of the institution's becoming a theological seminary. James Finley was also opposed to theological seminaries. His conclusions further reveal the Methodist sectarian hostility to theological training as such, as distinct from the growing denominational interest in liberal education. He came from an educated family, had received a good education for his time, and was ardently advocating better education. All people, he believed, should consider "improvement of the mind as the most valuable acquisition within their grasp, both for here and hereafter." In his opinion, if ever a poor man were justified in stealing, it would be to educate his children, for education raises man to "the exalted dignity of a rational being." Unlike many westerners, he was also a strong advocate of education for women.[22]

Before Finley joined the Methodists, he had asked a Presbyterian pastor about becoming a minister and was told that he would have to study theology at least three years before he could qualify. Perhaps the impatient frontiersman interpreted this friendly advice as a rebuff, and it may have strengthened his later opposition to ministerial education. Not the least of his arguments against professional training was the limited number of theologically educated men available for the ministry should Methodism ever have to rely upon them.[23]

Dependence on uneducated assistants, a necessity for John Wesley in England, had become a policy in America, particularly in the West. A letter in 1856, by Dr. John Dempster, "the father of Methodist theological education," makes vivid the vitality and emotional intensity of this antagonism to ministerial training:

For the last twelve years I have, from an overwhelming sense of duty, been occupied in an enterprise [to found theological seminaries] in the face of fierce opposition on the part of at least two-thirds of our entire ministry. Some of the highest dignitaries of the church have exerted official influence to embarrass and subvert the enterprise. Many friends of my tenderest rememberance forsook me for having allied myself to this cause, and even transferred their hostility from the cause to him who advocated it. To insure success to this persecuted enterprise I found such devotion to its interests indispensable as involved the almost total neglect of private friendships and the interchange of friendly courtesies.[24]

Significantly, it was the New England Methodists who founded the first theological school. New England was far from the centers of Methodist membership or wealth, but the region had educational standards and a tradition of having trained ministers. In 1839, a group concerned with improving the theological background of their ministerial candidates began classes in Newbury, Vermont. All three New England Conferences endorsed and supported the Biblical Institute, which later became the School of Theology at Boston University. A number of small contributions were received from persons all over the country, reflecting the growing individual approval. Naturally, most Methodist leaders elsewhere bitterly attacked it, even though they knew the founders were on the alert against the "dangers" of such a school. It was called a biblical institute in an attempt to minimize the opposition to theological seminaries. Dr. Dempster next helped to establish the Garrett Biblical Institute at Evanston, Illinois, with the financial assistance of Mrs. Eliza Garrett. Despite the existence of two biblical institutes, when the *Christian Advocate* published an article which appealed for a seminary in the middle Atlantic states, the journal was violently critized for publishing such a "dangerous" proposal. The editor hastily declared that he was merely introducing various views and assured his readers that he was absolutely opposed to the method of training ministers used by other denominations.[25]

Though one explicit reason given for the opposition to a learned ministry was that there was an acute shortage of itinerants — and this reason was supported in part by the evidence of a decrease in hostility with the lessening of pressure for additional itinerants — the great emotionalism aroused by the issue suggests that it involved basic attitudes and beliefs. Among the beliefs probably touched were: the fundamental importance of the conversion experience, the sectarian emphasis on lay leadership, the hostility to a priestly (or professional) ministry, and the deep faith that God never called an unprepared man. Perhaps it was felt intuitively that to remain a popular denomination a centralized denomination like Methodism had to maintain a free and easy democracy at the grass roots and readily accept converted men of ability into the itinerancy, whether or noth they had formal professional education. The Jacksonian exaltation of the untutored man of nature could well be a secular version of this outlook.

Ironical as it may seem, Peter Cartwright himself accepted a D.D. degree in 1842, regardless of his furious attacks on the "velvet-mouthed and downy D.D.'s." The eagerness of the early western preachers for "hollow titles" reached the point where at the 1832 General Conference some proposed a rule under which a preacher would automatically receive a D.D. degree on becoming an elder. This rather whimsical interlude emphasizes again the Methodist willingness to accept external trappings, even degrees and divinity "titles," as long as they were not construed to challenge the sectarian fundamentals, in this instance the rise of competent lay leadership or the equality of the members and the itinerancy. The acceptance of degrees also reveals the personal envy some circuit riders, even Cartwright, apparently felt toward the college-trained Congregational and Presbyterian ministers. Instead of helping the educated newcomers from the East as fellow workers, they took obvious pleasure in laughing at the initial mistakes the strangers naturally made.[26]

The Methodist flexibility in licensing and ordination was not without difficulties and some humor. William Cooper Howells tells about many Methodists being "vain" and wanting to preach. They claimed to have had a call which overcame all lack of talent, education, or intelligence, since God would put the proper words in their mouths. Besides engendering pride, "grammar and dictionary words" were hard for the poor to understand, they insisted, and "in fact, cultivated men were at discount." Quarrels arose, this Ohio pioneer noticed, because other Methodists objected to their attempts to preach.[27] In any case the similarity to the Baptist attitude is apparent, including its disadvantages. Congenial as the neighbors and relatives selected as local preachers and itinerants may have been, many would have the same limitations as fellow members and the same prejudices which prophetic religion claims to overcome. The growing demand by the socially rising membership for better-educated itinerants, however, markedly changed the situation over the next several decades.

The Friends did not have a professional ministry. Consequently they were not directly involved in the problems of professional training.

Even this brief sketch has shown the marked contrast between the Presbyterians on the one hand and the Baptists and the Methodists on the other in their attitudes toward formal, professional training for the ministry. Later in the nineteenth century the Presbyterian (and Episcopalian) insistence upon an educated ministry and also the rising economic and social status of the western Baptists and Methodists helped to change the Dissenting tradition. All the major denominations began to support colleges and theological seminaries and to encourage ministerial candidates to acquire professional training, but the original attitude long persisted among many members. Growing professionalization in the Dissenting ministry also symbolized the transformation from sects to more churchly denominations. This change, however, is still in process, and, to judge from the data on ministerial education among American Protestant clergy, it is thus far perhaps more fully realized in new attitudes than in actual standards.

CHAPTER IX

Attitudes toward Education

THE PRESBYTERIANS

Presbyterianism traditionally regarded the education of children as an inescapable religious and civic duty. Each session was to establish and assume responsibility for at least one school in a convenient place. Presbyteries also appointed committees to provide schools in vacant congregations. Whenever supplies were designated for such vacancies, they were expected to visit the schools and to report to the presbytery. Almost every western Presbyterian minister was also a teacher, a combination they deemed natural and desirable.

The Presbyterians provided far more than their proportion of the early western leadership and at first almost pre-empted the professions in several western states, partly because they dominated nearly all the frontier colleges. American colleges were generally established in frontier settlements to meet local needs. In the country at large, mainly on the successive frontiers, the Presbyterians founded forty-nine permanent colleges and helped to organize many others. Of the fourteen colleges and universities established west of the Alleghenies between 1780 and 1829, the Presbyterians founded seven and co-operated with the Congregationalists in founding another; the Episcopalians founded one; the Baptists, one; and the various states, four — all four under Presbyterian influence. In sum, the Presbyterians participated in organizing twelve of these fourteen colleges and universities and, under Philip Lindsley, helped to make Nashville an important educational center. The church became a virtual establishment as far as some state higher education was concerned and at one time

99

controlled Miami, Transylvania, Indiana, and Tennessee universities.[1]

Small sectarian colleges developed partly from the popular desire for local control, sectarian rivalries, convenience, and sheer absence of scholarly traditions. Philip Lindsley, as president of the University of Nashville, remarked in 1837 that the West had nothing approaching the European universities and wondered whether or not the "busy, restless, speculating, money-making" westerners would support such scholarly institutions if they should be established. Perhaps it was better to have many small colleges scattered throughout the West, he thought, since as a rule only young men under twenty-one years old attended colleges. Theodore Dwight Weld and Charles G. Finney, however, were able to induce men in their late twenties and thirties to enter Lane Seminary (see chapter xiv). Their success suggests that Dr. Lindsley may have been unduly pessimistic.[2]

The Congregational-Presbyterian understanding to co-operate in the West, the 1801 Plan of Union, extended to education. Lyman Beecher of Cincinnati became known in the East as a missionary to the West, much to the annoyance of the Methodists, who resented his criticisms of the western shortcomings in education and ministry and who certainly did not regard urban Cincinnati as a frontier settlement. Beecher agreed that the West would determine America's destiny. Mere prayers, charity, or colonial migrations alone would not suffice, nor would itinerant missions or distribution of Bibles and tracts. The West needed strong, permanent educational and religious institutions. A basic requisite was a learned and able ministry, for a country with such ministers "will of course be filled with schools, academies, libraries, colleges, and all the apparatus for the perpetuity of republican institutions," otherwise all too apt to be forgotten in the mad rush for wealth and power, Beecher insisted. "We must educate! We must educate! or we must perish by our own prosperity," asserted the great orator.[3]

Comment on the Presbyterians' interest in education and their pioneer role in founding and fostering colleges should not be permitted to obscure the marked deterioration in the intellectual standards of western Presbyterianism as compared with the best Presbyterianism in the East. We need only to contrast Samuel Miller of New York, his enthusiasm for the Age of Enlightenment, and his broad scientific and philosophical interests with such western Presbyterian leaders as Joshua L. Wilson of Cincinnati. Able and vigorous though the latter was, he revealed the far narrower intellectual and cultural horizon of the pioneer West.

The lower cultural level of the western Presbyterians, including the clergy, also manifested itself in bitter attacks on President Horace Holley of Transylvania University. As long as the university was virtually a Presbyterian denominational school, the cultured, religiously liberal elements in Kentucky could not realize their desire for a university able to promote literary and other cultural interests. Dr. Holley was impressed by the theaters, the painters, and the Athenaeum in Lexington. The conflict between the Presbyterians and the religious liberals centered on Dr. Holley after his election to the presidency. Should he succeed, the gayer society and culture of the gentry and the lawyers would prosper, and the "Christian society" which the Presbyterian clergy sought would never be attained. The president proved to be an able educator, and, by his vigor and his intellectual attainments, inspired a spirit of emulation in many who met him. Holley also attempted to improve the student social life and even offered to teach them proper manners. To broaden their lives he encouraged them to read novels. His students were permitted to bring their girl friends to his classes, apparently to help raise the quality of their social relations. His critics attacked all these activities as giving ministerial and academic approval to the "fashionable vices."[4]

A Yale graduate and minister, Dr. Holley accepted the Bible, broadly interpreted, as the sole standard of faith but regarded rigidly orthodox Calvinism as an obstacle to human development. Most other denominations did not find him a dangerous unbeliever. To attack him, Dr. Sonne records, the Presbyterians had to resort to distortions and falsehoods. They even accused him of salary irregularities. "It is notorious that President Holley is liberal and extravagant towards the Theatre, Ball room, Lotteries yet etc. [sic] neither he, nor his family ever contribute a cent to any charitable institution whatever," his critics said. Their statement was untrue, for Dr. Holley gave all the income from his law lectures to the university. In totaling the "extravagant" income which they accused him of receiving, the Presbyterians had included this very contribution.[5]

In Cincinnati, many Presbyterians joined with the Reverend Dr. Joshua L. Wilson in opposing the theater thereby helping to keep the city from becoming a good theater town (as were Lexington, Louisville, and Nashville with only half the population of Cincinnati). Its moralistic commercial rulers apparently saw nothing wrong, however, in conducting hangings as public spectacles before as many as 15,000 people. The crowds resented pardons which deprived them of "entertainment." At the same time, many Cincinnati citizens regarded the arts and creative scholarship as not only questionable but also sinister, for they were stepping-stones to aristocracy and anathema to religion. Pure and disinterested scholarship was but "avaricious accumulation of knowledge," a reprehensible zeal (presumably zeal should be confined to practical calling!). Presbyterian leadership was not conspicuous in expressing a more appreciative attitude. Joshua Wilson himself was opposed to the fine arts as transgressing the rule against graven images; even historical paintings were at best burlesques and at worst lies. The founders of the Cincinnati Academy of Arts faced considerable criticism, not mere indifference. A man could scarcely be an artist and not also be a blackguard. Italy exemplified the consequences of impractical education with its poor "painters, fiddlers, robbers, and lazarone," an astonishing but telling listing. It might be added that some of the pious who found the cultivation of the arts morally bad and the installation of a billiard table in the White House by President John Quincy Adams vicious — "a scandal, the abomination of desolation," Chevalier was told — never questioned the brutal treatment of the helpless Negro minority in Cincinnati and indeed supported the Ohio black codes.[6]

The very worship service of western Presbyterianism, while dignified and often intellectual, was aesthetically barren compared with Old World practices. Calvinism may not have belonged to the main liturgical tradition, but historical accidents helped to account for the virtual elimination in the West of whatever liturgical and aesthetic heritage Calvinism once had. A casual comparison with the Calvinistic church of the Huguenot migrants to America or with the Reformed Church in the Netherlands when the great Dutch school of painting was flourishing makes clear this western Presbyterian weakness. No one expects to find Rembrandts, Miltons, or Spensers in the new western cities, but Presbyterianism discouraged western cultural life more than we might expect, in view of the great Calvinist traditions. Many Scandinavian and German immigrants managed to enjoy at least some music, dances, drama, and poetry, often against popular denominational opposition, and successfully established themselves in the New World. That some community leaders classified the legitimate theater and opera with lotteries, and painters and musicians with robbers and demoralized beggars expressed a Dissenting sectarian outlook, far from the urbanity of early Calvinism.[7]

THE BAPTISTS

The western Baptists on the whole had a far more limited cultural outlook than the Presbyterians (see chap. xi). In general, Baptist initiative and support for education came more from the Baptists of New England and middle-states origin than from those with Kentucky and Virginia background even if many notable crusaders for education were of southern ancestry, as such names as Holman and Stott show. On the other hand, except for Campbell, the leadership and the rank-and-file support for the campaign against education and missions came almost entirely from former Virginians and Carolinians. The opposition was so great for several decades, notably around 1830, that even when the majority of a church or an association wanted to support educational activities, it could take no official action displeasing to the embattled anti-education elements. In Indiana some Baptists so distrusted "human learning" that they objected to having their children taught to read any book but the Bible. August, 1798, minutes of the Elkhorn Baptist Association in Kentucky records similar tendencies among some of its members.[8]

Fundamentally, Campbell was not fighting education itself, but he seemed to fear the use of educational requirements as an undemocratic device to bar competent but formally untrained men from the ministry. The less-educated settlers, however, interpreted his rather demagogic attacks as opposition to learning per se. In later years, when Campbell tried to raise money for schools, he discovered how widespread was the hostility to education in the West. Most Baptist meetings there did not dare to have even Sunday schools, for many western Baptists regarded such activities as desecrating the church. In 1831, when the Massachusetts Sunday School Union offered the Indiana Baptists $1,000 a year for two years if they would match the amount, the Indiana advocates could not raise the sum. In contrast, despite their smaller numbers, the Michigan Baptists were able to promote a variety of educational and missionary interests. The Michigan Baptists had come mainly from the middle Atlantic states and New England and had but little of the anti-mission and anti-education tradition.[9]

That some western Baptists questioned using any book but the Bible should not be too surprising when we see that in 1843 the national *Baptist Almanac* seriously featured the following story:

Doddridge's "Rise and Progress" a bar to ruin.

Mr. A——, a valuable officer in one of the churches in B——, stated at a meeting of the church to consider the expediency of establishing a *concert of reading*, that he came to that city in 1817, when a lad, and entered a store as clerk, where there were two partners. He had been religiously educated, and had a pious, praying mother. In the desk of one of the partners he found a copy of Shakespeare's works, and in that of the other the *"Rise and Progress."* He read several of the former, and had thereby a desire excited to see them acted. He had often left the store at night, and paced back and forth in front of the Federal street theatre, listening to the clapping and shouts of the multitude, and longed to enter; but his conscience and the thoughts of his mother's prayers deterred him. On other occasions he would read portions of

Doddridge, and would be led by that to the Park Street prayer-meeting. "Thus, for three months," said he, "my mind was swayed first by the influence of one book, and then of the other, my soul balancing between heaven and hell, till at last the question was decided. *Doddridge's Rise and Progress was the bar which God threw across my pathway to perdition*; and all that I am and hope to be, I owe to the Divine blessing on that precious book!" [10]

While the purpose of this story was to promote Baptist religious publications, it also perpetrated sectarian anticulturalism. As long as piety interpreted faith and cultural interests as incompatible alternatives, western Baptists as a denomination could not readily assume full leadership in educational and cultural life. Drs. Cox and Hoby, the British Baptist delegates, were aware of this outlook, but in 1836 they optimistically hoped that it would soon die out in America, since they felt that the cultivation of religion and literature was mutually beneficial: Religion "sanctifies and directs the mental culture" and literature expands the mind and "checks the excesses of enthusiasm." Drs. Cox and Hoby reported the over-all "superiority" of the New England Baptists precisely because of their better education and commended the successful efforts by the Maine Baptists, living in virtual wilderness, to establish Waterville (now Colby) College.[11]

We should also mention the Baptist Publication Society, the denominational agency for popular religious literature. It was founded in 1824, but its gross receipts for the sixteen years up to the 1839–40 fiscal year totaled only $86,048. In this period the Society printed approximately 3,342,000 tracts. The expenditure for the 1840–41 year was $11,428 and the property worth only $8,300. The editor, J. Newton Brown, deplored that these meager figures represented the "entire publication strength" of the denomination with 600,000 members and 3,000,000 attendants. Churches making systematic contributions, however small, he noted, were extremely rare. The little assistance received came from individuals, not churches. Within several years, however, the publication society was able to expand its work through the colportage system — itinerant missionary agents visiting various "desolate areas." By 1852 it had some thirty-four colporteur missionaries in the field. This slow progress by the publication agency of the then second largest denomination in the United States reflected the western anti-education and antimission movement.[12]

THE METHODISTS

John Wesley favored spreading not only specific religious knowledge, but also general "useful knowledge." He personally had widely diversified intellectual interests. He read continually such topics as physics, mathematics, philosophy, theology, drama, and poetry, and various works in Arabic, French, German, Hebrew, and Italian. In addition, he wrote 371 summaries, commentaries, and reviews of hundreds of different publications (his bibliography lists over 400 titles), and he founded a system of publishing and distributing low-cost books for mass circulation. Wesley's own writing covered such topics as theology, philosophy, poetry, grammar, medicine, and slavery.[13]

Until 1817, however, American Methodism failed in all its occasional efforts to found schools and colleges. All the schools that Bishop Asbury promoted either closed or were lost to the Methodists. Asbury sadly concluded, "People in general care too little for the education of their children." Their apathy toward his attempts to found schools was indeed discouraging to him. His attitude could scarcely be regarded as unappreciative of common schools.[14]

As we might expect, the New England Methodists founded the first permanent denominational school, Wesleyan Academy, in 1817 at Newmarket, New Hampshire. In 1825 it moved to Wilbraham, Massachusetts, its present site. While the Illinois Conference, encouraged by Peter Cartwright, agreed to found a college as early as 1827, McKendree College did not receive a charter until 1834. It was closed in 1835 and again in 1841 for five years because of insufficient funds. During that time, Wesleyan University opened in 1831, Allegheny in 1834, Indiana Asbury in 1837, and Ohio Wesleyan in 1842.[15]

The New England and New York conferences took the initiative on educational questions before the 1816 and 1820 General Conferences, and among other things requested permission for itinerants serving as school principals to stay longer than two years. A resolution was introduced in 1816 to have each annual conference establish a school under its control. Outside of New England and New York, the hostility to educational projects was still strong enough to paralyze all efforts to put the resolution into effect. The 1820 General Conference amended the *Discipline* to permit itinerants to serve as officers and teachers in colleges. Previously, the leadership had objected to circuit riders leaving the itinerancy. However, the opposition may not have been mainly to education as such but based on the shortage of trained itinerants, as one section in the 1816 General Conference Ways and Means Committee report makes clear. Many able circuit riders were forced to locate to support their families. If allowed to continue, this trend would leave only the second raters for the circuits, particularly since partial locations had also increased. The schools naturally would ask for the best-educated itinerants and would thus deprive the circuits of their essential services. By 1840 education had become so important that the conference advised the members not to object to Methodist schools calling ministers to their staffs, particularly since the number of itinerants in teaching would be small.

The increase in the number of Methodist schools after 1828 did not reflect any marked rise in the denominational interest in education. By then, the Methodist membership was rapidly expanding and the United States as a whole was improving its educational facilities. The growth of the Methodist schools did perhaps indicate weaker overt antagonism to denominational education among western Methodists. Most Methodist schools, however, survived only for a short time. Up to and including 1870, the Methodists had begun about 300 schools and colleges, but only 100 were still in existence as Methodist institutions. The others had mostly become insolvent and had closed. As late as 1861, eleven of the eighteen colleges had less than $4,000 total annual income. The median income was only $3,500. Three colleges had less than $500 per faculty member for all expenses, including maintenance.

The history of McKendree College, while not fully typical,

illustrates the difficulties faced by the less prosperous Methodist colleges. It had to suspend in 1835 and again in 1841 for lack of funds. It reopened in 1846 with a voluntary teaching staff paid a mere pittance. The presiding elder had to go directly to the individual members and personally beg them for food to feed the faculty. Only by assessing local class leaders twenty-five cents a quarter to be raised from their local classes could the college be kept alive. Even this sum was difficult to collect.

In Indiana, for some years at least, the Methodists preferred to co-operate with others to support Indiana University and consequently petitioned the legislature to change the law to enable Methodists to serve on the board of trustees and on the faculty, instead of continuing the then complete Presbyterian control. The Methodists' concern with higher education reflected their rising social status and they resented all the more what they felt to be Presbyterian arrogance. When the Methodists presented their petition to the legislature, Holliday reports:

A storm of indignation was raised among those who controlled the State University. . . . The movement was said to be an effort on the part of the Methodists to get a Methodist professor in the State University; and it was tauntingly said, in the halls of the Legislature, that "there was not a Methodist in America with sufficient learning to fill a professor's chair, if it were tendered to him." [16]

The Indiana Conference had no alternative under the circumstances but to found Indiana Asbury University at Greencastle, Indiana. Soon the presidency of Indiana University itself would be occupied by such Methodists as Drs. William A. Daily and Cyrus Nutt.

The original and persistent Methodist and Baptist apathy toward liberal education helps to explain the alarm felt by such Congregationalists and Presbyterians as Lyman Beecher, Samuel J. Mills, and John F. Schermerhorn with regard to western religious and cultural "desolation." With their higher educational demands and standards, they sharply questioned both the education and the religious role of the Methodists and the Baptists. When Dr. Bangs was not engaged in polemics, the Methodist historian freely admitted the Methodist weakness in education. After steps were taken to support schools, he happily remarked that Methodism at last was outgrowing the bad reputation it had, "not without some reason, that it had been indifferent to the cause of literature and science." The Methodists were prodded to face the serious need to raise far larger sums for schools.

Despite their opposition to formal theological training, the Methodist leadership came to regard general education as a great force for either good or evil, depending upon its supervision, and the bishops expressed their concern for better education for society at large. Their Message to the 1840 General Conference proposed a well-conducted system of collegiate education under General Conference control. It referred to the strong opposition which had existed among the Methodists to founding colleges, but noted the changing attitude. Since colleges had general importance and required large financial resources, they should not be left to local responsibility. Until colleges had sufficient endowments to support the faculty and similar direct outlays and the tuition was used only for contingent expenses, they were not financially safe. The schools were to be open to all, for Methodism was to be not a "bigoted sect" but an "enlightened and liberal Church." By 1862 all secondary schools were open to women, and the Methodists generally were ahead of the country in supporting collegiate education for women.

Although the 1824 General Conference had specifically urged the sponsorship of Sunday schools — in contrast to the eastern Methodists who had founded Sunday schools in the eighteenth century — the western Methodists did little at first. Many were decidedly opposed to the idea. The Ohio Conference journal for September 8, 1821, however, records the conference action ordering the book agent at Cincinnati to prepare "a Primmer containing suitable lessons for the early education of children" and the steps to appoint a committee to examine the text before its publication. According to W. W. Sweet, this was the first formal measure by the western Methodists for the religious education of the children.[17] The earliest Sunday school in Tennessee opened in Nashville, where the hostile local Methodists refused to let it use their church basement. The church displayed such signs as "No desecration of the holy Sabbath, by teaching on the Sabbath in this church." The class had to meet in pigsties, because no other places were available. It took the Sunday school advocates some years to overcome such antagonism.

A significant Methodist contribution to western education was the mass circulation of its low-priced books and pamphlets. An 1800 General Conference resolution called on the presiding elder, where no special book agent had been appointed, to distribute books in his district and to keep an account of the various items. Each itinerant in turn was to supply his circuit with books and keep a record of the sales and an inventory. The commission varied from 15 to 25 per cent of the wholesale price. The preacher received two-thirds of the total commission on all his sales and the presiding elder one-third. The itinerants thus automatically became agents for the Methodist Book Concern. The book sales provided sizable supplementary income for the poor circuit riders. We have seen that their nominal salary was only $80.00 per year from 1800 until 1816, when it went up to $100.00 per year, but many did not get more than a fraction of their stated pay, some receiving less than $20.00 per year. On the other hand, for the first two quarters of 1809, Benjamin Lakin's book commission totaled $36.75. In 1817 on the Limestone Circuit he apparently made only $17.83 on the 236 books sold. That year James Finley, as presiding elder of the Ohio District, received 1,203 books for sale in his district. The Book Concern profits went into the Chartered Fund for the relief of the circuit riders in financial distress, their widows, and their children. The itinerants had every reason to support the Concern.[18]

Methodists introduced books and pamphlets into areas almost destitute of reading matter, and they helped many westerners to develop the reading habit. Samuel Mills, otherwise often critical of Dissent in his report on western religious conditions, was impressed by the wide distribution of the Methodist publications. At first, however, the Book Concern in America either imported or reprinted material from England. Dr. Bangs gave the complete list of titles available in 1812 in order to show its meagerness at

that time. Except for Coke's *Commentary on the New Testament*
the full set could have been bought for $29.75. In addition to the
Discipline, the only three American publications were Abbott's
Life, Watter's *Life,* and *A Scriptural Catechism.* The Concern
made very slow progress until almost 1820 when the sales began
to rise sufficiently to encourage the 1820 General Conference to
open the western branch in Cincinnati with Martin Ruter as its
first agent. The first year he sold only $4,000 worth of books, but
before he left in 1828 to become president of Augusta College,
he had succeeded in sharply increasing business and in improving Methodist ministerial education in the West. By 1836, the
Cincinnati branch became independent of the New York office.

Promoting popular religious journalism was another Methodist contribution to western education. The earliest Methodist
publications, including the *Arminian Magazine* and the *Methodist Magazine,* failed, as did the first western periodical, *Western
Christian Monitor.* For some years the denomination had no
journal even to answer the attacks against Methodism. As a result,
the critics were even more inclined to regard the Methodists as
being indifferent to learning. The opposition within Methodism
was so strong that it prevented any action until 1818, when the
Methodist Magazine reappeared, followed in 1826 by the *Christian Advocate and Journal.* Both were widely read in the West.
The itinerants were also agents for the periodicals. By 1828 the
Christian Advocate had a circulation of 15,000, which was apparently among the largest in the world at that time.

The increase in the educated membership eventually forced
many opposed to higher education and theological training for
the ministry to reverse their positions. In addition, the Methodist
colleges had also introduced music, drawing, and other "ornamental" subjects into their curriculums, a curious inconsistency
since the Methodists generally frowned on secular music. A rather
typical pioneer account refers to many probationers dropping out
because they had "most willfully listened to the enchanting music
of the violin," a reprehensible thing to do since "more devils
lurked in catgut and horsehair than Luther ever dreamed of."[19]
This suspicion and disciplinary control applied to all music, not

merely to the violin, as the first of the two following stories illustrates.

One day when Bishop Asbury and James Finley stopped at the home of an old Methodist family, the Bishop noticed their young daughter playing the piano in the company of several friends. Her parents and grandparents soon came to greet the two men. Asbury looked at the grandmother to see if she resembled her "sainted" mother who was a first generation Methodist:

"You," said the Bishop, "and your husband belong to the second generation of Methodists. Your son and his wife are the third, and that young girl, your granddaughter, represents the fourth. She has learned to dress and play on the piano, and is versed in all the arts of fashionable life, and I presume, at this rate of progress, the *fifth* generation of Methodists will be sent to dancing-school." [20]

But John Wesley himself had once played the flute regularly. And Luther's interest in music and the great role of Bach and other music in European Protestantism are too well known to need any comment here.

This prejudice extended even more violently to the opera, drama, and theater, including Shakespeare, as Finley himself reveals:

As there are many professors [believers] who speak indulgently, if not encouragingly, of the opera, the theater, and the dancing saloon, it is time that a note of warning was sounded that would break like Heaven's loudest thunder on the ears of such.

"O, father," said a blooming girl of some eighteen summers, gentle and lovely as a rose of spring, "what harm can there be in going to the theater just once, to hear some of Shakespeare's best pieces rehearsed by star performers? Besides, haven't you got the works of that great author in your library?"

"I will answer your question, my dear," said the father, who was a minister, "by asking another. What harm would there be in letting this beautiful glass vase fall on the stone hearth just once?" . . .

"Why not? If it be true that, instead of being a 'school of morals,' it is a school of vice, and vice is contaminating to the soul, should it not be avoided? Can one take coals in his bosom and not be burned? Can one walk amidst a shower of soot, such as often falls in our city, and not have her garment soiled?" . . .

"The very form in which you have put this question shows that you are convinced of the impropriety of visiting such places, because you speak of a single visit, and seem to think that no harm can come of a single visit. You well know by your education, and I pray God it may never become part of your experience, that

> 'Vice is a monster of such frightful mien,
> That to be hated needs but to be seen;
> Yet seen too oft, familiar with her face,
> She's first endured, then pitied, then embraced.' " 21

These stories are perhaps more significant than they seem at first, since James Finley, as noted before, came from an unusually well-educated western family and was actively promoting education. Yet, obviously, he also shared the general Methodist antagonism to many of the arts. Perhaps Allen Wiley best summarized this attitude when he declared, "I have known of more cases than one, where men have passed for Methodists at home, and when they have gone to Indianapolis, they have attended a low, vile thing, called a theater." 22

These reactions are not personal quirks of individual Methodists, but definitely reveal the sectarian spirit of Western Methodism. In other words, despite the numerous resolutions on the need for more education, the very educators and the bishops had only a little, if any, appreciation for the arts and many types of literature, including much that was most significantly religious. Education was narrowly conceived, with no place for the imaginative, aesthetic, and spiritually creative aspects of life or for efforts to probe into the ultimate issues of life, or for real challenges to their naïvely simple image of the world. The Pastoral Address to the 1840 Conference typically denounced novels and thus automatically excluded many of the greatest works in literature and others of profound religious insight as evil, especially for the younger people, merely because of the form in which they were written. Novels "blast, wither, and destroy," induce "intellectual languor," and blunt "the moral feelings," the address insisted.

Some Methodist historians credit Charles Wesley's hymns with preserving their denomination's evangelical outlook. The importance of its hymnody for Methodism, therefore, can scarcely be exaggerated. Clearly illustrating again the cultural difficulties confronting early nineteenth-century American Methodism was the coarseness, if not the vulgarity, of many words and often the music in the western hymnbooks that were used in some places to the virtual exclusion of the original Wesley hymnal. Many hymns "possessed but little of the spirit of poetry," Dr. Bangs admitted, and they added "nothing to true intellectual taste," but they were useful for keeping excited those attending the revival meetings. The American hymnals not only lacked good music to go with the religious poetry, Dr. Bangs complained, but in many cases the "unskilled" editors had "mutilated" the poetry by "leaving out parts of stanzas, altering words, shortening or lengthening hymns, without much judgment or taste," and had left out many of the greatest European hymns. The Wesley hymnal, it would seem, influenced church music almost everywhere else, before it had further effect on American Methodism. In England, Samuel Wesley, son of Charles Wesley, composed the music for the Wesley hymns and was among the first to introduce Bach to England. His son, Samuel Sebastian Wesley, organist for Leeds Parish Church, 1842–48, and Gloucester Cathedral, is said to have initiated a new phase in the English church music.[23]

The low standards of many western Methodist songbooks also reflected to a degree the intense hostility many western Methodists had to formal church music. Eastern Methodists were more inclined to accept their Wesleyan heritage. As we might expect, Peter Cartwright furiously attacked all organs (he called them squealing gods), choirs, and instrumental and formal music, and he vigorously flayed the eastern Methodist churches for having them. In expressing this Dissenting sectarian attitude, he seemed to have conveniently forgotten that John Wesley, whom Cartwright liked to cite frequently as authority, loved Anglican liturgy and church music and had also prepared, in 1784, a service book for the American Methodists, adapted from the *Prayer Book* of the Church of England. The Christmas Conference of 1784 had officially adopted Wesley's Sunday Service, but the denomination soon abandoned it. It was not until more than a century later that the formal Wesleyan liturgy began to appeal to the western

Methodists. The *Discipline* also barred members from engaging in
"such diversions as cannot be used in the name of the Lord Jesus:
The *singing* those *songs,* or *reading* those *books,* which do not
tend to the knowledge or love of God."[24]

Any assessment of the Methodist role in the West, however,
must consider the unbelievably harsh and adverse circumstances
it confronted. The denominational task of helping to "civilize"
the West had to begin at the most elementary level of demanding
decency and order and even physical cleanliness. Full sponsorship of the arts understandably had to wait. The efforts of James
Axley were typical. Once this picturesque itinerant was chiding
members for straying from the paths of rectitude and for splatter-
ing the church floor with "tobacco juice." Then pointing to Judge
Hugh L. White, a leading jurist and one-time United States senator and presidential candidate, he concluded:

"And now I reckon you want to know who I do mean? I mean that
dirty, nasty, filthy tobacco-chewer, sitting on the end of that front seat";
— his finger meanwhile pointing true as the needle to the pole — "see
what he has been about. Look at the puddles on the floor; a frog
wouldn't get into them; think of the tails of the sisters' dresses being
dragged through that muck." The crestfallen judge declared that he
never chewed any more tobacco in church.[25]

In another mood, he supposedly wrote the following jingle on
women smokers:

> Tobacco is an Indian weed,
> And from the devil did proceed;
> It spoils a woman, burns her clothes,
> And makes a chimney of her nose.[26]

Considering the frontier hardships, we may wonder how Methodism was able to introduce such remarkable overt advances
among its members over the first half of the nineteenth century.
In part, the credit rests with the leadership, example, and discipline of the itinerants and the bishops, their sacrificial devotion,
and in part with the ambition of its essentially middle-class-ori-
ented membership. Many pleasant middle western towns and
cities, many colleges and schools, are monuments to their heroism
and achievement. Isaac Owen typifies the more ardent advocates

of education. His poor family could not provide him with any real schooling, and consequently he had to study even elementary grammar by himself in later life. While riding the frontier circuits, he learned Greek and other subjects of interest to him and also raised over $60,000 for Indiana Asbury University. Wherever Owen went, his enthusiasm for study inspired many poor youngsters to seek education. Later on, as a missionary in California, he was active in founding another college.[27] Such constructive personal influence goes a long way to substantiate the Methodist claims that the denomination was a great civilizing force in the West, as well as a dynamic faith for the settlers.

THE FRIENDS

The most important contributions of the western Friends to education were, first, their universal elementary schooling for children in the midst of a general apathy toward education and, later, their strong encouragement of secondary education for the greatest number possible. The 1840 Census record of only 0.4 per cent illiteracy in Wayne County, Indiana, the center of the Quaker settlement, as contrasted with almost 42 per cent illiteracy in Martin County and 14 per cent for Indiana as a whole, reflected this concern for common schooling. After liberal allowances are made for probable statistical errors, the difference is still striking. Unlike the Presbyterians, however, during the first decades of the nineteenth century the western Quakers had relatively little interest in college education. Earlham School was not elevated into a college until 1859.[28]

Whereas the western Friends concentrated on elementary schools at first, after 1850 their secondary schools became a significant factor in western education. At a time when both elementary and secondary schools in Indiana were woefully poor, the Quaker schools with their relatively high standards served as models to help improve the public schools. From the middle of the century the Friends became increasingly willing to permit their schools to join with the public schools, even if earlier they were opposed to such mergers, partly because the fines imposed on their members refusing to serve in the militia went toward the support of various "public seminaries." Their schools also avoided the violent and extremely autocratic treatment of children that prevailed in some other schools. The Quaker principles encouraged children to respect the rights of others and in turn guided adults in giving young people greater consideration as free personalities than was generally accorded them. Friends sought to inculcate in the children the sense of belonging to the Quaker community and the necessity for assuming their social responsibilities. In marked contrast to the general western contempt for teachers, the Society regarded the profession as honorable and the search for and the development of dedicated and concerned teachers was a major Quaker interest. Among the Friends able teachers could and did exercise community leadership.

Since the westerners were prejudiced still more against education for girls than for boys, the Quaker insistence on coeducation was all the more remarkable. It was another major contribution to the West. To illustrate the feeling against equal education for girls even among the parents interested enough to send their daughters to school, Dr. Boone tells about the non-Quaker parents in Livonia, Indiana, objecting to their daughters learning arithmetic or to use the pen at an academy taught by a Presbyterian minister. The Friends also helped to provide education for the Indians and Negroes at a time when the state authorities barred Negroes without question from the existing public schools.

For all their general interest in education, the early nineteenth-century Friends in the West shared, or even accentuated, the common Dissenting suspicion of the aesthetic and imaginative interests of man. Fiction was not considered to be "in Truth" by the Quakers; neither was music. Not until later in the century did the Friends begin to appreciate the arts. The common frontier attitude appears in the recommendation by the Education Committee to the Indiana Yearly Meeting that the youth be encouraged to cultivate and improve their minds "by useful reading; taking care in their selections for this purpose, to reject every thing of a light and chaffy nature, among which novels and tales may be particularly named," and that their attention be called to that "which may be permanently useful." Again, the Epistle of Advice of the 1839 Meeting stresses the great importance of good books, but adds, "Some books are pernicious; among which may be named all novels, romances &c."[29]

This critical attitude toward novels and drama among some Western Friends is not surprising, since in the early nineteenth century many eastern Quakers had similar views. As conspicuously illustrating an outlook combining breadth of learning with sectarian narrowness, Rufus Jones quotes at length from a letter by a well-known Friend, John Griscom, professor of chemistry at Columbia University, member of the faculty of Queen's College (Rutgers University) and several learned societies, and widely traveled. In his letter, Dr. Griscom explained why he was refusing an invitation to a lecture on Shakespeare, whom he had finally come to regard as the "prince of mischief" and commented that he would have been more inclined to attend if the lecture had been intended to show that exterminating all Shakespeare's works would help human morality. He felt that while Shakespeare's works contain "many noble thoughts, many humane sentiments, many profound and correct exhibitions of human nature, which may be culled, as the bee gathers sweets from poisonous plants," as a whole they demoralize society and in any case would never "aid a single soul onward towards the kingdom of Heaven." Rather, they encourage vulgarity and vice. It is by giving moral support to drama that Shakespeare is most pernicious, for plays are "among the most powerful engines of the Prince of Darkness," Dr. Griscom concluded. He realized that his opinions were extreme.[30]

To have a more balanced picture, however, we should refer to the Society's contributions to American literature. Beginning with William Penn, the Quaker writers include John Woolman, Thomas Paine, Charles Brockden Brown, James Fenimore Cooper, Walt Whitman, and John Greenleaf Whittier. In his study on Friends in American literature, Professor Hintz discusses Ralph Waldo Emerson as a literary figure greatly influenced by Quaker teachings, shown by the close relations between his and Quaker thoughts. Emerson's friendships with Friends and his serious reading of their writings are recorded in his *Journal*. They helped to shape such ideas as his rejection of church ordinances, priestly authority, and literal interpretation of the Scriptures. Quakerism was more in accord with his feelings than any other religious group. Whitman's writings also show Quaker influence. His mother and both his father's parents were Friends, and his father, nominally a Methodist, took young Walt to Society meetings, particularly to hear Elias Hicks.

This passing account of the Western denominational attitudes toward education would be incomplete without at least mentioning their ambivalent attitudes toward secular state universities. In some ways the Presbyterian efforts to retain their dominance over Transylvania University in Kentucky were typical of their activities in other states, even if the issues were not usually so clear or the conflict so bitter as in Kentucky. Not until the other denominations became influential and interested enough in higher education to end this virtual Presbyterian establishment were state and church in fact separated in higher education. In Illinois, Wisconsin, and Iowa, as well as in other states, sectarian opposition either delayed the establishment of the state universities or inhibited their growth after they were founded. The strong support for the state universities, which now characterizes many popular denominations, was a later development.[31]

PART III

SOCIAL AND CULTURAL HERITAGE OF
WESTERN POPULAR DENOMINATIONS

CHAPTER X

Sectarianism

In *The Social Teaching of the Christian Churches,* Ernst Troeltsch analyzes the decisive influence exerted by the Christian fellowship on the church organization and on the nature of the Christian faith itself. The very doctrine of the divinity of Christ, the "only peculiarly primitive Christian dogma," Troeltsch says, first grew from the worship of Christ, which in turn rose from the necessity felt by the new spiritual community for meeting together. Whether or not one fully agrees with his interpretation, the influence of fellowship is undeniable.[1]

Several previous chapters have emphasized the intimate fraternal relations within the four denominations, their common sense of responsibility for group life, their close watch over and mutual help for one another, and, except for the Presbyterians, their theory of the voluntary regenerate membership and their indifference or hostility to the secular culture. Emotionally, the "community" for the Dissenters was, first, the local fellowship and, second, the wider circles of each denomination, regional and national. The main stream of American Dissent, however, did not retain the sectarian indifference to the state and to economic activities, but instead helped to train the common people for active participation in community life. The Dissenters had accepted the concept of the calling and, to a lesser degree, the Calvinist interest in dominating the world (in Calvinism for the greater glory of God). In pursuing their callings, however, as we shall see shortly, the Dissenters were undermining some basic sectarian assumptions. The Presbyterians differed from Dissent in their continued insistence on an educated professional clergy, a more aristocratic polity, a systematic theology, and in their attempts even in the West to secure the prerogatives of a virtual establishment in higher education. Western Presbyterianism, nevertheless, exemplifies one way neo-Calvinism evolved into free churches and ascetic Protestantism. This particular approach intensified the fundamental asceticism in Calvinism to the point of rejecting much of the secular culture, in contrast to Calvin's own cultural interests and to early Calvinism, which was "distinguished precisely by its urbane refinement and humanistic culture."[2]

Perhaps the very personalities of the three previously mentioned Methodist leaders will illustrate this trend in Dissent, first toward sectarianism and then toward the acceptance of the calling. John Wesley had exceptionally diverse intellectual interests; he was absorbed periodically with many scholarly subjects, from Newtonian science and mathematics to classical literature, and he was a Fellow of Lincoln College at Oxford. When compared with some Anglican churchmen, he may have been found deficient in artistic sensitivity; nevertheless, at various stages in his life he played the flute, read numerous plays and poems, and enjoyed paintings. John Wesley loved the rich liturgical heritage of Anglicanism and, with his brother Charles, contributed to its church music. He was catholic in his attitude toward all who worked in Christian spirit and ecumenical in his approach to other churches.[3]

Francis Asbury was born to an English farm family and never had the advantages of a university education or of a literary and artistic life. He evidently did not share Wesley's interest in painting and music. Asbury, the father of American Methodism, though not as involved as Wesley was with scholarship, was well educated in comparison with the early nineteenth-century American circuit riders. He at least had elementary schooling, which was more than most of them had. His Greek and Hebrew were literally learned on horseback. At times before retiring, he apparently would read several chapters from the Old Testament in Hebrew. This background in itself, Bishop McConnell comments, would have placed Asbury in a unique position among the Methodist ministers of his day or indeed of today. Nor was his reading in the Bible always uncritical. For instance, he noticed that Matthew and Luke depended on Mark, a real insight for his time, when such interdependence of biblical passages was regarded not as indicating that one evangelist knew about another's writings but rather as revealing the Divine Spirit "dictating parallel utterances." His anxiety over the prosperity of the Methodists in some communities and their political prominence in other places rose partly from his sectarian tendencies. He preferred to have the Methodists withdraw from the world, and feared a possible decline in their piety and discipline with the coming of their material success. His *Journal* does not express conspicuously ecumenical attitudes toward other denominations.[4]

Our third representative personality might have been a frontier bishop, but Peter Cartwright is an equally representative, better known, and more dramatic figure. Not until he had become a circuit rider did he learn to study consistently. Cartwright probably never knew well a single scholar or artist, and he never had the opportunity to develop a taste for the arts or theoretical sciences. His sharp criticisms of other denominations were well known. Everywhere he was belligerent toward instrumental, organ, and choral music and formal liturgy, for all his professed admiration for Wesley. Cartwright's many contributions to the West, however, included years of actively promoting law and order, participating in public life and politics, and serving in the Illinois state legislature. In 1846 he was the Democratic candidate for Congress, defeated by a young Whig destined for greatness, Abraham Lincoln.[5]

These three leaders all belong to the Methodist tradition. The decline in its cultural and intellectual standards was cumulative. Unavoidable cultural deprivation was an important factor, but the sectarian attitudes, easily liable to extremism, accentuated the deterioration. Many Methodists rationalized this cultural weakness into a prejudice against learning and the arts, in part, perhaps, because they were on the whole an economically rising people who wanted no distractions from work and who needed justification for their intensive devotion to "duty." Wesley may not have been sensitive to the arts, but his love of liturgy and religious music and his amazingly broad intellectual interests make him an aesthete and a scholar in comparison with Cartwright. Cartwright was a practical farmer, a civic leader, and a politician engaged in the rough and tumble of party politics, and these roles symbolize the western Methodist emphasis on the calling and, in this case, also the so-called middle-class orientation of a rising membership.

The early nineteenth century was distinguished by the rise of numerous reformistic, enthusiastic, utopian, and ethnic religious sects and movements. These divisive influences affected even the existing organizations and co-operative ventures. After collaborating with the Methodists on camp meetings, the Presbyterians rejected these spectacular revivals and proceeded to eradicate the "Methodist tendencies" from their Tennessee and Kentucky presbyteries. Contemporary records, as diverse as Jacob Young's *Autobiography* and the report of the special synod committee to investigate the Cumberland Presbytery, indicate considerable Methodist influence on early frontier Presbyterianism. When David Rice, the pioneer Presbyterian minister, found a meeting too enthusiastic and "Methodistic," he "would rise to his feet, look over the assembly with great solemnity, and exclaim, 'High sail and little ballast!' then gather up his hat and cane, and take his departure." [6]

The Presbyterian scorn for the Methodists in some places almost approached persecution, the Methodists insisted. "They were the aristocracy, and we the poor people," remarks Jacob Young. James B. Finley speaks in a similar vein on interdenominational relations early in the nineteenth century, when there was more co-operation than somewhat later. The Presbyterians, Finley felt, regarded the Methodists as fit only for "hewing wood and drawing water" in the work of promoting religion. During the Great Revival (1801), when the Presbyterians and Methodists co-operated, the Baptists would not have communion with the others, though they joined in the preaching. "We kept up a constant fire upon the Baptists," William Burke notes, while Jacob Young mentions many bitter controversies between the Methodists and Baptists. According to Allen Wiley, James Finley's father once remarked in a sermon, "I will not say that any man who baptizes by immersion is an indecent man, but I will say, he has been guilty of an indecent act."[7]

These sectarian rivalries became sharper over the next several decades. The Methodists were typical in complaining about the unfair attacks on them by other denominations and in turn making but little effort to understand the others. Here again, Cartwright characteristically expressed the Methodist feelings as he deprecated all other denominations with such strong terms as "heathen," "wicked and high-strung predestinarian," and "corrupters" of morals. The Mormons he would treat as outlaws everywhere since in his view they were thieves and murderers. His attitude toward ministers sent West by the various mission societies and his glee when western ruffians "roughed" some of them were scarcely consistent with the presumably superior Methodist brand of Christianity. Even in his old age, Cartwright still insisted he did not know what the Baptists meant by a union (open interdenominational) meeting. Cartwright's message was so vital to him that he had to proclaim it without restraint and, consequently, he "did not hestitate to enter the pulpit of another denomination and there assail its theological teachings." This ardent free grace advocate looked on Calvinism as a major enemy which he must strike down wherever he could. "What had he to do with ministerial courtesy or denominational etiquette which denied his right — his call — to attack this slayer of the souls of men." This estimate by his admiring biographer, Philip Watters, helps us to feel the fervent sectarianism of the colorful itinerant, but it probably exaggerates his aggressiveness, for Cartwright was essentially kind except when engaged (as he often was) in polemics.[8]

The very hymns at the revival meetings, Dr. Nottingham found, increasingly stressed sectarian differences, some being "veritable batteries" of doctrinal arguments against other denominations, a tendency accentuated on the frontier by its "fighting spirit." Rough verses arranged for rousing tunes replaced the traditional eastern and Old World hymns. Group singing had an important social as well as religious significance for the western people, who for the most part knew almost nothing of the secular music and whose religion would have barred them from the concert hall had it existed.[9]

No wonder Allen Wiley, in 1846, was moved to remark, "The preachers and people of the present day can form no estimation of the asperity of feeling and language which prevailed in those days of bitter waters, even among good men and able ministers."[10] This sectarianism was not confined to the western preachers and people. The growing preference for denominational mission, Bible, tract, and Sunday-school societies paradoxically showed the national scope of sectarianism. The visiting British Baptist delegates, Drs. Cox and Hoby, wondered about the American Baptist withdrawal from the interdenominational Bible society, but the Presbyterians and the Methodists were hardly more co-operative. The Methodists believed that each sect should go its own way to spread the gospel, since joint work would, they said, lessen the support and since national religious organizations seemed "incompatible with the safety of our *free* institutions, both civil and religious." Whenever it was convenient to use national agencies, we might add, the Methodist did not find them incompatible with free institutions! While examining an enormous mass of source materials to write his Indiana Baptist history, John F. Cady found almost no references to interdenominational contacts. Accentuating strong denominational loyalty was considered an easy way to maintain local morale and to promote various activities; hence, there was no enthusiasm for interdenominational co-operation.[11]

Eventually, sectarianism weakened western popular denominations as a whole in many ways, not the least of which was by excessively multiplying local churches in some areas and totally neglecting other regions. Too many churches in a community meant that each church was too small and too feeble to satisfy the greater and more complicated religious requirements of the people later in the century. Charleston, Indiana, a village with a population of only several hundred in 1841, had six churches: two Baptists, two Methodists, one Presbyterian, and one Disciples of Christ. None of the congregations averaged more than forty-five at worship; four had only from twelve to twenty-five persons. Another and slightly better case was Huntington, Indiana, a town of 3,000, with eight Protestant churches.[12] So thoroughly was this division institutionalized that a century later it still remains a major western, indeed American, Protestant weakness. In 1935, about 75 per cent of all American Protestant churches were rural, following the old census definition of rural as the open country and communities with fewer than 2,500 inhabitants. Over 150,000 white churches had under 300 members, and only 18,000 had over 350 members. Instead of growing, the small churches were losing members. The distribution was even worse for the Negro churches which were more rural. The segregated Negro churches as such, of course, symbolize the sectarian separation originating in discriminatory non-religious social forces. Some country areas in 1935 still had three or four churches competing for less than 200 families, while at the same time millions of people in other areas had no access to any church at all. The problem is insoluble unless the major denominations de-institutionalize the early nineteenth-century sectarian pattern to pool their resources and co-operate, as they are now doing in some places. This institutionalized separation into sects, combined with popular denominational emphasis on individual conversion and local church discipline, delayed the Dissenting denominational efforts later in the nineteenth century to understand the nature of the rapidly developing industrialized urban society and to deal with it. Significantly, it was often the more churchly denominations, such as the Episcopal Church, which pioneered in confronting the problems of this later industrialized period.[13]

Before turning again to the earlier Dissenting indifference or hostility to many cultural activities, we should momentarily look at the western society as a whole, especially since this negative attitude toward cultural interests may at least partly reflect the prejudices prevailing in the larger community. The inhabited West in the 1830's was still mainly rural or even frontier, but already increasingly leavened by flourishing cities. People were on the move. The frontiersmen, including leaders, evidently moved three, four, or even eight or more times before settling down permanently. Thus, Turner found that in Wisconsin the 124 members of the 1846 constitutional convention had lived, on the average, in three different states and nations and probably in more than one place within a given state. Four had lived in eight states and countries, six in seven states and countries, sixteen in five or more states and countries.[14]

Denominational statistics also confirm this high mobility. Even many Friends moved a number of times, when their *Discipline*, we may recall, admonished them not to move needlessly but to consider the spiritual welfare of their children who must live in a stable Quaker community for proper development. The Whitewater Monthly Meeting, the first in Indiana, was organized in 1809 with 265 members, 170 being from Miami and West Branch Meetings which in turn had earlier received nearly all from other meetings, mainly southern. The Baptists and the Methodists had no such disciplinary inhibitions about moving and their church documents record the high turnover in membership. A neighborhood might have a flourishing class, wrote Allen Wiley, the pioneer Methodist presiding elder, but in a short time the members would be gone and often give place to a new group. "They might almost as well, like the Tartars, dwell in tents. Everything shifts under your eye," Timothy Flint reported. Caroline Kirkland, living in frontier Michigan, had further comments on this wanderlust and the hardships it created, particularly for women and children, all the more severe since the men obsessed with the future were insensitive to the immediate needs of their families.[15]

The popular denominations uniquely met a basic, probably a special, need of the moving frontier population, a significant but often overlooked contribution indirectly suggested by Robin Williams' thoughtful analysis of modern American society. On examining the present repeated large-scale American migrations, he asks whether they have not deprived the mobile people the membership in the intimate face-to-face (primary) groups that are essential for satisfying many emotional and social requisites of every individual, that give the individual the sense of belonging. Dr. Williams further asks if those on the move have not suffered psychological shocks as a consequence of not having these primary relationships.[16] Whatever may be the situation today, our previous data on the earlier nineteenth-century local classes and churches and their discipline clearly show how Dissent provided the constantly moving people with fellowship and primary relationships. American western society was also made more flexible in comparison with many traditional Old World societies in which only kinship or long established neighborhood groups can provide these close ties.

For the Dissenters, as many autobiographies and journals attest, conversion experience not only set them apart from the "world" at large, but joined them meaningfully in intimate fellowship. In Dissenting tradition, the Christian fellowship was a basic reason for organizing a church. To promote discipline, the local class or meeting inquired regularly into each member's conduct and personal condition and heard his open testimony. This practice could readily accelerate understanding and friendships and, at times, serve as mental therapy to relieve certain anxieties and aggression. The tearful farewells to members and families moving farther west and the personal ties revealed by the various Methodist and Baptist records suggest the close relationships within these denominations notwithstanding the repeated migrations. Wherever the members went in the West, they could join the local church of their denomination or co-operate to organize one and soon be a part of its fellowship. The popular denominations went far to satisfy both the religious and the interpersonal needs of their members. Early in the twentieth century, long after the various denominations had ended their disciplinary practices, the continuing value of being a member in good standing impressed Max Weber. In several sections of this country, he discovered, membership still meant friendly social contacts for comparative newcomers and was still significant enough for local banks and business firms to grant the newly arrived residents, who were relative strangers, more favorable terms.[17]

The moving and rapidly growing western society had low educational standards. In 1830, the Kentucky House Committee on Education reported that in thirty-four of the counties in the state fewer than 11,000 of the almost 52,000 children were attending schools. The very groups whose children were denied education seemed the least interested. Because of the strong opposition, much time and heart-breaking effort was required barely to begin the public school system in the American West. After a strenuous campaign, Ohio enacted a public education law in 1825, but the widespread hostility against it blocked its enforcement for many years.[18] In many Indiana communities the public school advocates were considered dangerous subversives. In the middle of the century, the free school was often still regarded as "dangerous to the State and subversive of the highest individual good. It was undemocratic." The state itself had received 576,000 acres of land from the federal government for education. Theoretically, the state constitution allocated substantial blocks of additional land for schools and set up a comprehensive educational system, beginning with the local township schools and culminating in a great state university with free tuition, equally open to all. It further assigned 10 per cent of the proceeds from the new county seat town land for libraries. The abstract provisions consequently seemed ample to realize the acknowledged purpose of this education, the "preservation of a free Government." Little was done, however, to put these pious sentiments into effect. Seemingly adequate laws had broad loopholes. As R. G. Boone shows in his history of Indiana education, up to 1849 Indiana had no real school system. No amount of references to ordinances, laws, and constitutional clauses for education altered the reality: education existed only on paper. It was but a casual afterthought and "learning was at a discount," he concludes.

Only the best counties opened schools, and then seldom as long as three months a year. Despite the federal land grant, by then worth about $1,250,000, the Indiana schools had no actual revenues, and mismanagement dissipated what little had been scraped together. Not one county in all the West in 1835 raised as much as $1.50 per pupil for public schools; most private schools were equally poorly supported. In Indiana in 1842, James Eastbridge of Orange County received only $36.50 for teaching three months, $25 in state scrip, $2.00 in Illinois money, and $9.50 in currency. Johnson County paid a teacher

$19 for three months, a dollar each for nineteen pupils. Vincennes University had no tax support and no endowment. Tuition was its only source of income. Governor Harrison proposed using it for training officers for Indian wars, which again indicates the low status of education. When Wabash College tried to secure a charter for "literary training," it had to appear practical or add practical features because of the "prejudice against colleges, pianos, and Yankees." [19]

Even where schools existed, educational standards were not established, still less enforced. The local township examiners were ignorant, sometimes illiterate, men; they are amusingly described by Caroline Kirkland:

Our law prescribes examinations, but forgets to provide for the competency of the examiners. . . . We know not precisely what were Master Horner's trials; but we have heard of a sharp dispute between the inspectators whether a n g e l spelt *angle* or *angel*. *Angle* had it, and the school maintained that pronunciation ever after. Master Horner passed, and he was requested to draw up the certificate for the inspectors to sign, as one had left his spectatcles at home, and the other had a bad cold, so that it was not convenient for either to write more than his name.[20]

This particular teacher rose as high as a district teacher could ever hope to rise, because he owned a farm and did not board around. He was the "preeminent beau of the neighbourhood, spite of the prejudice against learning." Among the reasons Mrs. Kirkland advanced for the inadequacies of the schools were the deduction of charges when the pupils were absent — such deductions encouraged parents to keep their children home, while technically they could still claim they were sending their children to school; the erratic changes in books and methods, a result of having new teachers every few months; the hostility or indifference of the parents to education; and the sheer ignorance of the teachers (many of whom could not even speak correct English). Competent persons had no incentive to teach:

What man in his senses who is capable of earning a decent livelihood . . . will undertake a most vexatious and thankless task, for wages inferior to those of a common laborer? . . . And what inducement can there be for study or any effort at improvement on the part of such young persons as may wish to become teachers, when they know that it will probably be their fate to be "examined" by persons totally incompetent, and that these posts are usually let out, like railway contracts, to the lowest bidder? [21]

While boarding at the Kirkland home, one teacher apparently learned more in a week than he usually did in a season. He was surprised to see a "pi-anner," perhaps his first, and went down on his knees to examine the revolving piano stool. Finishing his meal before others had even begun, he asked the Kirklands, "Jest play on it, will ye?" Even the carpets had to be pulled up for him to see how they were woven. No one had peace because of his insatiable curiosity. The Kirklands rather liked this young man, but they realized that his ignorance was typical of nearly all teachers. The situation was natural, Mrs. Kirkland felt, as long as the teachers had a lower social status and less income than unskilled workers: "A school in the country is only another name for starvation, and not reputable starvation either." [22]

In Indiana, on the basis of the 1840 Census, Wayne County had the best literacy record, supposedly 0.4 of 1 per cent of the populace illiterate. It was the center of the mass Quaker settlement, and, as we have seen before, the Friends systematically established schools along with their meeting houses and required at least common schooling for all their children. In contrast, Martin County had almost 42 per cent illiteracy, Jackson County over 41 per cent, and Indiana as a whole 14 per cent illiteracy. We may question the actual percentages, since standards of literacy were vague, but the basic differences among these counties are obvious. The ex-Kentucky and ex-Virginia Baptists were concentrated in the southern third of the state, which had the higher illiteracy rates and was the center of the hostility against public school education. Dr. Boone refers to the strong prejudice of the earlier Virginia migrants to Kentucky, which persisted in their descendants who in turn settled in Indiana. This prejudice was one factor responsible for the pathetically poor Indiana education so vividly dramatized in Edward Eggleston's *Hoosier School-Master*. The very arguments against public schooling included charges that it was a priestly scheme designed to "traditionalize" the children religiously to prepare for the merger of church and state. These statements have familiar eighteenth-century Virginia Baptist overtones.[23]

Indiana public schools generally excluded Negroes, as did those of Illinois and many in Ohio. The 1853 Indiana House Committee on Education did not even pretend to believe in racial democracy. It was better "for the weaker party" not to have any privilege which might "induce the vain belief that the prejudices of the dominant race" could ever be so modified as to remove the "rugged barriers that must forever exist between their social relations." Legislators in favor of the admission of Negroes to the public schools supported them with ulterior motives. An educated Negro would be aware of his "degradation" in the United States and would search for another country where as a man he might "breathe the free air of social as well as political liberty."[24]

The general indifference or hostility to education reflected the frontier "disdain for intellectual attainment," concludes Dr. Rusk in his history of western literature. The cultured were virtually compelled to act as if they had no education if they wanted to have their neighbors' confidence, and they often tried to imitate the crude speech of the illiterates to avoid being thought undemocratic. Caroline Kirkland found that the people in her frontier community had only contempt for books, above all novels. If a story was not literally "true," it was "condemned as 'a pack of lies.'" Some settlers asked regarding Cervantes whether it were not disgraceful to "write anything that a'n't true." Apparently, objection to "lies" did not prevent their having some interest in the stories of the Revolution and Indian wars if they were bloody enough. The populace habitually turned away from anything requiring imagination for its production or enjoyment. The people, Mrs. Kirkland goes on to say, were generally intelligent about practical matters, but did not at all realize their loss of "literary advantages." A friend told her that "he finds himself in a country where 'the reputation of having written a book is equivalent to that of having picked a pocket,' or something to that effect." Many settlers complained about the extensive free time they had to spend by themselves, but whenever she suggested reading, they would tell her they had no books and never did read much anyhow. Far from reading, they would condemn others for "wasting" time reading for amusement, especially fiction, while they would spend the entire day in petty gossip. "The time which is squandered in eternal visiting would give a good course of reading, both useful and cheering, to those who had a taste for it," she thought, while opening libraries in towns would perhaps end as many as nine-tenths of the quarrels in the settlements.[25]

This antagonism represented a sharp change from the late eighteenth-century culture in the old seaboard states. Many leaders of the Revolutionary War period, many Founding Fathers, among them Jefferson, Franklin, Madison, and Adams, were intellectualistic, rationalistic, cultured, and cosmopolitan. The religious leaders of that era also shared (in varying degrees) this outlook. The Declaration of Independence embodied and appealed to the intellectualism and universalism of that age (hence its lack of appeal to many present-day "professional patriots"). To appreciate the drastic change in the later nineteenth-century American cultural attitudes, it is necessary only to examine the intellectual vigor and honesty of the Founding Fathers, the literature they read and wrote, their broad interests, and in some cases their personal contacts and correspondence with the European minds. They were at home in all the Western world and its Enlightenment culture.[26]

Petty provincialism, pious sentimentality, and intellectual flabbiness were frequently encountered in the subsequent period. As illustrations Ralph Gabriel cites the Parson Weems stories and others like them, on which generations of nineteenth-century Americans were raised. We might also compare the relative urbanity of the Virginia gentry with the emerging Dissenting sectarianism which eventually triumphed. The rise of Dissent nationally was a factor in this profound social and cultural transformation. The Dissenting insistence on the equality and worth of each individual, on lay leadership, and on responsibility encouraged the common man to participate actively in the public and economic life of the young nation. By the 1830's, the so-called evangelical, mainly Dissenting, Protestantism and its secular (and political) counterpart, the democratic faith, had replaced the rationalism and cosmopolitanism of the Founding Fathers. In Dr. Rusk's estimate, the Protestant denominations succeeded in the West in "inverse ratio to their intellectual attainments, and in direct ratio to their emotional appeal." One reason for the antagonism toward educated people, Mrs. Kirkland thought, was that being too few to influence society in the West, they were suspected of being proud and unwilling to conform to the crowd.[27]

In keeping with their originally negative attitude toward intellectual and cultural interests, the popular denominations, as we have already seen, generally lagged far behind the Congregationalists and Presbyterians in fighting for higher educational and cultural standards. In this role, Presbyterianism was beginning to reveal, however faintly and narrowly, its older churchly tradition rather than its frontier sectarian tendencies. Before the popular denominations could effectively assume cultural responsibilities, they obviously had to change some basic sectarian assumptions, as well as raise their ministerial standards. The earlier Dissenting trust in competent, even if formally uneducated, leadership had congealed into mistrust of learning and preference for an unschooled ministry. Timothy Flint, an admittedly biased critic, stated openly what many Yankees in the West felt, that Dissenting ministers as a rule were so lacking in education that they were beyond criticism. More specifically, Mrs. Kirkland regretted that polemics constituted a large part of the little reading done by the frontier preachers because of the resultant increase in sectarian disputes among the people. Yet the pulpit was perhaps the best means for educating the populace on the frontier, she thought, and hence the necessity for proper training. Many ministers, however, were decidely inferior to their members in general education and often in their religious knowledge. Some merely strung words together and terrorized or excited people into religion, Mrs. Kirkland noted. Flavel Bascom, a Congregationalist missionary, often met men of this type, who indiscriminately quoted passages from the Bible with no logical connection.

These men, he felt, in "bellowing and blowing through the Bible" threw "no more light upon the passages quoted, than the roar of artillery does upon our declaration of independence." Some people, however, preferred such preaching to the Yankee ministers who, they said, were "always proving things, just like Lawyers." [28]

Concluding from her firsthand experience of living on the frontier, Mrs. Kirkland agreed with Tocqueville on the potential danger of what he considered the rising popular materialism. Pioneer hostility to supposedly non-practical things extended sometimes even to the cultivation of flowers and trees. A few would deliberately cut down the trees and shrubs retained or planted by the interested minority. Sometimes they chopped down shade trees protecting schoolhouses. Yet such behavior was not necessarily characteristic of frontier life or of sectarian religious discipline and asceticism, and certainly not of the system of calling. The very effort by a small minority of settlers to beautify their surroundings demonstrated the real existence of a different cultural outlook.[29]

Another type of ascetic sectarianism on the frontier is illustrated by the celibate Rappites who lived communally. This austere sect which first settled in Harmony, Indiana, saw no inconsistency between religious rigor and appreciation of natural beauty. Its members loved flowers and decorated their buildings and machines with bouquets. Outside their settlement they had a labyrinth of shrubs and vines surrounding a summer house with a rough exterior and an attractively finished interior. It symbolized their belief that the hardships in the world were but prefaces to the beauty and happiness of the hereafter. When Karl Bernhard, Duke of Saxe-Weimar Eisenach, visited the Rappite settlement, by then in Economy, Pennsylvania, he too noticed the beautiful flowers and gardens and the tame deer kept as pets. Some buildings had places for musicians to sit and play for the benefit of those working. The Duke attended a musical program given by the Rappite girls and praised the arrangement of their music, which included both religious and gay, secular compositions, and their excellent singing. Rappite wine also tasted good to him.[30]

On the other hand, an amusing item in the minutes of the Elkhorn Baptist Association of Kentucky for August 12, 1805, suggests the extremes to which western Dissent sometimes went:

> Quere from Glens Creek Is it right for Baptists to join in & assemble at barbacues [sic] on the 4th of July?
> Answered No.[31]

As further demonstrating that the western Dissenting hostility to many cultural interests had no vital correlation with either sectarian rigor or the system of calling, we might consider the corresponding Moravian attitudes. The Duke of Saxe-Weimar Eisenach twice visited the Moravian settlements around Bethlehem, in 1825 and 1826. Although the town had hardly more than 700 people, its church had an excellent organ, which the Bishop himself played for the Duke. The community enjoyed a weekly concert by a small orchestra of eleven musicians. Wherever he went the Duke heard good music and fine voices. He visited the schools and commented on the addition of music, drawing, and crafts like embroidering to the usual courses for girls. Some were interested in nature study. The students invited him to a delightful musical program. At receptions the Bishop played beautifully on the piano, his own compositions as well as those of the masters. In visiting various families, the Duke found a piano in nearly every home. Bishop Hueffel showed him a fine collection of sketches and reprints of paintings by the great masters, which had been selected for the settlement with much taste. The town also owned several original paintings and drawings.[32]

Certainly by the 1820's Bethlehem was an established settlement. Cultural amenities might be expected. This condition, however, does not alter the significance of the Moravian attitude toward music and the arts, an attitude going back to eighteenth-century frontier days. What is more, Methodists at that very time, and many in that very area, were still antagonistic to music and the arts. The Moravians, continuing their great history and heroic tradition despite their small numbers in this country, supported more missionaries than any other denomination in the early settlement of America. Their very success with the Indians was responsible for their expulsion from Connecticut where the pious authorities obviously did not want the Indians converted. The Moravians were noted then for their piety, religious fervor, rigor of their religious discipline and expectations, and devotion to duty, and, indeed, they were responsible for John Wesley's own conversion. Their sacrifices for their far-flung missionary and educational activities were probably more burdensome than those that Dissenters made, and yet they saw no conflict between their beloved music and art and their religious duties, discipline, simplicity, and calling.[33]

Obviously the Dissenting definition of religious life and attitudes incorporated as much the personal prejudices and accidental cultural limitation of particular leaders and members as they did any basic sectarian qualities, let alone churchly traits. Without discussing the alternative Christian approaches to secular life, we can readily realize as intimated previously that in accepting the system of calling popular denominations had undermined some fundamental assumptions regarding their faith and order. In an essentially Calvinistic type of calling, everyone had an inescapable duty to devote his whole life in this world to a calling, and some retained the original Calvinist concept of glorifying God by this calling and by shaping society to divine ends. Significantly, early Calvinism had included the system of calling in its total social program, which was designed to permeate and regulate the entire life of a nation; and in turn early Calvinism accepted and was noted for its urbane humanistic culture. Calvin was not acting irrationally or compulsively in searching for the best scholars for the university, even while hostile armies were besieging Geneva. Rather, learning and scholarship stood high in his hierarchy of values.

Western popular denominations were here involved in a contradiction. Despite large numbers, nationwide scope, and distinguished memberships—a striving, rising, middle-class oriented people among whom were many wealthy and influential community leaders—the popular denominations often felt, thought, talked, preached, and at times behaved (or at least reacted) as if they were still small persecuted or withdrawn groups of regenerates. A denomination cannot successfully seek to permeate the secular society through the system of calling and simultaneously assume that that society is the sinful world from which its members have withdrawn. If such a society is vulgar and materialistic by Dissenting religious standards, perhaps popular denominational hostility to cultural activities helped to make it so. We should keep in mind, however, that the members of the popular denominations also came increasingly to support programs for improving and spreading basic and practical education, which was proving to be more useful for their callings and for their higher economic statuses. The early frontier colleges provided the essentials for the frontier professions and some "ornamental" courses which also had value for their graduates in their relations with the more sophisticated minority. It was the higher scholarship and the serious pursuit of the arts which the popular denominations continued to regard with suspicion for some decades longer. In time the rising general educational standards apparently helped to create a growing appreciation for higher learning and the arts.

If popular denominational anticulturalism was based on assumptions contrary to their actual social roles and was not inherent in sectarian vigor, we still have to ask if this attitude was necessary at this stage of the general frontier development. Here we may conveniently refer to the observations of various European visitors, among them Fredrika Bremer, a leading Swedish author and social critic who traveled widely over the United States in mid-nineteenth century. She saw how markedly the German immigrants with their music, dances, art, and even metaphysical discussions over their beer "as in their old Germany" differed from the Anglo-Americans who had "no other pleasures than 'business,'" even in cities like Cincinnati. Later, in the Wisconsin wilderness, the excellent meals and the joyful atmosphere of a home in a Swedish settlement delighted her. One leader of the group wanted to found a new Upsala upon a lovely promontory on Pine Lake, which the company went to see. Returning to the log house, the twenty-one Swedes spent the evening dining, dancing, singing, and playing games. At one point she read stories to them "exactly as if in Sweden." Everyone had an exuberant and joyful time; the American guest tumbled down, overcome with laughter. Finally, they danced around and around the house and afterward went down to the lakeshore where they sang the star-song of Tegener under the stars. Later she asked Mrs. Petterson to sing a Swedish evening hymn, and "all joined in as she sang—'Now all the earth reposeth.'"[34]

The Swedish settlers could make a great contribution to the West, Fredrika Bremer concluded:

Heartfelt kindness and hospitality, seriousness and mirth in pure family life; these characteristics of Swedish life, where it is good, should be transplanted into the Western wilderness by the Swedish colonists, as they are in this instance. . . . The Swedes must continue to be Swedes, even in the New World; and their national life and temperament, their dances and games, their star-songs and hymns, must give to the western land a new element of life and beauty. They must continue to be such a people in this country that earnestness and mirth may prosper among them, and that they may be pious and joyful at the same time, as well on Sundays as on all other days. And they must learn from the American people that regularity and perseverence, that systematising in life, in which they are yet deficient.[35]

Near Koskonong, Wisconsin, she came upon a log cabin of the pastor to some Norwegian settlers. He was out, but his "pretty, refined, and graceful" wife was delighted to welcome Miss Bremer. Next day the guest was entertained "with the songs of her native land, sung to the guitar with a fresh, sweet voice."[36]

Her experiences may have been exceptional but are nevertheless indicative of the possibilities open to settlers. No one could have conceived of some Methodists dancing, playing games, reciting, and setting poems to music and singing as they enjoyed the beauty of the landscape and the stars. Nor could anyone have imagined the wife of a Baptist minister entertaining a visitor with songs "sung to the guitar." The popular denominations forbade such recreation, and later, when the less traditional members began to tolerate greater range of amusements, the people at first did not have the background to participate. It was not possible to eradicate musical and artistic heritage from the populace and then with a change in outlook to expect the cultural desert to flourish.

Undoubtedly pioneer life was lonely, harsh, and exhausting, at least during certain periods and seasons. An unspecialized sub-sistence economy was a cause of those hardships which fell most heavily on the women. They bore many children; their tasks never ended. Woman's place may have been at home then, but it should be emphasized that on the frontier the home was also the factory, mill, cannery, and general workshop. Not only did the women have to care for the family — cook, keep house, look after the children, nurse, wash, sew, and knit — but also spin, weave, make clothing and simple household equipment, can and preserve food, bake, and often tend to the domestic animals, poultry, and garden. Foreign travelers were depressed by the extremely rapid aging of frontier women as compared with European women. As Frederick Paxson, historian of the frontier, says, "The frontier graveyards show how hard the early life was on the women of the family. The patriarch laid to rest in his family tract, beside two, three, or four wives who had preceded him, is much more common than the hardy woman who outlived her husbands." Nearly everyone aged early, Elizabeth Nottingham concludes, but "the tombstone records show that more men outlived two or three wives than women two or three husbands." [37]

Nevertheless, visitors also observed the frontiersmen, particu-larly at certain times of the year "wasting" not merely hours but days. The English agriculturist Morris Birkbeck was shocked by the loafing he saw everywhere. "Indolence is the epidemic evil of the Americans," he wrote; "Life is whiled away in a painful state of yawning lassitude." But it was then relatively easy to earn sub-sistence and the people lacked the tradition necessary to enjoy healthy recreation or to develop more formal cultural interests. It "grieved" Timothy Flint "to see so many fine young men ex-empted from labour, having no liberal studies and pursuits to fill up their time, and falling, almost of course, into the prevail-ing vices of the West — gambling and intemperance." The in-habitants were "imprudent and lazy beyond example," thought Richard Lee Mason. Characteristically, before James Finley be-came a Methodist (like Cartwright and Young before their con-version), he enjoyed dances, shooting matches, and "frolics," as well as gay holiday parties. The rise of Dissent virtually ended these pleasures for its members.[38]

The Presbyterians and even New England Puritans sometimes shared almost the same attitude as Dissent toward some forms of recreation, as distinct from their more favorable attitudes toward intellectual and theological interests. Here, of course, comparisons are relative and William Cooper Howells, for one, refers to the gaiety of the Presbyterians in Ohio as compared with the Methodists. In their history of Congregationalism, Drs. Atkins and Fagley find that Puritan spiritual "frame" was not large enough for life, especially in frontier settlements deficient in cultural resources. A broader outlook would have lessened the harshness and cruelty of existence and would have given the people a fuller life, they add. If earlier Puritanism with its far more profound intellectual and cultural heritage still could not provide an adequate "frame" for the whole of frontier life, obviously sectarian Dissent with its much narrower horizons could still less comprehensively fulfil western emotional, recreational, and cultural requirements. Thus, the western Methodists never tolerated dancing and music as did the nineteenth-century Connecticut Congregationalists. Among the Congregationalists, music and dances were acceptable entertainment, and Connecticut families held receptions and dances which "sedate churchmen, their wives and daughters, attended without a qualm of conscience." [39]

The frontier is hardly the place to foster artists, musicians, and poets. This is not the issue. The relevant emphasis is that at least some German, Swedish, and other Continental settlers on the frontier had occasional songfests, plays, dances, and music. Where Germans were present, Avery Craven writes, time and taste for good music were found: "When German social habits were no longer considered of the low, sordid, animal kind, both his beer and his Beethoven gained in favor." Fredrika Bremer and Harriet Martineau pointedly suggested that the Americans would have done well to learn the value of feasts and dances from the Indians and Negroes. The very insensitivity of the settlers to the beauty and power of American Indian arts and designs, as distinct from "useful" Indian crafts, in itself symbolizes this older aspect of the Dissenting tradition. [40]

CHAPTER XI

The Baptist Anti-mission Movement

The great movement within the western Baptist churches against missions, education, Sunday schools, Bible and tract societies, and state and national conventions — as some critics said, against "human effort" — reached its peak between 1820 and 1840. It had various causes; consequently, any purely religious approach to this campaign may obscure its social, economic, and political factors. Indeed, the movement may be regarded as a combination of several distinct crusades, some by the ultraconservative predestinarians among the less-educated rural Baptists and others by the opposite wing, those essentially opposed to dogma. This chapter will focus on several main leaders and their influence on the Indiana Baptists to illustrate the developments of the movement.[1]

The dramatic appeal by Adoniram Judson and Luther Rice for Baptist support for the mission in Burma brought Baptist leaders together in May, 1814, for a general missionary convention. Thirty-three delegates representing eleven states attended this first national Baptist meeting and organized the Triennial Convention. Its constitution provided for official delegates from societies contributing one hundred dollars or more and a board of twenty-one commissioners responsible for conducting the business between the conventions. Luther Rice proposed missions in the West as one of the Baptist objectives. The board began by supporting Isaac McCoy of Indiana as a missionary among the Indians and John Mason Peck and James B. Welch as missionaries to the settlers in the St. Louis area. Peck, later known as an outstanding Baptist missionary in the West, had impressed on the commissioners the requirements of the region, but they soon ceased making further contributions. The board publicly announced that it lacked funds and that the migrating Baptist preachers would satisfy the western needs. The real though unstated reason was the increasing western Baptist opposition to the missions. Eventually, in 1822, the Massachusetts Missionary Society decided to assist Peck, while Welch returned East to join the Sunday School Union staff.

The very enthusiasm of the eastern Baptists had helped to create the opposition. Spurred by their own zeal, they promoted an extensive national program that was not understood by the western and southern Baptists. The easterners were accustomed to working together through local and state missionary and education associations. The Massachusetts Baptist Missionary Society had been organized in 1802. The eastern Baptists collected books, set up libraries, helped to support the education of ministerial candidates and ministers, established colleges and seminaries, conducted missionary activities, and published such periodicals as the *Massachusetts Baptist Missionary Magazine*. They were unaware of the profound ignorance and provincialism of many western and southern Baptists, who in some instances still nursed bitter memories of their Virginia experience. Although he was an outsider, Allen Wiley, the pioneer Methodist presiding elder, understood that it was mainly the less-educated rural Baptists who were the anti-missionites. In towns and cities the Baptists worked to some extent with other denominations and had learned to appreciate these "benevolent" societies. To educate and to interest the rural Baptists in what was happening in the world, Wiley urged the urban Baptist churches and ministers to circulate religious periodicals among their rural co-religionists.[2]

The seeming failure of the three major projects which Luther Rice had undertaken, the Columbian College at Washington, D.C., the *Columbian Star*, and the Tract Society, complicated the issue. They absorbed a portion of the mission funds and their collapse weakened the missionary movement. Many western churches and associations did not have one member sufficiently educated to understand the situation and to refute the widespread rumors of graft, exploitation, and luxurious living attributed to the mission leaders. Consequently, many western Baptists looked on all the missionaries and mission agents as "blood-sucking leeches," an opinion not unrelated to the strong western Baptist antagonism to stated financial support for the ministry.[3]

As demonstrated by the Baptist activities in the East, their tradition as such need not have engendered hostility to missions and welfare causes. In the West, the Maria Creek (Indiana) Church and other societies, where Isaac McCoy served as pastor, enthusiastically supported missions. These McCoy churches never deserted the cause and promoted pro-missionary interest throughout southwestern Indiana. Unfortunately for the mission movement, there was only one McCoy family. Many Indiana settlers hated the Indians and some wanted to exterminate them. Should the Indians become trained agriculturalists and citizens, the frontiersmen would be unable to seize more Indian land. Any reform would also disturb those influential pioneer families who had vested interest in whisky distilling and trade with the Indians. The very inability of most pioneer Baptists to respond to McCoy's ethical challenge to foster friendship with the Indians apparently intensified their hostility to the missionary cause and made them seek additional arguments against it.

In the meantime, Jacksonianism was spreading rapidly in the West, more markedly after the 1819 economic depression. The Jacksonians won a plurality of the votes in Indiana in 1824 without any organization and swept the state elections in 1825. The party represented the poorer section of the Indiana populace, the same elements that also formed the main Baptist constituency. Daniel Parker, John Vawter, Thomas Lincoln, and many others were enthusiastic Jacksonians and active anti-missionites. The anti-mission Baptists extended the sectional jealousies of the western Jacksonian movement to their own campaign. Both the religious and economic activities of eastern origin they denounced as schemes advanced by ambitious and wealthy easterners to betray American democratic liberties. The Triennial Convention had provided for the representation of societies contributing more than one hundred dollars. What clearer proof was needed to show that the mission system was an eastern financial instrument? The strenuous efforts by Luther Rice to raise money for missionary purposes were condemned as shameless and indecent tricks designed "to overthrow the democratic institutions of the nation."

Another reason for the anti-mission sentiment was the personal jealousy of some western preachers. At an Illinois association meeting, reports John Mason Peck, one minister expressed a typical objection to the missionaries: "We don't care any thing about them missionaries that's gone amongst them heathens 'way off yonder. . . . We don't want them here in Ilinois." When pressed by the moderator for his reasons, he eventually admitted, "Well, if you must know, Brother Moderator, you know the big trees in the woods overshadow the little ones; and these missionaries will be all great, learned men, and the people will all go to hear them preach, and we shall all be put down. That's the objection." A circular letter of the White River Association in 1844 embodied the resentment felt by many Baptist preachers: some members neglect their own pastors who have been working for them for years but give generously to the visiting missionaries and mission agents.[4]

The very inclination by the more prejudiced to see in the greater learning of the missionaries a criticism of their own preachers and possibly of themselves also stimulated anti-missionism. All proposals to educate the candidates for the ministry were denounced as attempts to change "graceless and lazy young men into clerical parasites." Many able but uneducated preachers shared with their less competent associates this hostility to the missionary movement, as is exemplified by John Vawter, an outstanding Indiana Baptist, whose family as a whole was prominent among the older western Baptists. John Vawter at various times had been an innkeeper, surveyor, proprietor of the local store, magistrate, member of the state General Assembly, state senator, United States marshal for Indiana, frontier ranger, sheriff of Jefferson and Clark counties, vice-president of the national convention that nominated Zachary Taylor for the presidency of the United States, founder of Morgantown, preacher of the local church, and "nabob of Vernon." He was perhaps the most influential leader among the southern Indiana Baptists. A mature man of his ability and experience would resent the implication that a young missionary fresh from a New England college and a theological seminary could advise him and his church on their problems. Not until late in his life did Vawter become a mission supporter.

The final reason for the objection to the mission movement to be considered here was, as previously mentioned, the assumed unscripturalness of "human agencies" that would deprive the church of its unique position. Wilson Thompson, for one, had once accepted McCoy's invitation to join the Indian mission, but the members of Thompson's church pleaded with him not to go. While he was walking home one day, the expression "Who hath required this at your hands?" flashed through his mind and satisfied him that the mission system was "human." Having rationalized his unwillingness to work among the Indians on the basis of not having a direct call from God, Thompson then looked for a scriptural justification of his refusal. In the process he readily convinced himself on the necessity for narrowly defining "Gospel preaching" and restricting it to "God's elect creatures." Anyone overstepping these rigid limits and preaching to others was against God. To most frontiersmen the Indians were obviously not among "God's elect creatures." Missionary churches in any case were not organized scripturally, and what is more, usurped God's direct missions. Thompson next elaborated predestinarianism into a strong argument against the missionary system. All human efforts to salvation were sinful and insulting denials of God's sovereignty. If God wanted to save the world He could and would.[5]

Daniel Parker (quoted in chapter viii) was a more widely active anti-mission leader. In his view, the Baptist Board had usurped Christ's authority and was openly violating the Scriptures in helping to train ministers and assigning them to various posts. The education and colonization of Indians did not concern religion, and, if anything, was contrary to God's will, Parker insisted. He also appealed to the frontier racial, religious, and sectional prejudices. His famous "two-seeds-in-the-spirit" doctrine sought to explain physiologically the existence of evil and election and also rationalized his hostility to "benevolent" efforts.

God saves the predestined in His own way. Those born of Satan's seed will and ought to return to their true father in hell. Hence, Parker declared, it was positively against God's will to preach the Gospel or give Bibles to people born of Satan. Through his periodical, the *Christian Advocate*, first issued in 1829, he stirred up the more ignorant people against educated ministry and missions. His election to the Illinois State Senate, where he served from 1822 to 1826, indicates at least some general popularity, and his influence extended to Kentucky, Tennessee, and Indiana, including the Little Pigeon Association in which Thomas Lincoln's church was for a time a Parker stronghold.[6]

Alexander Campbell was a leader in the "liberal" wing of antimissionism. His publications, including the *Christian Baptist* begun in 1823, helped to spread his views widely. By rejecting creeds, mission system, and predestination, he won many followers. To clarify their position, the regular Baptists insisted upon acceptance of five fundamental doctrinal points: total moral depravity, effectual calling, predestination, perseverance of the saints, and the believer's baptism by immersion. Their very action drove into the Campbell ranks some Baptists traditionally opposed to all doctrines. The theologically liberal minority and many antipredestinarians also joined Campbell, especially in areas dominated by the Parkerites and other extreme predestinarians. The whole Campbell movement ultimately became a western religious version of rationalism and liberalism, sometimes regarded as a rough and later parallel to New England Unitarianism. The missionary board Campbell viewed as a new "Holy Alliance" and an embodiment of "Jesuitry" founded solely by and on money to undermine religious liberty. Unless the people stopped the salaried priests on the mission board, they would establish an ecclesiastical hierarchy and destroy church democracy. The only legitimate missionary activity was the migration of a whole congregation to a heathen land where individual members would continue to labor in their secular occupations and set an example before the people. The idea of merging the various sects, which Campbell advocated, attracted many followers despite his origi-

nally negative position. Eventually, as he became more concerned
with uniting all sects, his anti-missionism faded away.[7]

The bitter factionalism aroused by Thompson, Parker, Campbell, and others shattered many western churches and associations.
The churches and associations that still seemed united had to
avoid commitments to escape the aggressive anti-mission attacks.
The Indianapolis Association, for instance, had to proceed cau-
tiously even after it had expelled both the extreme predestinari-
ans and the "reformers" (Campbellites). Royce McCoy and his
pro-mission group had to leave the Silver Creek Church when it
became Campbellite. They formed a new church and joined the
Lost River Association, only to be isolated again when the assoc
ciation became Parkerite — that is, anti-mission on the extreme
predestinarian wing of the movement. Eventually they organized
the Bethel Missionary Baptist Association in 1837. These controversies consumed time and energy of the mission supporters who
would have preferred doing constructive work.

Throughout the bitter conflict Isaac McCoy continued to minister to the Indians and speak for their welfare. He expected little
or no encouragement in Indiana for his work. The bulk of his
support came from Kentucky and Ohio, aside from his own Maria
Creek Church, the Blue River Missionary Society headed by his
brother James, the Aurora Missionary Society led by Judge Holman, and a "non-Christian" merchant named Phillips. The federal government did not pretend to keep its solemn agreements
with the Indians. It violated its stated policy to train them as
agrarians by canceling their titles as rapidly as possible. At least
once a government interpreter flatly refused to translate McCoy's
words to the Indians because "none but a fool would attempt to
instruct Indians." McCoy went to the Fort Wayne area in 1820
to be free from the unscrupulous settlers, but by 1822 he had to
move again, after the influx of whites who had no respect what-
soever for Indian rights.

His greatest contribution to the Baptists was possibly to practice charity instead of arguing over divisive doctrinal issues that
few Baptists understood in the first place. Under his leadership,

the pro-mission churches collected food, clothing, money, and other necessities. Individuals and societies engaged in these activities lost interest in sterile controversies. His was a worthy program in which local churches and missionary societies could participate and by their very participation develop common interests and learn to co-operate. Furthermore, he and his family suffered great hardships for their ideals. Their lives gave direct lie to the lurid stories of missionary dishonesty, extravagance, and greed for power. Their work appreciably helped to promote Baptist unity, notably in organizing the state convention in 1833. The very name, "The General Association of Baptists in the State of Indiana," instead of "The Indiana State Convention," was chosen to minimize the prevailing anti-mission prejudice against state conventions. Its employees were to be members in good standing with no special educational qualifications. The association was to pay no salaries to its officers aside from the actual cost of the supplies used in business, to accept delegates regardless of the amount or lack of contribution to it, and to have no authority over any church. Its constitution specified it was to employ for preaching only those regularly ordained. Despite the restrictions imposed on the General Association and its small income, averaging less than three hundred dollars per year between 1833 and 1839, it helped to break down provincialism by making possible yearly assemblies and contact with outside Baptists.

Perhaps the most ambitious pro-missionary project in Indiana was to found Franklin College. To minimize the social prejudice against academic pursuits and to help finance the school, its supporters decided to set up a manual labor college. The college was constantly in financial difficulties, for it was almost impossible to persuade the members at large to accept a denominational school. Besides the prevailing contempt for scholarly activities, more antagonism existed specifically against educational requirements for ministers than against any other feature of the missionary program. All this hostility forced the Baptist pro-mission leaders to promote the vital activities as individuals, since the Baptists as a denomination were virtually paralyzed. The General Association in Indiana did not dare for years to sponsor education, not even

Sunday schools, although the leaders were aware that the perennial bickerings rose mainly from the sheer ignorance of many ministers and members alike.

The Baptist refusal to support their preachers financially seems to have been an important reason for the scarcity of competent men. The Aurora Church was the first to pay a regular allowance. It was only a dollar and a half per month and this sum was withdrawn later. A preacher was not even reimbursed for his travel expenses as an itinerant. An agent for a northern Indiana Bible Society reported in 1826 that he had not received as much as fifteen dollars from the people for three years of preaching.

With the spread of the post-1839 depression, those advocating co-operative religious work were able to secure a hearing. The missionary question was becoming less of an open issue, while at the same time the center of Baptist influence in the state shifted from southern to northern Indiana, where the Baptists had come from New England and were as a rule friendly to the missionaries. In contrast, many ex-southern Baptists abused them personally as Gospel speculators "laboring for the fleece and not for the flock." Often the missionaries had difficulty in finding lodging in Baptist homes in southern Indiana and were frequently denied the pulpit merely because they were missionaries. Dr. William H. Pratt typically received greater welcome from the Methodists and Presbyterians than he did from the Baptists.

As elsewhere in the early West, Indiana Baptists were weak in the larger towns and consequently the missionaries had to take the initiative. This statement does not refer to churches founded in small villages which later grew into cities, but to the already thriving population centers as yet without Baptist churches. The Baptist Home Mission Society nominally assigned its missionaries to specific places, but in reality they served as itinerants and worked in several communities. The above-mentioned Dr. Pratt, a Colgate graduate, helped to found churches in Crawfordsville, South Bend, Mishawaka, Logansport, and Lafayette. The Chicago churches received direct missionary aid. When not missionaries, the city church pastors were usually professional or business men, not farmers.[8]

Thus far we have briefly reviewed some more obvious reasons for anti-missionism, such as ignorance, greed for land, personal jealousy, sectional bias, and alleged lack of scriptural sanction for the missions, but these factors were essentially symptoms or, as we have seen, rationalizations after the fact. The opposition sprang from more basic, often unstated but emotionally and socially significant, causes implied by the very nature of the mission movement. In *The Genesis of American Anti-Missionism*, B. H. Carroll, Jr. strongly supports the pro-mission Baptists and in the process, perhaps without fully appreciating their importance, indirectly brings to light the fundamental dynamics of the hostility. As his main proposition and general conclusion, Dr. Carroll states that the foreign missions system had made its greatest impact at home — it has incalculably benefited the American Baptists, since it has been the main force holding the Baptists together as organized denominations, mainly through the southern and northern conventions, and countering the "centrifugal force" of isolationism, local church sovereignty, and divisiveness. The fundamental reason for anti-missionism, we might therefore suggest, was probably this very point. Those opposed to missions wanted to retain their familiar small sect practices and ideals, their own congenial, independent, intimate, and relatively withdrawn fellowships. Missions, education, Sunday schools, Bible and tract societies, state and national conventions, and other organizations would inevitably transform their face-to-face local lay fellowships into far more impersonal and less localized and less democratic denominations with professional ministries. Again, Dr. Carroll indirectly raises the mission issue by asserting as his secondary thesis that the foreign missions were the wellsprings of "education, organization, home missions and other denominational activities," the very development which the anti-missionites opposed.[9]

Typically, John Taylor of Kentucky, an outstanding early anti-mission leader, expressed this very fear. "The deadly evil I have in view, is under the epithets or appellations of *Missionary Boards, Conventions, Societies*, and Theological Schools, all bearing the appearance of great, though affected sanctity." The Mission Board, not God, called the candidates, Taylor argued, and, to make matters worse, it assigned missionaries to specific places and supported them. The Board not only subverted God's sovereignty, religious liberty, and democracy but also was unscriptural. The mission supporters would create a Baptist papacy, Taylor charged, and he professed to see parallels between their aims and the Jesuit missions in Paraguay, the archetype of the development he feared. His concern led him to see sinister implications in matter-of-fact statements, as shown by his misinterpretation of Judson's appeal to the Baptist Board for men with "amiable, yielding temper, willing to take the lowest place." Judson wanted men submissive to his grandiose pretensions, asserted Taylor, when, of course, Judson had in mind men able to work cheerfully under harsh conditions in Burma.

The mission advocates began with mission societies and then created a great board with officers who selected "the most vigorous and artful agent" they could find to organize various types of societies, such as Female Societies, Children's Societies, and "even Negro Societies, both free and bond," Taylor charged. He then compared Luther Rice with Tetzel, since Rice's aim was "through sophistry and Yankee art" to raise funds for missions in which he would have a part. "I did begin strongly to smell the *New England Rat*," he said. Each local church organized by the home missionaries in the West provided additional authority and glory for the Mission Board which would also control every church thus established. The very correspondence by the board members with various churches and their personal contacts as such were dangerous, for this connection gave these men power and money. They were becoming an aristocracy, seeking to undermine the Baptist republican church government, Taylor insisted. "The highest court Christ has fixed on earth, is a worshipping congregation, called a church." [10]

The anti-missionites focused their attacks on education, in particular theological training. An educated ministry was "an abomination unto the Lord." To them theological seminaries, Sunday schools, and mission and welfare societies were all Satan's devices to ensnare and corrupt the church. On the other hand, the pro-mission groups invariably supported education. The anti-mission movement also opposed state conventions and other organizations designed to promote denominational work. Conversely, in almost every case, state conventions stressed education and missions among their main objectives, which would also lead to a professional ministry and a more formal church organization. Yet the survival of the denomination depended upon furthering these co-operative efforts. Although the mission and anti-mission Baptists split into almost equal factions in the nineteenth century, Dr. Carroll states, the regular Baptists have grown into major denominations with millions of members, while the old anti-mission group totaled only 126,000 in 1902. To use the political analogy, the missionites reinterpreted the western Baptist democracy from a rough parallel to the most limited concept of Jeffersonianism (much narrower than political Jeffersonianism which was national in scope and continental in outlook) into an equally rough parallel to Jacksonianism using organizations democratically controlled and led and responsive to popular will to achieve hitherto unobtainable objectives which the members wanted. In contrast, even while supporting Jacksonianism, the anti-missionites stressed its negative sectional and class bias — they were fighting the organizations and programs which, many thought, were fostered by the eastern moneyed interests.

The common principle, then, held by such otherwise conflicting anti-mission leaders as Alexander Campbell and Daniel Parker was their opposition to innovations which would inevitably change the familiar sect into a more churchly denomination. The virtually independent intimate local fellowship would become a part of a more institutionalized, more formal associations influenced by distant national offices and committed to programs outside its immediate control. Significantly, the anti-missionites were the poorer, less-educated rural Baptists — the very elements even then less confident of rising socially and economically and similar to the less privileged groups which to this day find sects and holiness groups more congenial than the more impersonal middle-class denominations. On the other hand, the pro-missionites were generally better educated and more prosperous, that is, more explicitly middle-class oriented, rising economically and socially, and more optimistic about their future. Many originally opposed to missions who later changed their opinion and became pro-missionites were the prosperous minority among the anti-mission-ites. Others, including the Campbellites, never accepted some of the specific sectarian traits, since they had a more liberal outlook and soon began to support education, missions, and other de-nominational activities.

This period marked the turning point for the Baptists. They had to decide whether to remain essentially a sect, or perhaps more accurately, a group of sects, appealing on the whole to a more humble and less prosperous membership, or to become increas-ingly large-scale, middle-class oriented, more churchly denomina-tions. The present survey also demonstrates the value of making analytical distinctions between church and sect, each with its par-ticular attributes, since the issues involved the very qualities — or-ganizational, social, cultural, psychological, and theological — which distinguish sects from churchly denominations.

American histories, religious and secular, have generally cor-related the rising political democracy in this period with the grow-ing popularity of the free-grace doctrine, particularly Methodist, and the decline of rigid predestinarianism in the denominations which originally emphasized this view. Some correlation existed, but this interpretation probably oversimplifies the complex inter-action. It was precisely the more prosperous and better-educated Baptists who joined Campbell for his more liberal position, where-as it was definitely the less privileged Baptists who supported the strongly predestinarian side of the anti-mission movement. The ardent faith the poorer elements had in undemocratic ultra-predestinarian views requires further investigation, but perhaps a brief tentative speculation is possible here.

The popular denominations often correlated assurance of salva-tion with conversion commonly gained at revival meetings. Com-pared with this conversion, culture, wealth, and worldly honors were deemed secondary in value. The conversion experience itself became the criterion of the new elite. The extreme predestinari-ans, as the poorer and less-educated elements, were more likely to need compensatory rationalizations for their unfavorable status, all the more since the prosperous at times equated the state of their grace with their worldly prosperity. Since their conversion experiences "assured" the underprivileged their salvation, they could deprecate others' worldly attainments. The humble would get to heaven, but not many of the mighty. Such beliefs would be consistent with the extreme emotionalism which permeated their attacks on education, "benevolent" societies, and "Yankee agents." The underprivileged saw no reason to support education to produce people scornful of them. It was outrageous to send missionaries to the "heathen," because only the elect could and ought to be saved. The very idea was disturbing, for they would not be any more the elect than the despised Indians if, as the missionaries asserted, the heathen were also saved. To remain a sect, members withdrawing from a growing denomination with a strong emphasis on winning converts, as many American Baptists then had, would find an essentially aristocratic belief, such as extreme predestinarianism, helpful, if not necessary, to justify their decision.

The combination of free grace and popular democracy suited the rising lower-middle classes optimistic about achieving appreciable worldly success and more fully imbued with middle-class outlook. As their denomination grew, it inevitably changed from a sect-like group to more churchly denominations. Conversely, extreme predestinarianism with revivalistic assurance would seem more assuring to those who were without such expectations of material achievement and were partly isolated from the larger community. For the anti-missionites, predestinarianism as a compensatory belief perhaps belonged in the same category as modern racism, which often gives the less-favored classes of one race a feeling of superiority over another race (and here also the anti-mission opposition to the work among the Indians was relevant), and as extreme isolationism which creates in other less favored people similar illusions of superiority over "foreigners."

CHAPTER XII

Revivalism

Revivalism deeply permeated the religious and to a lesser extent the secular life in the West and was at the same time an expression of western religion and sociability. An analysis of revivalism as such is beyond the scope of this chapter, which will refer to only a few of its many features. Ironically, revivalism of the type with which this study is concerned first became prominent between 1720 and 1740 in certain Presbyterian and Reformed churches in the Middle Colonies when the so-called New Lights captured several presbyteries. The New Lights concentrated on conversion experience and evangelical fervor and were less interested than the orthodox in the formal church polity and doctrines. Thus, the New Brunswick Presbytery, which came under New Light control, defied the synod rule limiting ministerial ordination to graduates of recognized European universities and New England colleges. Instead, it accepted some students from the "log college" at Neshaminy, Pennsylvania, with religious "experience" rather than formal academic training as a criterion. The rising New Light influence accentuated the existing sectarian tendencies within American Presbyterianism. Some historians believe that later in conquering Dissent the revival-minded leadership altered the course of Dissenting history.

Many enthusiastic New Lights did not hesitate to invade recognized Presbyterian and Congregational parishes and to denounce non-revivalist pastors. Their reported censoriousness, self-righteousness, and petty moralism reveal traits often ascribed to the nineteenth-century western revivalists. Gilbert Tennent castigated the "unregenerate" ministers as "plastered hypocrites," "caterpillars," and perhaps his strongest condemnation, "moral negroes." This racism confused with "pure religion" exemplifies the spiritual and ethical obtuseness frequently attributed to revivalistic moralism. Tennent may not have been a racist, but his name-calling cruelly insulted the helpless Negro minority in the colonies.[1]

At the June, 1741, session of the Synod, the conservative Old Sides formally protested against the revivalists for invading the existing congregations and condemning all who did not agree with them as "carnal, graceless, and enemies to the work of God." The New Lights taught the people, so the Old Sides declared, that any preaching by ministers regularly ordained but unconverted was worthless and that the call of God consisted of invisible "workings of the Spirit," which only the person himself sensed and concerning which he may have been mistaken. Furthermore, the revivalists preached in such a terrifying manner that the weakminded would "cry out in a hideous manner" and have convulsions. The New Lights then boasted that this hysteria was divinely inspired when, the Old Sides insisted, it probably had pernicious origins.[2]

From its beginnings, revivalism has been highly divisive. It became a widespread social phenomenon in America, but many studies on the subject deal almost exclusively with its individualistic manifestations. Yet the very forms of the hysterical agitation which "seized" persons attending the revivals spread with the news about their occurrences. Typically, the general public first became interested in the violent "jerks" around the turn of the century during the Great Revival in eastern Tennessee. As long as a person had the jerks, parts of his body would snap back and forth with such rapidity that the long braids of hair cracked like whips. Stories about this particular hysteria circulated widely and thereafter it became so popular that safety zones had to be established at some meetings to enable the victims to have their jerks with less danger. Allen Wiley mentions the first appearance of the "laughing jag" and comments on its rapid spread. Physical displays, in brief, had definite origins, widespread publicity, and growing popularity (even if involuntary) as the latest fashion in revivals, and then declined in public interest. Many western revivalists regarded these physical phenomena as "heavenly visitations," while they consciously resorted to time-tested techniques to induce them in susceptible persons. On the other hand, the better-educated Presbyterian and Congregational ministers denounced them as vulgar "animal displays." [3]

Revivalism was also a force for democracy in the eighteenth and early nineteenth centuries. As we have seen, the conversion experience itself became a basic criterion for the new regenerate elite. Wealth, family, and learning were considered of secondary importance, if not a positive detriment, to attaining this vital experience. The chapter on Dissent in Virginia has already mentioned the increasing participation in religious organizations by the common people directly under revivalistic stimulus. They also became active in the political life of the Old Dominion, originally to defend their religious rights, and helped to alter the state socially and culturally. The New Light triumph over the orthodox Presbyterians against the latter's rigid polity and aristocratic outlook again illustrates the democratic influence exerted on religious organization by the revival movements. [4]

Since the more naïve revivalists assumed that only one way to grace existed, revivalism tended to be anti-intellectual and anti-cultural. Robert E. Thompson, a leading nineteenth-century Presbyterian historian, complained that "instantaneous, conscious conversion, preceded by an overwhelming sense of personal guilt, and followed by a joyful assurance of acceptance" by God was the only form of salvation revivalism recognized. Religion thus had no relation to a man's past, Dr. Thompson protested, but came to him "like a bolt from the blue." [5] To the ardent revivalists, the conversion experience became at once a criterion of salvation and their one certainty amidst the worldly confusion. Theology, philosophy, art, and science might lure the faithful from salvation. In a typical revivalist story, a "master and lover" of Greek classics long resisted conversion since he did not wish to surrender his classics, but he finally gave them up and was thus happily converted. [6] One may wonder how Calvin, a classical scholar, would have reacted to such a peculiar interpretation of salvation.

At any rate, the Congregational and Presbyterian doubts regarding revivalism become understandable. To their more learned ministers, even the regular Dissenting preaching often seemed but "animated noise." To meet the competition, the Congregational ministry learned to make their sermons more popular but without vulgarity.

John Mason Peck persuaded some Baptist ministerial candidates to spend a few months studying the Bible, the rudiments of English grammar, and other subjects necessary to handle the Bible with some understanding, only to encounter the hostility mentioned above (chap. XI) from many Baptists. Some applicants still open-minded enough to attend the school expected to learn everything in a few months. When no "bolt from the blue" enabled them to master every branch of learning, they became discouraged. Revivalistic emotionalism was not conducive to long systematic study. Perhaps Dr. Mecklin is partially justified in his witticism concerning one consequence of revivalism, that Americans "have never been able to forego the exquisite pleasure of prostituting their intellects to their feelings. It is so much easier to feel good than to think straight." [7]

Revivalistic anti-culturalism vulgarized the very worship services of many popular denominational meetings. Dignity and beauty were often lost. The change in the American Methodist services before the denomination was ready to reclaim its older heritage illustrates the trend among Dissenters in general. In 1784, as mentioned before, John Wesley prepared for the American Methodists an abridgment of the Anglican Prayer Book, concerning which he wrote, "I believe there is no Liturgy in the world, either in ancient or modern language, which breathes more of solid, Scriptural rational piety than the Common Prayer of the Church of England. . . . Little alteration is made in the following edition" for American usage. When Wesley sent Coke to America, he had Coke take unbound copies of the *Sunday Service* with him. The 1784 Conference, which founded American Methodism as a separate denomination, adopted the *Sunday Service* as the "ark and covenant for the Methodist Episcopal Church." Yet the service book never became popular. William

Burke was astonished to see Vasey using it, since the service did not seem Methodist to Burke or other Americans. The book went through only one more edition in 1786 and was then promptly forgotten, except that in 1792 such offices as the communion, baptism, marriage, ordination, and burial were incorporated into the *Discipline*. The haste with which American Methodists discarded the *Sunday Service* was symbolic, as were the painful efforts by the prosperous Methodists in later years to rediscover their Anglican background. In the meantime, the great religious architecture, paintings, and other arts had also disappeared from western popular denominations.[8]

Pageantry, festivals, folk music and dances, and the formal arts and music would probably have curtailed the vulgarity and the extremes of revivalism. The great leader of the Danish spiritual rebirth, the Lutheran Bishop Nicholas S. F. Grundtvig, emphasized on the one hand practical agricultural and technical training and on the other hand adult education, community recreation, music, dances, arts, and similar activities as essential requisites for the spiritual as well as the social and economic regeneration of the Danes. The intuitive revivalist hostility to these recreational interests is consistent.[9]

In some instances, revivalism apparently accentuated the emotional instability of both adults and children. Richard McNemar, a Kentucky revival leader, describes a twelve-year-old boy speaking with tears streaming from his eyes to a highly excited audience. Some members at the peak of excitement "fell like those who are shot in battle." This is an extreme case, but illustrates the emotionalism often prevalent at revivals. Another correspondent reports, "One little boy in my congregation, one night, was crying bitterly. 'O!' said he, 'I am lost forever. I am going right down to hell. O, I see hell, and the breath of the Lord like a stream of brimstone kindling it.'" Still another contemporary writes that "little children . . . were to be found in every part of the multitude . . . crying out for mercy in the most extreme distress."[10] Exciting children was essentially inconsistent with the popular denominational insistence on adult conversion and membership. A comparison with the still earlier New England Puritan practices, however, may temper present-day criticisms of the way the Dissenters treated their children, since at first the Puritans, regardless of their better education, apparently did not hesitate to resort to terror to discipline their children — perhaps literally driving the "fear of God" into them. In contrast the Anglicans showed a greater understanding of their children, while the gentle and humane way the Mennonites dealt with their children is praised by some present-day educators.[11]

Many adults, it is said, also developed permanent emotional or nervous peculiarities from continued attendance at revivals. The fear engendered by some fiery sermons, the superstitious belief in the physical displays as "heavenly visitation," the mob excitement, and the prolonged lack of sleep and rest at camp meetings drove large numbers close to hysteria. In his study on revivalism, F. M. Davenport believes that there is a direct correlation in some nineteenth-century communities between the number and intensity of their revival meetings and the frequency of their lynchings. If such a correlation existed even partially, it meant that the people most susceptible to revival hysteria were also the most susceptible to impulsive mob action and weakest on rational ethical control — hardly an ideal Christian personality to foster. Indeed, such loss of self-control violates the Calvinist ideal of the disciplined and rational Christian engaged in his calling, an ideal essentially adopted also by the American popular denominations.[12]

It was the successful preachers at camp meetings, Cartwright and Finley among them, even more than the opponents of revivalism, who most vividly described the hysteria, turbulence, confusion, and noise at these meetings with hundreds or thousands shouting, bellowing, and screaming, others in convulsions, and at times many in free-for-all fights. Cartwright, like others, dealt summarily with trouble makers, often by cracking their skulls together. The whisky dealers who set up stands nearby were blamed for some of the wild fights.[13] Today it would be almost impossible to imagine such agitated scenes as ever being regarded as religious. In the backwoods of the Lincoln country, Herndon found people at revivals "hugging each other and singing in ecstasy that was half religious, half sexual — 'I have Jesus in my arms / Sweet as honey, strong as bacon ham.' " [14] It became necessary to post guards to prevent affected couples from going into the woods. In their hysteria some women would throw themselves on the ground, tear open their clothes, and hug and kiss every one around them. Such strong opponents of revivalism as the Reverend Mr. John Lyle, a Presbyterian, actually listed girls who became pregnant at the camp meetings. With some basis, but probably with unfair exaggeration, some cynics have said that "more souls were begotten than saved" at these meetings. [15]

This emotionalism spread from camp meetings to regular religious activities. F. C. Holliday, a pioneer Indiana Methodist presiding elder, describes a session at Concord. The preacher began to read the text, Job 19:25:

"I know," and then said, "Glory!" Repeating, "I know," he said, in a louder tone, "Glory!" Again repeating "I know," he shouted, at the top of his voice, "Glory, glory, glory!" and, covering his face with both hands, wept like a child. The presiding elder, Rev. Robert Burns, asked him if he should read the text, to which he assented. He then introduced his subject by saying that "Job was no Campbellite — glory! — for he knew — glory! — that his Redeemer lived — glory!" and preached a melting sermon to a weeping congregation. [16]

Here we see that both the emotionalism and the sectarianism of revivalism (in this case, an attack on the Disciples) have permeated a meeting. As to similar excitement in western politics, Turner and Paxson point to parallels. Politicians often attended camp meetings and spoke on the outskirts. Indicative of the revivalist emotionalism affecting the regular circuit riders, Allen Wiley, himself a rather restrained Methodist presiding elder, comments on the fervor of several frontier itinerants. "I well remember . . . Thomas Hellums, who was a most grave, zealous, affectionate, and weeping preacher." Again, "Hugh Cull, or Hugh O'Cull, as his name was originally, could exhort most feelingly, and weep showers of tears all the time; so that he made powerful impressions on the people in this new country, where they had not much able preaching." [17]

The fundamental assumption most revivalists held that only

one road to salvation existed was a basic factor in what several critics, including Dr. Thompson, regard as the deterioration of American religious and cultural standards. The extreme revivalists tended to isolate Christian experience from life and to concentrate on inward emotions. This negative outlook may seem paradoxical against the active popular denominational participation in contemporary economic and community life, but it was the Dissenting denominational discipline and organizational activities which stressed the calling in contrast to the revivalist emotionalism, introspection, and individualism. That is, revivalism as such had tendencies conflicting with or subversive of popular denominational ideals. Even in the eighteenth century, to the extent that in his more revivalistic moments he emphasized personal salvation, Jonathan Edwards also deviated from the great Calvinistic accent on the church triumphant.

Indirectly, Timothy Flint brings out the limitations inherent in the extreme revival theory. A Kentuckian whom Flint met explained that he did not swear in the presence of ministers and told him:

That all his relatives were religious, and that he was almost the single stray sheep from the flock; he had often tried to "get religion," as the phrase is here; he had laboured as hard for it, as he ever had at rolling logs, and that whatever was the reason, do all he could, to him it would never come; and now, if it would come to him of itself, good; but if not, that he meant to try for it no more.[18]

Regardless of the prominence given to revivalism, the popular denominations considered it essentially a technique for gaining new members and for revitalizing the faithful. Many later accounts equate the camp meetings with western religion, when in reality such gatherings were outside the official denominational life. In all his research Professor Sweet has been unable to find any references to them in the Methodist *Discipline* and in the Methodist General Conference legislation. The Methodists had no church laws on revivals and camp meetings; they were extracurricular activities. Local sponsors and regional committees, however, prepared rules for governing the camp meetings. The regular Methodists clearly understood that without the subsequent membership in an established denomination with its organized fellowship conversion could be meaningless. The formal classes and societies and their systematic discipline constituted the heart of the Methodist and Baptist religious life, not the spectacular revivals. The Presbyterians, of course, had early rejected the camp meetings even as extracurricular devices. The Friends ignored the whole system, and consequently some Methodists were furious with them.

After the initial period of the Great Awakening in the middle eighteenth century, the popular denominations gained very substantial numbers through revivalism. This growth was an outstanding achievement in the face of both the Enlightenment culture of the great Founding Fathers and the long persistent popular indifference to organized religion. Among the Mayflower group, only twelve of the one hundred and one were church members, and one person in five in the Massachusetts Bay Colony was a "professing Christian." As late as 1760, New England still had the highest ratio in the colonies with about one out of eight residents being a church member. In the Middle Colonies the proportion ranged from one in fifteen to one in eighteen, while in the South it was only one in twenty. The over-all colonial average was roughly one church member among every twelve people.

Although the popular denominations gained vast numbers through the revival meetings and thus appreciably overcame the handicaps arising from the continuous large-scale population movements which broke many traditional ties, their success does not prove that other means might not have been as effective or better, particularly in the long run. Drs. Reed and Matheson, the British Congregational delegates to America, reported in 1835 that the Dissenters paid little or no attention to such alternative approaches as systematically visiting the homes of prospective members in the more permanent settlements and providing religious education for all the children. Many people deliberately waited until the camp meeting period before seeking church membership, since it was fashionable to go to the revivals first and then apply. Revivalism consequently was credited with winning members who had already intended to join. What is more, some churches were actually losing members because of the revivals. In 1803 the Presbyterians had 31 presbyteries, 322 ministers, and 48 probationary ministers in Kentucky and western Tennessee. A year later after the great revival these figures had dropped to 27 presbyteries, 130 ministers, and 33 probationary ministers. "The general result of this great excitement was an almost total desolation of the Presbyterian churches in Kentucky and part of Tennessee," reported Dr. Alexander to the Synod.[19]

Reed and Matheson in general accepted Lyman Beecher's conclusion that revivalism impoverished western religious life in many ways. As an eastern missionary to the West, Dr. Beecher was hardly unbiased, but his remarks seem at least partly valid. In his opinion, if revivalism had been entirely successful, it would have stopped all progress in science, education, and religion, thus causing a new Dark Age to fall on the United States. Even when the "burnt-out areas" exhausted by repeated revivalistic excitement became indifferent to religion, they definitely retained their hostility toward learning, educated clergy, and organized churches. Such regions, Beecher felt, were much worse off than if revivals had never taken place. Perhaps we should add that not all burnt-over areas remained apathetic. Upstate New York was frequently swept by religious excitement until mid-nineteenth century, but became a center of many reform movements. There, however, it was Charles G. Finney and his colleagues who were responsible for many revivals. Their approach differed appreciably from the usual western revivals and will be discussed below.

Independently of Beecher, the British Baptist delegates, Cox and Hoby, who came to America shortly after Reed and Matheson, reached similar conclusions regarding the western type of revivalism. They too deplored what they described as the detrimental effects of revivalism and prolonged meetings on the American Baptists and other Dissenters. Western revivalism subtly affected the very spirit and outlook of Dissent, but many studies on the subject have concentrated on the more concrete features instead of analyzing the changes.

The western revival system, it has been suggested, served as a convenient means for recruiting new members in a moving society, for democratizing religion, and for stimulating the interest of the active members. At the same time, as many have asserted, it tended to vulgarize the worship and other religious services, to make religion more emotional and less thoughtful, and to accentuate the existing doubts about intellectual and cultural pursuits. To the extent that revivalism of the previously discussed type helped the popular denominations to win substantial numbers of new members, it also complicated their discipline and local religious life. Sudden influx of religiously ignorant and not clearly committed members would inevitably dilute the quality of denominational life. Even on the frontier, thoughtful leaders like Allen Wiley had moments of doubts about the value of revival meetings. Present-day Methodist and Baptist leaders who deplore what they consider to be the lack of discipline, commitment, and religious knowledge of their denominational membership might assess to what extent, if any, these trends continue the earlier dilution of the local church religious life.[20]

We might consider several less frequently mentioned revivalistic influences as well: weakening the Dissenting ideal of sober, responsible citizenship and disciplined, self-controlled devotion to the calling by continually emphasizing the introspective and emotional factors; making religion, as Drs. Cox and Hoby thought, alternate between wild excitement and cold apathy; and interpreting salvation as a purely "spiritual" process in which the environment supposedly belonged to the "sensual" or "material" realm and was thus irrelevant to spiritual development. The latter tendency blunted the popular denominational understanding of slavery from the first and later in the nineteenth century almost disastrously delayed their understanding and efforts to confront the spiritual and moral crisis which all churches faced when the United States rapidly changed from an essentially agrarian to an urban industrial nation. As a consequence, for a time Dissent lost both influence and members among the working classes and other urban residents.[21] It would be difficult to assess the extent to which Dissent inherently had this outlook and how much revivalism had affected the popular denominations, but in any case revivalism did much to promote a narrower definition of religious responsibility than they would otherwise have had. The popular denominations paid a very high price for revivalism, a price often overlooked by its enthusiasts.

On the other hand, earlier in the century the emotional certainty associated with conversion experience, the disciplinary control, and the system of calling, in combination, encouraged the ambitious lower-class members to raise their economic and social aspirations. All three factors were essential, the discipline and the system of calling no less then the conversion. The conversion experience and discipline alone could lead to a sectarian withdrawal from life. The denominational discipline and teaching stimulated many who had originally joined as a result of revivalist excitement into "bettering" themselves. Thus, Methodist records refer frequently to converted individuals becoming Methodists and acquiring ambition and more and more substance through hard work, thrift, and devotion to business.

Finally, a few words on the Congregational and on Finney revivals will help to distinguish them from the western Dissenting revivals. Aside from the temporary excitement inspired by Jonathan Edwards and some early eighteenth-century revivalists during the Great Awakening, New England Congregationalism did not tolerate wild meetings. Edwards himself preached soberly. During the second great revival in the early nineteenth century, the Connecticut Congregationalists stressed reason and education, not excitement. Generally, small Bible study and prayer groups met regularly for a period prior to the larger gatherings. The one evangelist assigned to stimulate special interest, the Reverend Mr. Asahel Nettleton, preached only the "soundest of doctrines." He urged the people to meet quietly, to be orderly in their assemblies, and to disperse immediately afterward without disturbance. It was not his emotionalism but his sincerity that encouraged his listeners to try to lead a quickened religious life. Except for Nettleton, no special evangelists toured Connecticut. He worked entirely under the arrangements made with local pastors. Naturally, many ministers exchanged pulpits, as agreed upon in the church associations, but no lay preacher, no itinerant, no minister from outside the state was used. These revivals were successful mainly because of the preparation and subsequent religious activities. Not only in New England but also on the western frontier, the Congregational services retained their dignity.

The Charles Grandison Finney revivals were far more emotional than the usual Congregational and Presbyterian meetings, but they too differed appreciably from those of the Methodists and the Baptists. By 1825 the reports of his upstate New York revival meetings began to trickle eastward to New England. Finney was a Presbyterian and subsequently a Congregationalist, but it was rumored that as he approached the climax of his dramatic discourse, many in the audience would begin trembling and shrieking. Mr. Finney, it was further said, was denunciatory. Again, reports had it, he would pray for "sinners" by name, and his helpers, a "holy band" of recent converts, were a sore trial to the local ministry because of their enthusiasm. The institution of the "anxious seats" (a row of seats in the front for the worried sinners) was permitted, and so were public prayers by women. The news disturbed the New England orthodox who in 1827 sent delegates, including Lyman Beecher, to confer with Finney and to end irregular practices. In comparison with modern Congregational and Presbyterian standards, Finney's meetings were apparently "extravagant." At that time, however, the Baptist and Methodist revivalists appealed immediately to the emotions, while, in contrast, Finney first reasoned closely with the "anxious sinners." Only after he had convinced them rationally did he resort to his hypnotic eloquence, and this power he used in moderation. He never lost control over the emotions of his converts. His followers, it should be said, were not necessarily as restrained.[22]

Granting that many regarded Finney as the most powerful contemporary speaker, it is not his eloquence but his teachings that concern us here. For him, original sin was simply a deep but mainly voluntary self-interest, not an inherent depravity causing the actual transgressions. Virtue was disinterested benevolence, and sin was selfishness. To Finney, revival conversion was not supernatural but came from the "*right exercise* of the powers of nature." The released emotions stimulated these powers, but they should not be deplored on this account, since people will not "act until they are excited." How many persons, he asked, procrastinate about doing the right thing until they are so aroused that they "cannot contain themselves any longer"? It was the sinner himself who carried out his own conversion, not some miracle of the Holy Spirit.[23]

His message changed the religious outlook of his followers. American revivalism had tended to make personal salvation the primary aim of the saved, while for Finney salvation was the beginning of religious experience, not its end. Far from escaping life, converts began a new life of greatest possible service. Hence the Finneyites threw themselves into various social movements, from education to penal reform, from abolition to better training for the clergy. Theodore Dwight Weld was perhaps the greatest Finney convert. He may well have been the outstanding abolitionist leader. In addition, he was partially responsible for founding the women's rights movement in upstate New York, which became its center. Finney's other conspicuous friends included the then famous members of the interlocking directorates of the major national benevolent associations promoting education, abolition, missions, Sunday schools, seamen's welfare, temperance, and other causes. Among these directors, the leading spirits were the Tappan brothers, especially Arthur and Lewis, wealthy Presbyterian businessmen and philanthropists. In every community Finney left a group interested in entering the ministry. The men began to exchange confidences through Weld as their leader and formed a loosely knit circle of friends who agreed to meet some time for theological training. Weld himself repeatedly refused influential offices and remained a student for many years, while Dr. Finney later became a professor of theology and president of Oberlin.[24]

This brief and necessarily oversimplified summary has shown some basic differences between the Finney and the typical Dissenting revivals. Finney held his meetings under control and appealed to reason, as well as to "sympathy." He seemed to understand the natural basis of the revival phenomena. If the Finney revivalists retained the petty moralistic elements common to contemporary evangelicalism, they generally had no direct anti-intellectual bias. Instead, many, including Finney himself, became outstanding educators and promoted education. In contrast to the Dissenters, their ministerial candidates patiently undertook regular studies in colleges and theological seminaries. Finally and perhaps most important, the conversion experience of personal salvation was not the end of religious life, but the beginning of an active career in disinterested benevolence.

In later years, the Finney revival and similar schools of revivalism aroused in many Protestants — from Dissenters on the one hand to Episcopalians on the other — a driving interest in reform and welfare. Many publications on revivalism have confused the highly emotional, sectarian popular denominational revivalism in the West discussed in the previous pages with this later (1840–60), more sober, more socially oriented, and more ecumenical form. The western Dissenting revivalism helped to win members on the moving frontier but contained negative implications for the popular denominations. Often associated with the growing social reform emphasis, the new revival movement, in which the Finney group also participated, began mainly in the eastern cities among the relatively better-educated middle classes. Compared with the frontier revivals which appealed on the whole to a more rural and more humble people, the newer revivalism functionally served the interests of somewhat more secure professional and business groups. The new form spread westward and began to leaven the Methodists, Baptists, and other Dissenters in the West, many of whom by then had begun to "arrive" economically and socially. In spirit, practice, and perhaps motivation it differed appreciably from the older sectarian Dissenting revivalism. Thus, in Methodist circles, if the frontier revivals are associated with such names as John Grenade, James Axley, and Peter Cartwright, the later movement suggests Mrs. Phoebe Palmer, William Arthur, and possibly Bishops Matthew Simpson and Leonidas Hamline.[25]

CHAPTER XIII

Attitudes toward Slavery

In no other Western nation have slavery and race relations affected the religious organizations more profoundly than they have in the United States. None of the larger denominations, not even New England Congregationalism, was free of slaveholding members. The good Puritan felt that God had given him the heathen as his heritage and in enslaving the Indians and later the Negroes he was merely claiming his inheritance. As H. R. Niebuhr has found, racial prejudice was so respectable in America that the various denominations openly accepted it as a sufficient reason for separation and segregation, whereas they nearly always resorted to theological rationalizations to conceal other social causes of their sectarian differences.[1] Of the four denominations under consideration here, only the Friends confronted slavery directly on religious ground and they too had to be prodded by their German brethren and by their leaders like John Woolman.

Aside from economic interests, one reason for this relative indifference to slavery was the influence of their origins on the Dissenting groups. Sects may limit their community to their own brotherhood. Depending on their experience, leadership, and outlook, they may also define the community more broadly or have more inclusive concerns, as did the Friends. In addition, as we have observed, western revivalism also focused on individual conversion rather than that of the general society. Revivalism and sectarianism could become preoccupied with minute personal habits and almost overlook many larger issues, a tendency which some churchly critics have regarded as petty moralism. At the same time, the remaining traces of pietistic dualism, especially in western Methodism, discouraged a more serious concern with social institutions not directly associated with its then narrowly conceived "gospel message." Ultimately, in this dualistic tradition Christian faith transcends the mundane limits and as long as religious observances are possible, a Christian should care little whether or not he is free. The historic German Lutheran inclination to endure tyrannical governments as ordained by God illustrates one type of dualism in a church that was not generally considered narrowly moralistic.

In the early nineteenth century, various European travelers recorded that the United States treated its Negro population with callousness, if not with calculated cruelty. The endless humiliations imposed on the Negroes even in New England indicated that the custom was national and not merely southern. The virtually complete disregard for their personal feelings as well as the more obvious brutality that some citizens inflicted on them merely for "amusement" shocked many foreign visitors, who were often told by Americans that American democracy and morals were superior to European standards.

If racial prejudice was national, the West was possibly more biased than the East. Some seaboard states accepted free Negro voters, but all the early western states as a rule barred them.[2] The Indiana, Illinois, and Ohio black codes reflected the popular will. Similar sentiments were widespread in the West regarding the Indians. Anglo-Americans found the Indians repugnant even when they maintained nominal peace with them, Timothy Flint insisted, whereas the French learned the Indian languages and customs and, to his disgust, even lived with them. This chapter will not attempt to analyze slavery or race relations as such, but will be concerned mainly with the western denominational attitudes toward slavery and to a less extent toward race relations.

THE PRESBYTERIANS

Early in the nineteenth century, David Rice, a pioneer Presbyterian minister in Kentucky, actively encouraged antislavery movements. He addressed the Kentucky Constitutional Convention on "Slavery Inconsistent with Justice and Good Policy," using economic, moral, and biblical arguments to support his position. His plan would gradually emancipate the slaves already in the territory and prevent further importation of others. The proposal lost in the convention, but many in the slave states held this gradualist position against slavery. In the 1820's and 1830's, Tennessee was an important center of antislavery movements, frequently under Quaker and Presbyterian leaders.[3]

The most spectacular and influential western Presbyterian antislavery movement originated among the students of Lane Seminary, near Cincinnati. On Theodore Dwight Weld's recommendation, Arthur Tappan of New York undertook to endow a professorship at Lane Seminary if Lyman Beecher, then a nationally known pulpit orator, would accept it. Beecher agreed to join the faculty and to serve as the seminary president. It was perhaps the first institution of higher learning in America open to a Negro. Its first theological class included James Bradley, a Guinea Negro who had been kidnapped as a child and sold into slavery in South Carolina. His master had moved to Arkansas and he had permitted Bradley to purchase his own freedom from his earnings.[4]

The Seminary opened in 1832 with ninety-six students — forty enrolled in the theology school and fifty-six in the undergraduate literary department. The theology class was not only large but also mature and unusually well qualified. Thirty students were over twenty-six years old and all the forty had college education or its equivalent. Some already had extensive professional experience. Thirty-one, among them Finney converts, originally came from New England or New York where Weld had known most of them. Weld enrolled in the Seminary as a student and refused the appointment to the faculty which was offered to him in recognition of his ability and his contacts with the Tappan brothers. According to President Beecher, the class regarded Weld as the president: "He took the lead of the whole institution." Of Massachusetts birth and Yankee antecedents, he had previously studied at Andover, Hamilton, and Oneida. Today, Weld is little known partly because he was extremely self-effacing, asserts a recent biographer who also says that on the basis of his influence Weld was not only the outstanding abolitionist but also a major figure in his days.

Weld had previously discussed with the Tappan brothers the possibility of interesting the Lane students in abolitionism. None (except Bradley, the former slave) had ever been concerned with the issue. With his usual effectiveness Weld converted William T. Allan of Alabama to the cause, and together they won over several others. Finally, they asked for and received permission from President Beecher to debate the question. The discussion turned into a protracted meeting continuing for eighteen nights and as a result almost all the nearly hundred students were converted to abolitionism. In typical Finney tradition, the students immediately proceeded to carry out their convictions. They sought to improve the condition of the Cincinnati Negroes by establishing reading rooms, schools, and other means of self-help. Some lived in Negro homes to understand more clearly the problems confronting the Negroes, to win Negro confidence, and to express their equalitarianism. In the meantime, this successful conversion of the southerners at Lane had aroused the eastern abolitionist hopes for winning the South. All the officers of the Lane anti-slavery society were southerners. Among them, William T. Allan, Augustus Wattles, Marius R. Robinson, and James A. Thome became well known as abolitionist leaders.

Many Cincinnati people were actively opposed to their efforts to befriend the Negroes and brought pressure on the students. These citizens insisted that the students were promoting "social amalgamation" — an old and irrelevant charge. Perhaps the hostility was inevitable since Lane students intended once and for all to disprove the stereotype of Negro inferiority through education and training. The students were not content with mere patronizing "charity"; they wanted to apply their Christian principles.

During Dr. Beecher's absence, the trustees dissolved the student abolition society and placed all future discussion under the board censorship and right of dismissal. Inevitably a storm broke out. The students refused to be suppressed and nearly all withdrew. Not even Beecher was able to persuade them to return. Under great hardships, the majority spent the following year teaching each other and especially the Cincinnati Negroes and doing welfare work in the community. Eventually, in 1835, many former Lane students went to Oberlin College for the spring semester, taking with them the Reverend Dr. Asa Mahan, the only Lane trustee to support them, and Professor John Morgan, their faculty friend. The students accepted the invitation from Oberlin, however, only after they had negotiated at length to secure equality for Negroes, presidency for Dr. Mahan, and faculty appointments for Morgan and Weld. Mahan became president of the new college in the virtual wilderness. Weld did not feel that he could accept the professorship, but he recommended Charles Grandison Finney, whom the Tappan brothers eventually persuaded to go to Oberlin. Their financial contributions reflected their satisfaction at finding simultaneously a home for their ex-Lane protégés, a school open to Negroes, and a nursery for abolitionism.

The wholesale transfer by the Lane students, their vigorous and persistent fight for principles, including their prolonged negotiations with the Oberlin trustees for Negro rights, and their work with the Cincinnati Negroes reveal the effectiveness of their conversion. Only two of the forty in the theology department and five of the fifty-six in the literary department remained at Lane. Of the sixteen new students who arrived during the dispute with the trustees, eight withdrew after listening to the discussion. Eventually, thirty former Lane students (nearly all had moved to Oberlin) became the most effective abolitionist group developed in the country up to that time. Using the Finney technique to gain converts, the Weld team campaigned throughout Ohio and western New York and Pennsylvania, associated their cause directly with religion, and called upon everyone to help eradicate the "sin of slavery" from the country.

At first, the Lane abolitionists carried on their crusade largely within Presbyterianism, many meetings being held in Presbyterian churches. Hostile citizens often mobbed the sessions at which Weld and his associates spoke, and in places the "better elements" incited rowdies to assault them, but their heroism was equal to the task. Typically, Weld would conduct a thorough discussion, continuing from six to thirty days, until he had won nearly everyone in a given community to the cause. He and his associates began "another Great Revival," this time in abolitionism.

The less orthodox New School Presbyterians became the main supporters of the cause. Weld himself attended the 1835 Presbyterian General Assembly and had personal conferences with the commissioners from every state represented at the meeting. The various delegates were questioned as to their position on slavery and as to the progress of abolitionism in their home communities. These activities apparently had considerable impact — thus, in December, 1835, the Synod of the Western Reserve unanimously adopted the antislavery resolution which it had voted down only a year earlier. The 1836 General Assembly received twelve separate petitions asking it to act against slavery. After a prolonged debate on the subject, the assembly indefinitely postponed the whole issue, presumably because of other business and insufficient time. This delay was attacked by various leaders, including the outstanding orthodox spokesman, Joshua L. Wilson of Cincinnati. The debate shows that at least by 1836 an antislavery faction had risen to challenge the current Presbyterian position, granted that many against slavery were "moderates" who favored emancipation mainly in theory and supported the American Colonization Society. The outright abolitionists, as noted before, became increasingly critical of this society and its interest in expatriating the freed slaves because they felt it was distracting the public from the basic issue of freedom. In 1837, the Presbyterians finally split into the New School and the more conservative Old School churches. Slavery was not officially mentioned as a cause of the separation. The two factions disagreed over many issues, among them mission boards, theology, discipline, and eldership. An immediate factor was the action of the Old Guard majority in exscinding the synods of the Western Reserve, Genesee, Geneva, and Utica over issues of polity, but these synods were also nationally known at the time as abolitionist strongholds.

This brief sketch does not suggest that western Presbyterianism, as a whole traditional, agreed with Weld and his associates, for this was far from the case at least for some years. Since the eighteenth century, the denomination usually had a conservative attitude toward slavery. Samuel Davies, the great colonial Presbyterian leader and president of Princeton, had seen no wrong in slavery. The order of Christian providence established the master-slave relationship, he declared, and far from seeking to abolish it, Christianity would merely regulate it. The master would gain from Christianizing the slaves, since those Christianized were more diligent, faithful, and honest — and more profitable for the masters![5] On the other hand, many early western leaders, including David Rice, worked ardently to end the system, and Presbyterians were prominent in the various antislavery organizations in Tennessee and the border states. Nevertheless, while western Presbyterianism generally opposed slavery and disagreed with the later southern Presbyterian argument favoring slavery as a virtually divine institution beneficial to the slaves, many western Presbyterians were decidedly hostile to Negroes as individuals and as a race. Others, possibly the majority, were too indifferent to counter the widely prevailing western prejudice against Negroes.

THE BAPTISTS

The early centers of the western Baptist antislavery movement were first Kentucky and then Illinois. The outstanding abolitionist among the Kentucky Baptist clergy was David Barrow, formerly of Virginia, often regarded as the ablest pioneer Baptist minister in Kentucky. His fifty-page pamphlet published in 1808 and entitled *Involuntary, Absolute, Hereditary Slavery Examined on the Principles of Nature, Reason, Justice, and Scripture* circulated widely in Kentucky. Other pastors began to preach against slavery as well. The opposition immediately accused them of perverting the Negro minds and in 1805 Barrow had to explain his activities to the North District Association. The association at first took no action, but several churches were dissatisfied. Since he refused to give up his antislavery campaign, the association expelled him in 1806 for "preaching the doctrines of emancipation to the hurt and injury of the brotherhood."[6]

The emancipationists organized the Friends to Humanity Association in September, 1807. They accepted the principles — later known as Tarrant's Rules — formulated by Carter Tarrant, Barrow's associate. The Friends to Humanity Association resolved in 1808 that the relation of their church organization to slavery was unscriptural. They then organized the Kentucky Abolition Society to conduct their antislavery activities, while the Friends to Humanity Association continued as the religious association of the antislavery Baptists. The Abolition Society would give free Negroes practical training and moral instruction, ameliorate the condition of all Negroes, and seek justice for those held contrary to the existing laws. In 1816 it petitioned the legislature to support a plan for colonizing the free Negroes on public lands and sent additional memorials to the legislature and Congress the following year or two.

The Abolition Society and the Friends to Humanity Association represented but a small minority of the Kentucky Baptists and both organizations had ceased to exist in Kentucky by 1820. The Kentucky Baptist interest in abolition declined for various reasons, among them the War of 1812 and the loss of Carter Tarrant's leadership, for he became an army chaplain and died soon afterward. Furthermore, Baptist associations were reluctant to do anything which might disrupt the tenuous ties among the Baptists. Thus, the Illinois and Indiana Baptists who refused to admit slaveholders still corresponded with the slaveowning Kentucky associations instead of supporting the Friends to Humanity Association. Another factor was the traditional Baptist belief in the separation of church and state while slavery was considered a secular question. Perhaps the most direct cause of the declining abolitionist sentiment was the increase in slaveholding among the Kentucky Baptists. John Taylor, for one, had only four slaves in Virginia — and they were inherited, but in Kentucky he acquired 3,000 acres of land and twenty slaves.

The antislavery provisions of the 1787 Northwest Ordinance

did not prevent the French residents in Illinois from retaining slaves they already had, and the territorial administration in reality permitted slavery everywhere in Illinois. When Illinois was separated from Indiana in 1809, the territorial indenture law remained in effect in Illinois, whereas Indiana rejected the act in 1810. In the meantime, the uncompromising refusal of James Lemen, the father of the Illinois Baptist movement, to retain fellowship with the slaveholding Baptists led to his expulsion in 1809. Presumably encouraged by Thomas Jefferson, he then founded a small church at Cantine Creek, which was viewed from its inception by most Illinois Baptists as schismatic. At first the pro-freedom campaign seemed a forlorn cause; the Cantine Creek Church consisted of merely the seven members of the Lemen family. In 1815 the movement still had less than twenty members. By 1833, however, stimulated by the struggles over slavery in the state, the Friends of Humanity Association, organized in Illinois in 1820, had grown to thirty-nine churches and 1,347 members. In the campaign to elect the delegates to the 1818 constitutional convention, prominent anti-slavery Baptists included Edward Coles (later governor), John Mason Peck, and James Lemen. Between 1820 and 1824 the proslavery elements made their final major efforts to call another constitutional convention to broaden the indenture system. The anticonventionists successfully opposed them, and the Illinois Friends of Humanity next turned its attention to such activities as supporting the American Colonization Society. After 1835 the antislavery fervor waned.[7]

Since the American Baptists emphasized the separation of church and state, the visiting British Baptist delegates, Cox and Hoby, observed in 1836, they should have opposed the secular laws interfering with their religious rights, just as they had done so vigorously in eighteenth-century Virginia. On issues involving religious freedom, the Virginia Baptists had not hesitated to organize and vote as a church. Cox and Hoby reminded the American Baptists that in accepting the southern laws proscribing literacy for Negroes who were consequently denied direct access to the Scriptures, the Baptists were contradicting their professed

veneration for the Bible as the book of God. Moreover, the Negroes could not participate actively and were not permitted to
exercise leadership in church affairs, regardless of the Baptist
claims to being in conformity with the Primitive Church tradition. When Cox and Hoby proposed immediate freedom for the
slaves, their American hosts insisted that the Negroes were inferior and unable to live as free citizens. If the British Baptists
expressed concern for the "degraded condition" of the slaves,
the Americans would then tell them not to waste their sympathies
because the slaves were "remarkably shrewd" and doing well! [8]

The prevalent racist outlook can be seen in this typical appeal
by a woman missionary to Burma to the Philadelphia Baptist
women in 1835 for funds to publish tracts in Burmese:

> O, my sisters, in all I have suffered on leaving . . . my own beloved
> country; in all the dangers . . . I have experienced among the bar-
> barous, degraded heathen; nothing has wrung my heart with such bitter
> anguish, as to be obliged to deny even a single leaf containing gospel
> tidings, to a perishing fellow creature.[9]

Similar pleas appear frequently in the current religious periodicals, curiously combining dedicated concern, cultural imperial-
ism, compassion, arrogance, and racism. Nevertheless, compared
with the anti-missionites, the mission groups on the whole had a
far more sympathetic attitude toward the "heathen," and some,
like the McCoys of Indiana, a genuine friendship for other peoples. The mission movement became a significant force, if not
the most important influence, in American Protestantism for
more friendly interracial and international attitudes later in the
century.

After 1830 the far northern and New England states became
the center of Baptist abolitionist activities. Thus, in 1836 the
Maine Baptist Association formally denounced slavery as the
most abominable system of "iniquity that ever cursed the world."
The active majority of the abolitionists in New England was
apparently Baptist and Methodist, not Unitarian and Congregationalist, as sometimes assumed. Mainly because of this growing
northern Baptist sympathy for freedom, by 1845 the southern

Baptists withdrew from the Triennial Convention and the constituent home and foreign mission organizations.[10]

A short summary of the national Methodist policy on slavery will help to clarify the western Methodist attitude. The 1780 Conference denounced slavery and required the itinerants to promise to free their slaves, but the regulations were not fully enforced. The 1784 Christmas Conference again passed an antislavery resolution and specified the procedure to be followed by the members in freeing their slaves. In the light of the unsuccessful 1780 legislation, the 1784 action would be difficult to understand were it not for the strong antislavery position of Wesley, Coke, and Asbury. Wesley regarded American slavery as "the vilest that ever saw the sun." The initial attempts to apply the ruling aroused hostility in several slave states, and within six months the resolution was suspended.[11]

One obvious reason for the Methodist failure was their haphazard approach. They relied almost entirely on sporadic preaching instead of systematically educating their members in the local classes — perhaps reflecting their naïve faith in the providential power of preaching. In contrast, as several Methodist scholars have asserted, the Quaker leadership strove to have all the monthly meetings examine the subject fully. Concerned members pleaded patiently but persistently with slaveholding Friends to consider the harmful effects that their practice had on the spiritual welfare of both the masters and the slaves: the slaveholders had to justify their position to God. The Quaker success in eradicating slavery from the Society, these Methodist authorities insist, shows that the Methodists too could have enforced the 1784 legislation and thus could have circumvented many subsequent denominational crises. But the American Methodists had no John Woolman, while the aged John Wesley was far across the Atlantic in England. This comparison between the Methodists and the Friends may not be entirely valid because of the larger Methodist membership in the South, but Quakerism too had a substantial southern following at the time they made their decision.

The 1784 resolution, however, helped to free many individual slaves. Cartwright claims that thousands were emancipated over the years in conformity with its spirit. What is more, the ruling stimulated the thinking of many Methodists, above all southern itinerants. Freeborn Garrettson, a leading early Virginia circuit rider, for one, had never questioned slavery until it was discussed at several conferences. When convinced that it was evil, he freed his slaves. Many southern Methodists moved north to avoid further entanglement with the institution.

Whatever interest many individual Methodists may have had in the Negro members, Methodism as a denomination did not grant the Negroes any real rights and treated them as inferiors even at the worship services. As early as 1787, therefore, some Philadelphia Negroes withdrew (beginning the major separations) to organize their own chapel with a Negro minister ordained by Bishop White of the Episcopal church. Not until 1800 did the General Conference agree, and then most reluctantly, to ordain Negroes as local deacons. To mollify the strong opposition to this step, the conference suppressed all publicity concerning it. The *Discipline* did not mention the new provision. Only the unpublished conference journal was to record the decision, further indicating the Methodist confusion regarding Negro membership, even if the antislavery faction did manage to retain the clause requiring itinerants who married slaveholders either to free the slaves or to be dropped. Circuit riders in North and South Carolina, Georgia, and Tennessee were exempt from this ruling, since their state laws allegedly made emancipation very difficult. Cartwright pointedly reminded his colleagues some years later, however, that these laws did not prevent manumission; they required the owners to provide assurance that their freed slaves would not become public charges. He himself served as surety for a large number to enable them to become free.

Negroes in many Methodist churches in the West as well as elsewhere could not take the sacraments until all white members had been served. In some churches the whites treated the Negro members unkindly and "even pulled them off their knees" while they were praying and "ordered them back to their seats." Perhaps a remark by Peter Cartwright illustrates how completely the anti-Negro prejudice had affected many Methodists. One day, when informed that General Andrew Jackson had come to hear him preach, Cartwright deliberately asked in a loud voice to be overheard by the whole church, "Who is General Jackson? If he don't [sic] get his soul converted, God will damn him as quick as he would a Guinea negro!" This story has been cited as an evidence of Methodist democracy when it is flagrantly racist. Harriet Martineau heard similar expressions, such as that God cared as much for Negroes as he did for the "wisest" and "best" whites. No one could even understand her protest at such "wanton insult." [12] The automatic categorization of a whole race as sinful or contemptible shows how deeply racism had permeated even Cartwright. It was a spiritual prejudice all the more infectious because this courageous crusader for faith and freedom was unaware of it. He had moved his family north to live in a free state and had said he would rather send his children to Calvinistic schools in free Illinois than to Methodist schools in a slave state.[13]

In 1804, 2,000 copies of the *Discipline* containing no rule on slavery were printed for the South. The 1808 General Conference ordered 1,000 copies of the *Discipline* without the section on slavery for distribution in the South. Instead, the ministers were periodically to "admonish and exhort all slaves to render due respect and obedience to the commands and interests of their respective masters." According to J. J. Tigert, a Southern Methodist bishop and authority on Methodist constitutional history, this "dangerous and unjustifiable act of 1808" was an important cause of the ultimate split. The 1808 General Conference also removed all restrictions on slaveholding by ordinary members, although the annual conferences could still legislate regarding members engaged in the slave trade. The Tennessee Conference, for one, retained no regulation against slaveowners as members. In 1820, however, Henry B. Bascom and other delegates from the Tennessee Conference persuaded the General Conference to assume the legislative power over slaveholding. At this time, Tennessee had nearly one-fifth of the total national membership in anti-slavery societies. It would seem that Bascom and his colleagues wanted to protect Methodist slaveholders against the local emancipationist influence.[14]

In his rationalization of the 1808 compromise, Bishop Asbury shows how dualistic piety may confuse religious understanding:

Would not an *amelioration* in the condition and treatment of slaves have produced more practical good to the poor Africans, than any attempt at their *emancipation?* The state of society, unhappily, does not admit of this: besides, the blacks are deprived of the means of instruction; who will take the pains to lead them into the way of salvation, and watch over them that they may not stray, but the Methodists? . . . What is the personal liberty of the African which he may abuse, to the salvation of his soul; how may it be compared? [15]

By 1836, the General Conferences were officially voicing sentiments which today would seem virtually pro-slavery. Most strongly disapproving abolitionism and the antislavery lectures by two delegates, the 1836 Conference disclaimed wholly "any right, wish, or intention to interfere in the civil and political relation between master and slave." The conference message from the bishops emphasized their "duty" to oppose emancipationism, although the episcopacy sympathized with the preachers led astray by the antislavery agitation. Neither as ministers or as private citizens should the circuit riders participate in abolition movements, since emancipation was a "matter of state power." Indeed, the itinerants were not even to subscribe to or patronize antislavery publications. The slaveholders would stop the Methodist missions to the slaves if the preachers were suspected of having abolitionist sentiments, the bishops continued. In essence the bishops asked the circuit riders not to support even legal abolitionist organizations and not to hear or read emancipationist arguments. The episcopal message did, however, strongly condemn all mob violence and self-appointed tribunals seeking forcibly to suppress differing opinions because a nation based on freedom of speech must have mutual forbearance. Far from opposing slavery, official Methodism was actually discouraging abolitionism.[16]

The western leaders in the main did not actively reject the conference position, if the opinions of such spokesmen as Peter Cartwright and the widespread western hostility to Negroes and to abolitionism were representative. Cartwright openly criticized slavery as a grave evil, but he also deplored abolition movements as sinister and un-Christian: they would lead to the dissolution of the federal union and to a civil war that would not help the slaves, for it was the masters who had to be persuaded to Christianize and to free the slaves. Furthermore, he insisted, the abolitionists had no interest at all in the welfare of the slaves. Again reflecting the prevailing prejudice which Cartwright had unconsciously absorbed along with other westerners, he often referred to Negroes in derogatory ways. His remarks were apparently intended to be humorous, but even in his day visiting Europeans immediately sensed the cruelty inherent in expressions he used while biased westerners never realized they were insulting.[17] Negroes had no feelings, human dignity, or rights which westerners were bound to respect. Today, the average northern American, let alone an outstanding church leader, would be embarrassed to make such gross remarks. Actually, Cartwright was well intentioned and the Reverend Mr. Oliver Spencer of Cincinnati better exemplifies a Methodist with strong pro-slavery views than Cartwright. Besides being one of the twelve leading Cincinnati citizens who called on the local abolitionists to demand that they stop their antislavery activities, Spencer personally taunted them for not going south to die as martyrs. Because the "best elements" in Cincinnati were opposed to abolitionism, they did not seriously attempt to maintain freedom of speech. As one consequence, a hostile mob destroyed the abolitionist property, while the mayor watched this destruction with approval.

As we have noted, the denominational attitude toward slavery stemmed partly from pietistic dualism and sectarianism which could look on slavery as a civil institution not directly relevant to religion, an outlook found in the General Conference reply to the 1840 fraternal message from the British Methodists urging greater efforts to eliminate slavery. Slavery was deplorable, the American Methodists admitted, but they would "regard it a sore evil to divert Methodism from her proper work of '*spreading Scriptural holiness over these lands,*' to questions of temporal import, involving the rights of Cesar [*sic*]." The various states of the Federal union were independent, and national legislation to abolish slavery would not be effective. Therefore, the American statement continued, it would be "wrong and unscriptural to enact a rule of discipline in opposition to the constitution and laws of the state on this subject." Besides, abstractly considering the question is quite different from having a disciplinary rule to be enforced "contrary to, and in defiance of, the law of the land." To be consistent, the Methodists should not have campaigned against alcoholic liquor, for their own arguments against abolitionism were almost equally applicable against their antiliquor movement.[18]

The 1840 General Conference endorsed the controversial American Colonization Society. Whether or not this society was effective, the conference action seems scarcely consistent with the previous Methodist arguments on the separation of church and state. Apparently, Methodism could endorse those civil organizations approved by slaveholders. The General Conference also sustained the appeal by the Reverend Mr. Silas Comfort, who had been condemned by the Missouri Conference for permitting a Negro to testify in a church trial. It then accepted Dr. Few's resolution forbidding Negroes to testify against whites in church trials in states where the civil courts did not permit Negro testimony. To quiet the continuing agitation over the Comfort case and the Few resolution, the conference then passed three additional resolutions. The first was that the conference in supporting Mr. Comfort did not endorse the resort to Negro witnesses in states where they could not testify at law. The second motion was that in adopting the Few resolution, the conference was not barring Negro witnesses in states where they customarily testified in church trials if in the opinion of the church judicatories Negro testimony would not disturb the church. The final resolution was that conference action did not imply any distrust of Negro piety or integrity. The three resolutions were confusing, if not contradictory. Abolitionism, the conference contended, was Caesar's prerogative and hence outside the responsibility of the church, but in some states the Methodists were to suspend their church rules because civil laws restricted Negro testimony in the civil courts. In other words, the church was not to deal with basic moral issues if they could be assigned to Caesar, but Caesar's practices could apply to strictly religious affairs.

By this time, northern Methodists were becoming dissatisfied with the denominational position and many had become aboli- tionists. Finally, in 1844 the General Conference took the fateful step of separating northern and southern Methodism. The threat of further northern withdrawals to the antislavery Wesleyan Con- nection, the changing public opinion in some northern communi- ties (which Methodism had to meet if it were to thrive in these towns), and the southern stand hastened the decision. The anti- slavery Methodists discovered, however, that the separation did not open the way for abolitionism since the denominational au- thorities insisted on placating the pro-slavery border-state Meth- odists. Instead of shaping public morality on slavery, official Methodism was pushed by it. From the beginning the Methodists had justified their inconsistencies mainly on their need to have free access to the slaves to convert them. The slaveholders would not allow the Methodists to preach to their slaves if they suspected Methodism had any abolitionist sympathies. Numerous itiner- ants and laymen gave last full measure of devotion to the mission- ary work, and the Methodists rightly claim to have been a major agency in Christianizing the slaves. To be consistent, the Method- ists should also have appointed Negro members to offices suitable to their talents and should have insisted on the right of their members to read the Bible and therefore on the revocation of the laws against teaching slaves to read.[19]

In many cases the masters permitted the Methodists to evange- lize their slaves because converted slaves showed "distinct improve- ment in their moral character and habits, making them sober, industrious, honest, and contented." In brief, the itinerants la- bored sacrificially to bring religion to the slaves and incidentally to make the slaves more profitable to their masters. Unwittingly, the missionaries were, one may say, not only religious apostles, but also production engineers raising the economic efficiency and out- put of the slaves to the greater profit of their masters. Peter Cartwright again spoke for many Methodists in naïvely remarking on the financial value of preaching to the slaves, as well as expressing concern for their religious welfare:

On week days they were . . . not permitted to hear preaching. Sundays they were out drinking and trading, selling brooms, baskets, and the little articles they manufactured. [He began to convert them]. . . . These two old Methodist . . . [masters] said I had . . . bettered or enhanced the value of their servants more than a thousand dollars; they ceased getting drunk, stealing, and breaking the Sabbath.[20]

At first, the masters preferred to have the Negroes in the same churches with them to prevent the slaves from having direct contacts with Christianity. To segregate the slaves into independent organizations seemed dangerous to the whites. The church was another instrument of control, not freedom; it encouraged the slaves to accept their lot as divine will. As a result, H. R. Niebuhr concludes, the first step toward religious equality ironically required the racial separation of the churches. The one-time superintendent of the Methodist missions among the slaves, Bishop William Capers, regarded the slave traffic as "providential" for it made possible their "exodus" to the United States to work under "the light and saving influence" of Christianity. The western Methodists generally, often vigorously, opposed slavery, but many were at the same time highly prejudiced against Negroes. This western bias and discrimination stemmed essentially from the same racism as did Capers' defense of slavery, the same unquestioning assumption that the Negroes were "unfit for political freedom" and "unable to govern themselves" because of their color, caste, and "intellectual inferiority." Religious education itself, Capers insisted, must be adapted to their limited "mental capabilities." [21]

Once Methodism had consciously or unconsciously adopted the un-Christian, undemocratic, and unscientific racist dogma of Negro inferiority, the denomination could readily discriminate without much scruple. Regardless of the strenuous efforts by farsighted individual leaders, more noticeably after 1865, the denomination has been unable to restructure the institutionalized discrimination incorporated into its polity and life. The original missionary work among the slaves was itself not without some negative consequences. The more astute European observers, including Fredrika Bremer, for instance, saw that the Baptist and Methodist attempt to suppress the slave interest in music and the dance at least initially further deculturalized the slaves, even when the preachers were sincerely trying to promote their welfare. At any rate, such efforts may have weakened the spiritual independence of the slaves and made them more inclined to obey their masters without question as their divinely ordained duty — that is, reduced them further to the status of draft animals or tools.

Notwithstanding the confused denominational attitude, many individual Methodists were greatly concerned with the welfare of the slaves and free Negroes. Some itinerants in the slave states, among them Thomas Rice, courageously continued to speak for freedom. More southern circuit riders moved to the North because they were against slavery. William Cravens of Virginia went to Indiana where he repeatedly criticized the settlers who had hired out their slaves in the South and were drawing their wages. Others had sold their slaves and had purchased property in Indiana with the proceeds. At the same time they were deploring slavery. All such persons were denounced as "blood-stained hypocrites," worse than the masters who were treating their slaves kindly.[22]

An account of the long-standing Methodist interest in the Indians is outside the limits of this study, but, ironically, it was a poor underprivileged Negro, John Stewart, who in 1815 began the first full-time Methodist mission among the Indians. He and Jonathan Pointer, his interpreter and fellow Negro collaborator, carried on the work from 1815 to 1820 among the Wyandots on their own initiative without any denominational support. Finally, in 1818 with several of his converts who commended his services, Stewart came to the Quarterly Meeting near Urbana, Ohio, to ask for ordination as a local preacher. Bishop George approved. The incident aroused Methodist interest and as a consequence the Ohio Conference took steps in 1819 to send John Montgomery to the Wyandots. The 1820 Ohio Conference authorized its mission committee to give Stewart and Pointer necessary support. When Stewart was married that year, Bishop McKendree collected money to purchase a small farm for the couple near the Wyandot settlement where the Stewarts lived until his death in 1823. In addition, Bishop McKendree solicited aid for Stewart from Negro Methodists, many of them slaves and all desperately poor. In common with most other denominations, frontier Methodists tended to confuse Christianity with the elements of secular culture accidentally associated with religion, such as their inclination to measure Indiana conversion by the extent to which the Indians rejected their culture and accepted American customs. Nevertheless, the sympathy such frontier Methodists as McKendree and Finley had for the Indians stands out in sharp relief against the widespread western prejudice. The denomination as a whole pioneered in its concern for the Indians, and this interest was another influence on its growing social awareness.

THE FRIENDS

The historic Quaker concern for the Indians and Negroes has already been discussed in chapter vi. The western Friends were not free of prejudice against slaves and Indians, but they at least partly sensed their own shortcomings. The 1840 Indiana yearly meeting reminded every member that he should "know his Lord's will," find his personal role, and fearlessly promote freedom; "a sense of the enormity of the evil urges us to persevere" in the task. Time was short, slavery was expanding rapidly. The Friends were

to labor for the removal of all those unjust laws, and . . . the unwarrantable distinction of color . . . which has brought so much suffering upon those settled in different parts of the Union, and which we think, must conduce to the strengthening of the prejudices of former years, and to retard the work of Emancipation.[23]

This statement reveals an important insight into the social and psychological factors which in recent years American social scientists have begun to understand more clearly: discriminatory practices and laws not only humiliate the victims but also help to create the very prejudice in the dominant group which in turn is then used to justify the overt discrimination.

Friends thought of Indians and Negroes as human beings endowed with the same natures and rights as they themselves. They rejected as outright sin such racism as expressed by William Capers. Slavery was so vast an evil that merely ameliorating the plight of its victims, while helpful as long as the institution existed, was not a substitute for efforts to bring freedom. To the Society, the pietistic and sectarian indifference to the evil institution was a gross evasion of the basic Christian duty, for all Christians "should break every yoke, undo the heavy burdens, and let the oppressed go free." Although many Quaker groups may have lagged far behind their leading spirits, as a denomination the Society pioneered in arousing the public conscience instead of only following public opinion. Their concern suggests that sectarianism does not inevitably involve social ethical indifference. Rather, much depends on a sect's definition of what is religiously relevant and the emphases its leaders may give.

Several leaders of the popular denominations mentioned slavery in other ages and places to justify their position, but usually overlooked their differences from the American situation.[24] In the ancient societies to which some referred, free men became slaves and many slaves became free. This mobility was all the more meaningful since these historic societies were scarcely democratic, as the Dissenters understood the term. Among the slaves were famous teachers, philosophers, and occupants of responsible positions. In contrast, the American South legally forbade teaching slaves, and in some cases free Negroes, to read and write, let alone to become scholars, refused to recognize slave marriages, and placed barriers to their freedom. Western states generally excluded free Negro children from public schools, and popular prejudice often barred the free Negroes from all but menial occupations.

Early nineteenth-century Latin America had extremes of poverty and wealth. Poor Latin Americans, free and slave, may have fared worse than many American slaves, as some popular denominational leaders said. Here again, these leaders ignored the differences, At least in some Latin American states, the church and the government encouraged the masters to free their slaves and facilitated the procedure. State and church agencies protected the slaves from their masters' excesses and legalized slave marriages which masters had to recognize. Slaves owned and sold private property and had a legal right to purchase their freedom. If a master and a slave could not agree on the price, the authorities set an attainable figure. All holidays and certain number of hours during the working day belonged to the slave who was often urged to seek outside employment or conduct business during his free time to earn the money for his freedom.

Many slaves were encouraged to become artisans. In some places, free Negroes dominated the skilled trades, and as American visitors observed, some were prominent in the professions as doctors, lawyers, teachers, and priests. A number of Negroes and persons of part Negro ancestry became outstanding as military officers, judges, and high officials even before slavery was abolished. Mobility and contacts existed between the slave and the free. Prejudice was also widespread, but it was flexible and limited compared with the rigid American racism. Stanley Elkins reminds us in his study on slavery that the Latin Americans significantly did not stereotype Negroes as childish, shiftless, and lacking in initiative as did the Americans. The differences, which he believes existed in the personalities of some slaves in the two continents, reflected the destructive impact of the harsh North American conditions and attitudes.

In conformity with their active moralism and without attacking slavery, the leaders of the popular denominations could have campaigned for the right to preach to the slaves and to teach them to read and write, for legal recognition of marriages, and for better procedures to enable slaves to purchase their freedom. The major popular denominations could have persuaded their own members to mitigate the harsh discrimination against the free Negroes in the West. To change the existing social order would have been extremely difficult, of course, particularly since Dissenting institutional strength was based on their disciplinary control over the members and slavery was not even a disciplinary question for most denominations. A possible alternative was to make clear their views to the membership and the public, as perhaps established churches might have attempted. The larger Dissenting denominations, while criticizing the state churches as morally decadent, upheld attitudes toward slavery and free Negroes that the established churches might have regarded as appalling. The Dissenters had traditionally opposed special privileges for aristocracy, formal clergy, or elite and had insisted on each member assuming active responsibility for their religious life. Yet, they did not curb the power of their slaveholding ordinary members over their slaves, a far greater power than the supposedly undemocratic and decadent established churches tolerated.

Perhaps, we should ask again how the strongly democratic popular denominations developed attitudes and practices which seemed to violate Christian principles, and in any case, were less democratic than the conservative church practices. One reason was that the popular denominations had apparently taken for granted their prejudices and social origin which did not affect them directly, as well as their economic interests, and had incorporated them into their denominational structure. In contrast, the Friends increasingly questioned slavery and began to oppose it at considerable cost to their members. Their decision indicates that the popular denominational position was far from being inevitable, if they had had the insight and the will to examine it critically. Another reason was that Dissenters used the separation of church and state to classify slavery as a worldly institution not directly relevant to religion, a view illustrated by the previously mentioned American Methodist answer to the 1840 British Methodist protest against American indifference to abolitionism. In contrast to the later Finney and eastern reformistic revivalism, western revivalism indirectly strengthened this outlook by interpreting conversion as a spiritual experience leading the new elite away from worldly evils. To bar such ideas, the Friends made testimony against slavery a religious and disciplinary requirement and assistance to free Negroes an important moral objective.

Still another reason for the institutionalized discrimination within the larger popular denominations was their emphasis on intimate local churches composed of like-minded congenial members (originally without racial overtones). Sectarian rivalries accentuated this practice, since persons with differences in background and outlook were expected to find other sects with which they presumably had more in common. This objective, in conjunction with the open prejudice against Negroes, moved the popular denominations away from having Negroes in some places in a subordinate status to virtual segregation and discouraged any serious thought on the consequences of this trend. Once incorporated into the denominational structure, segregation in turn encouraged separation of interest. Negroes were "obviously" outsiders. Not surprisingly, it is still being said to this day that Sunday morning at eleven o'clock is the most segregated hour of the week in the great heartland of America.

CHAPTER XIV

Popular Denominations and Jacksonianism

The major Dissenting denominations accepted the system of calling, encouraged their members to participate in civic life, and actively sought to win new converts. Although some of their early leaders (among them Asbury) feared that Dissenters would lose their religious fervor with their rising status, many members became outstanding in the community and state, while the membership as a whole was rising to middle-class respectability.[1] The popular denominations influenced the secular society, including such political movements as Jacksonianism, and in turn were affected by the secular trends.

Western Dissenters, of course, did not have a homogeneous background. The Baptist anti-missionary controversy, for instance, revealed the influence of their Virginia or New England and New York origins or, more particularly, the influence of their immediate cultural heritage on the western Baptists. The pro-mission former-Virginia leaders often had personal ties with the more cultured plantation or professional families, in contrast to many anti-mission Baptists who came from humbler classes in Virginia. Nevertheless, though the Dissenters had a more diverse background than sometimes assumed, by and large during this period they shared an appreciably similar religious and social outlook. On the whole the western Baptists were an economically rising group and, whether from Virginia or New England and New York, valued religious freedom and voluntarism. The New England Baptists had struggled for freedom somewhat as the Virginia Baptists had. Their outstanding spokesman in Connecticut was the same John Leland who had successfully led the Virginia campaign. He urged the Baptists and all other Connecticut Dissenters to ally themselves with the Jeffersonian party to fight the ruling elite. Nearly all the Methodists were Jeffersonians, recalled Alfred Brunson, an early New England itinerant, who wrote that if a person had not previously opposed the existing interests, he joined the democratic party on becoming a Methodist.[2] By 1803, most non-Congregationalists in Connecticut, except the Episcopalians, could be regarded as Jeffersonians. In contrast, close ties frequently existed between the Federalist and the Congregational and Presbyterian clergy in seeking to retain old prerogatives and to maintain the Federalist ascendancy. In Kentucky also, Dr. Sonne found, many Presbyterians were actually Federalists and were so considered by others regardless of their nominal Jeffersonianism. They were opposed to the French Revolution and the War of 1812, agreed with such New England leaders as Timothy Dwight, and criticized democracy at home. In the West, from the first a substantial proportion of the Presbyterians belonged to the upper classes.[3] Even before their major westward expansion, then, the Dissenters were more closely associated with the Jeffersonians than they were with the more conservative parties, while subsequently in the Old Northwest many pioneer Jeffersonian leaders were active Dissenters.

By winning the migrating people on the frontier as well as in towns, Dissent strengthened the western inclination to use voluntary organizations to promote objectives beyond the reach of discrete individuals. This voluntarism is often regarded as being conducive to, if not essential for, modern democracy. Granted that the Dissenting denominations had no inkling of all its varied consequences, in popularizing the system of calling they also satisfied some other basic needs of their economically rising members and gave them moral support in their efforts to overcome obstacles. The Dissenters were able, individually and collectively, to aid many new migrants to adjust to the new western environment and later to the changes introduced by rising industries.

More specifically, the popular denominations familiarized many westerners (and to a degree, many of the humbler easterners) with the requisites for conducting and leading group activities. This experience was valuable for their personal development and often for their economic and political life. A recent study of sectarian Protestantism in a middle western town, for example, showed similar processes at work even now.[4] For a review, perhaps we should briefly list some of the ways the Dissenting denominations, from the colonial days through mid-nineteenth century, enhanced the secular life of their members as a latent function (as a "by-product") of their religious duty. The first was their emphasis on the system of calling with its ideal of strenuous and systematic devotion to secular responsibilities which helped them to advance occupationally. If they were interested, members could also apply some of this energy and systematic effort to their political activities.

Members had to learn to organize groups, arrange religious programs, and conduct business meetings of their local churches and related societies. For some, this duty meant learning proper procedures for meetings, give and take of committee operations, and even how to keep written records and financial accounts. Obviously, they also had to acquire some fluency in speaking in public. These responsibilities, at least in many instances, assumed the ability to read and study religious tracts and the Bible, and to speak on these topics. This study is far from academic scholarship, but it does mean reading with understanding and thinking about popular publications, and if interested, political articles and tracts, and speaking about them. The members therefore learned not only to be more fluent, but also to have more to say. As members of denominations seeking new converts, they were occasionally expected to call on their neighbors and strangers to persuade them to join. Again, as a result, a number of members learned to converse more persuasively, a skill that was also useful in their business and in politics. Their faith probably gave many believers inner confidence which was reflected overtly in greater poise and assurance, in itself a valuable social asset. The custom of holding various church programs, ranging from formal Methodist classes to more informal committee meetings, in the homes of members also meant that the more ambitious members of simple background could observe the social behavior and perhaps even social niceties when the more cultured members were entertaining them. Finally, it should be noted that Dissenters maintained social control through peer groups. Theirs was not the continuation of the old feudal or authoritarian tradition, but essentially volunteer peer group discipline of equals, a vital factor in the growth of voluntary groups.

It is scarcely necessary to suggest further that politically concerned Dissenters could benefit appreciably from their religious organizational experience. Some historians have marveled at the organizational vigor of Jacksonianism in the West, which obviously reflected the familiarity of many people with group activities. We have already referred to the enthusiastic support many Indiana Baptists gave to the Democratic party. Again, busy as he was, Peter Cartwright served in the Illinois state legislature and was the Democratic nominee for Congress in 1846, when Abraham Lincoln as a Whig ran successfully against him. Before the 1860 Illinois Democratic Convention, Cartwright reminisced on the sturdy development of the state and humorously added, "Yes, my friends, for seventy long years, amid appalling difficulties and dangers, I have waged an incessant warfare against the world, the flesh, and the devil and all other enemies of the Democratic party." [5] Yet, more significant than any temporary popular denominational and Jacksonian association with the same constituents in many localities and perhaps as important as the organizational training provided by the popular denominations was their impact on the popular attitudes to which Jacksonianism appealed. Such Dissenting fundamentals as equalitarianism and insistence on lay participation and leadership preceded, paralleled, and interacted with the secular equalitarianism and the growing participation by the common man in the nation's political life. The two movements had similar faith in his capacity and worth. [6]

Pioneers in the Old Northwest did not seem averse to having the government intervene in certain crises, regulate monopolistic utilities (including such private ventures as milling) in public interest, or support various public services. Aside from mentioning the frontier responsiveness to leadership and the rapid rotation of offices, Turner did not fully account for these "centralizing" tendencies, which he also strongly emphasized. While he often visualized the settlers as discrete individuals rather than as parts of organized groups and society, he and other historians sometimes attributed a national and centralized, rather than individualistic or even state-rights, outlook to the frontier and regarded it as a product of the development of the Old Northwest directly under the national government. This background was significant, but can the actual day-by-day western experience with voluntary associations be overlooked in an account of this aspect of social history? Many Dissenters had given devoted service to their own sects and had seen them grow from struggling and often persecuted local meetings to nationally prominent denominations. It seems unlikely that all the larger implications of their group experience, even to having delegated assemblies and constitutional procedures in their church and affiliated societies, would be lost on the settlers. Many were capitalizing on their experiences in their community and local political activities. As suggested before, such organized aspects of the frontier life as the centralized Methodist structure require more attention than most accounts usually give.

In the light of some modern political theories, Jacksonian ideas on governmental responsibilities may seem limited. Nevertheless, unlike many Jeffersonians, the Jacksonians would have the government assume a more positive role. To the Jacksonians a strong leader and executive was not necessarily a detriment to democracy. Instead, effective democracy required leadership. This leadership, however, had to be responsive and responsible to the people, had to help formulate their vague aspirations into realizable terms, and had to stimulate and utilize local talents. Earlier, the Dissenters had rapidly developed similar leadership for their denominational and related organizations for promoting religious and social interests, locally, regionally, and nationally. Lay leaders and preachers came from the rank and file and were encouraged by the members. Regional conferences brought together these leaders and the more active members for common counsel and group action. From them came the representatives to the state and national organizations and their leaders. Denominational vitality depended on a fruitful interaction between the leaders and the active membership. Methodist bishops claimed to represent the over-all denominational interests in contrast to the more limited views of the local preachers and circuit riders, while at the same time the episcopacy was sensitive to the wishes of the individual members and the local meetings. At least overtly, in Jacksonian terms, the Methodist bishops were democratic, but they nevertheless had authority and exercised it to advance denominational welfare. The Baptists, too, learned to appreciate large-scale efforts after they had overcome the opposition by the "anti-effort" elements. As with the Dissenting equalitarian attitudes discussed above, popular denominational experience with organizations and leadership preceded, paralleled, and interacted with the Jacksonian experience.

Participation in political and civic organizations which were community-wide, state-wide, and nationwide in scope probably broadened the outlook of many Dissenters. At least some must have found in these wider activities additional possibilities for self-realization. Because candidates were often so eager, the local campaigns and changes in offices, as pioneer records confirm, were in retrospect often tinged with humor and irony. If originally Dissent helped to train its members for more effective public life, Jacksonianism and civic movements eventually encouraged them to transcend sectarian limitations, and also strengthened the voluntary feature of the western society.

Dissenting ambivalence toward slavery and racial discrimination had its secular parallels in the relative Jacksonian indifference to Negro and Indian rights. Some Jacksonian groups may have been interested, but the party on the whole showed little inclination to battle for democratic principles when they involved Negroes and Indians. Slavery and conflicts with the Indians obviously conditioned — some would say corrupted — the racial assumptions of both Jacksonianism and Dissent (except for such denominations as the Friends), while their provincialism insulated them from those world-wide intellectual trends which were increasingly critical of slavery. Both movements tolerated, if they did not earlier accentuate, racism and slavery which had persistent institutional consequences for them and for the United States.

The popular denominations also helped to shape the current political mythology and its emphasis on nature, providence, and will. One aim of the religious discipline and teachings was to fortify the Dissenter's will. Under divine scrutiny in his calling through strength of character, the faithful overcame all obstacles and circumstances. Contemporary lore portrayed Jackson as a man with an unbreakable will, a will strong enough to shatter the British invaders at New Orleans. True to the religious element in this party tradition, popular accounts dramatized his later decision to join the Presbyterian church, a step symbolizing to many the principle that even the strongest human will must ultimately submit to the divine. The concept of the spiritual elite which overcomes all difficulties to glorify God may have had Calvinistic and Puritan origins, but the popular denominations helped to spread it and in the process gave it a more democratic turn. The increasingly secular version of this idea became the esteem for the self-made or successful man. Jacksonianism upheld this hard-working, productive citizen against what it denounced as the wiles of the exploitive financial manipulators.

The Jeffersonian faith in the natural man and in fostering a natural aristocracy by selecting and educating talent changed to the Jacksonian faith in the man of nature. In shifting from the Jeffersonian concern for education, many Jacksonians were inclined to dismiss formal scholarship as being only ornamental at best and more generally as tending to corrupt natural reason and wisdom into mere understanding and knowledge. For many, Andrew Jackson personified nature's man with uncorrupted reason and wisdom, in contrast to the formally educated John Quincy Adams. Artistic, literary, and intellectual standards some Jacksonians attacked as impositions by vested interests to strengthen the plutocratic ascendancy over the common people. They felt that it was as important to abolish "special privileges respecting cultural property" as those involving physical property. One obvious reason for this hostility was that some wealthy easterners were using cultural standards essentially as weapons for attacking democratic trends and for retaining their own privileges. Unlike many leaders in the Enlightenment era, these businessmen had, as such foreign observers as Grund and Tocqueville noticed, very little intrinsic appreciation for intellectual and artistic pursuits. Even granted that the more cultured at that time came mainly from the old ruling classes, it may be observed that the Jacksonians gave little thought to the possible necessity for a democracy to have more, not fewer, persons of intellect and culture than an aristocratic society.

In many ways, their outlook seemed to be a secular parallel to the earlier sectarian Dissenting hostility to cultural interests and to formal theological education and to the earlier Dissenting preference for an untrained and essentially lay ministry "uncorrupted" by human learning. Yet, we should note that this heritage also strengthened the existing practical American approach to political problems, as distinct from the more doctrinaire politics found later in some Continental countries. Several European critics have admired this American refusal to be imprisoned by abstract political dogmas or to be lured by extreme ideological utopianism. The Dissenting emphasis on direct experience, practicality, and the innate ability of the common man was congenial to the concept that politics is the art of the possible. In contrast, the theology-like ideologies, these European commentators feel, may readily ignore practicality or human needs and if at all realizable can be put into effect only through absolutism.[7]

Perhaps the original Dissenting preference for an untrained lay ministry more explicitly paralleled the Jacksonian approach to civil service and government administration. Dissent insisted on the right to call any person whom his peers considered competent whether or not he had any formal training. It eliminated nearly all the invidious discrimination within its ranks. The Jacksonians upheld the view that any reasonably intelligent man could discharge the duties of any public office. The party infused the government system with a new vitality by opening the way for the many, if not for talent as such, and not merely for the "well born and the well to do." The spoils system served also to minimize any tendency by the officeholder to regard his position as personal property or right. The view was not unrelated to the Baptist custom of ordaining fellow members, electing them annually, and changing them often. For the Methodists, the ready ordination as a local preacher and even as a circuit rider and the appointment each year to a new circuit may have acquired comparable effects, notwithstanding that their original purpose in rotating the circuit riders was quite different. Dissent regarded ministers as servants of the people and not authoritative dignitaries separated from the rank and file by ordination and office. Worthy pastors confirmed their tenure by faithful service and spiritual leadership. Dissenting tradition, then, did not even exempt the clergy from popular criticism and responsibility to the people. The Jacksonian attitude toward the public officeholders paralleled and interacted with this earlier Dissenting outlook.

The widely held faith in the American mission to plant freedom everywhere seems at least partly a secular adaptation of the popular denominational teachings on providence, grace, and evangelism. The altruistic aspects of this belief led in later years to the unprecedented American concern for all peoples and to the vital American interest in extending democracy. We may find religious parallels, for example, in the Methodist zeal to propagate the doctrine of universal free grace and to encourage charitable and reform measures, as well as to support the growing missionary movement. On the other hand, the more nationalistic interpreters of American destiny or mission utilized the idea to justify their dream of a United States reaching not only from the Atlantic to the Pacific, but also from the Arctic Ocean to the Isthmus of Panama, if not to the very tip of Cape Horn. Some advanced this imperial vision as an American religious duty to plant vigorous popular Protestantism in the farthest reaches of the world. Often inherent in their views was a strong contempt for the Old World culture, a contempt which was as sectarian as it was vehement and which ignored the dependence of any society and its attainments on its cultural heritage. One of the first publicists to use the term "manifest destiny" declared that the advocates of "human liberty, civilization, and refinement" could not review the history of past monarchies and aristocracies without deploring their existence and without considering the older civilizations merely as examples of what should be avoided. The "vestigial" remains of European culture found in American legal, educational, and social institutions he found regrettable. Such views reveal both sectarianism and the idealization of the natural man and also seem to have been somewhat later and more aggressive parallels to the charges which earlier Dissent leveled against secular culture, orthodox religious traditions, and established churches. They expressed similar feelings.

The Jacksonians successfully translated the democratic creed into the reality of popular rule and appreciably advanced democracy, Ralph Barton Perry believes, but at the same time they often also revealed such "inherent and besetting evils" of democracy as the "envy of superiority, and the compensatory pride of inferiority," the virtual disregard for standards of excellence, the removal of political authority from man's higher faculties to his "baser passions," and the demagoguery by which the ambitious gain power. Whether, as Dr. Perry says, such setbacks inevitably beset a democracy is open to question.[8] The Scandinavian democracies and to a degree the British have had somewhat different experiences. We have already seen the Presbyterian and Congregational leaders time and time again advance similar charges against the popular denominations and accuse them of resorting to demagoguery and to "baser" passions when the Dissenters were democratizing the religious life of the people. The more conservative churches also criticized the popular denominations for retaining their hostility against intellectual and cultural responsibilities for years after they had accepted the system of calling and after their members had been actively participating in the community life.

Any evaluation of the supposedly lower western standards in religion and politics, however, must take into account the character of the frontier life, its inadequate formal education, and its simple economy, which often called for practicality and versatility rather than trained professionalism. Local denominational histories, such as Holliday's *Indiana Methodism*, contain biographical sketches of men who had engaged in four, five, or more different occupations — as hunters, farmers, wheelwrights, millers, carpenters, tanners, surveyors, storekeepers, and sometimes as pharmacists, physicians, and ministers. Regardless of the simpler requirements of those days, not even the more talented could have done well in all these occupations. William Dean Howells, for one, emphasizes the reverse side to the present-day myth of western versatility when he discusses his own father, an able Ohio pioneer who was so long forced by circumstances to be satisfied with make-shifts that this practice had become habitual and mediocrity expected. Mrs. Kirkland and others have recorded the difficulties that the better-educated pioneers faced whenever they wanted to have quality work done.[9]

In both religion and politics, this indifference to quality delayed the development of thorough professional training and high standards. The popular denominations gave a positive impetus toward democratizing leadership in public affairs, not the least by familiarizing their membership with organizational activities, but on the intellectual and cultural bases of public life, their influence was often negative, except for the strong emphasis on the value and ability of every person. Sectarian hostility to intellectual and cultural growth, which may have been consistent with the aims of a small sect trying to withdraw from active life, was obviously inconsistent with the responsibilities of a large national denomination, and still more, of an aggressive political party attempting to dominate a nation. The Congregationalists and Presbyterians (and later the Episcopalians) exerted continuous pressure on the popular denominations to raise ministerial and educational standards. They denounced Dissenting practices, set examples, and attracted many better-educated Dissenters into their churches. The popular denominational emphasis on achievement eventually helped them to change their attitude. In secular life, the growing complexity of the governmental responsibilities and the industrial pressure for better-trained men also encouraged the populace to raise the standards.

Both the popular denominations and Jacksonianism incorporated to an appreciable degree the so-called middle-class aspirations of the common man. Basically, the two movements appealed to those whom they regarded as the hard-working, productive, and democratic classes — that is, as the virtuous elements which created the real wealth, in contrast to those whom they denounced as parasitical speculators and aristocratic money-power. Here again Jacksonianism was partly stating a secularized version of some Dissenting ideas. At noted before, however, it was the Dissenting influence on the outlook and practices of its members and the larger society which was significant, rather than any temporary or partial association of its following with any political party. Other parties had to take the resultant situation into account to meet or outdo the Jacksonians in their appeals (as in the 1840 Harrison campaign). Later in the century, of course, many heavily Dissenting regions in the upper Middle West became prosperous Republican strongholds.

PART IV

CONCLUSION

CHAPTER XV

The Heritage of the Popular Denominations

In the first decades of the nineteenth century, the small struggling Dissenting sects grew rapidly to become the largest Protestant denominations in the West and in the United States as a whole. As it happened in the Old World, so too on the seaboard, the established churches and educated upper classes modified Dissent in the East. In the West, Dissent was freer to realize its potentialities. The Dissenting denominations were formed primarily to satisfy the religious aspirations of their followers. At the same time, however, they influenced the secular society and helped shape its institutions and in turn were affected by it. Indeed, even before their great expansion in the West, the Dissenting denominations had been in the forefront of the struggle for religious liberty and had helped to found what has become the American pattern of organized religion, the coexistence, with mutual toleration, of many denominations and sects. The United States, as a number of observers have noted, has a new pattern of organized religion which differs from both the medieval and the Reformation churches. It involves both the unique values or beliefs of each denomination and the common body of values which all the major denominations share.

The first major thesis of the present study concerns the over-all organizational and social aspects of the popular denominations and their implications for western society. Contrary to popular tendency today to correlate the frontier with dissociated individuals, many western Dissenters were in fact conforming members of society and disciplined formal organizations with definite personal and social standards. The material on the church organizations and discipline examined in the previous pages supports this thesis. A corollary to this statement is that the popular denominations helped to create a western society experienced in using voluntary association to promote aims and mutual welfare not attainable by separate individuals. Dissent expected its members, however humble their circumstances, to assume responsibility for its activities and thus trained many in organizational leadership. The Dissenters then extended their experience with religious associations to secular organizations and to politics to realize additional objectives and to influence the government.

A concrete social contribution made by Dissent, as the result of a basic organizational purpose — the formation of a vital fellowship — was to provide a means for hitherto complete strangers, migrants on the frontier, to establish close personal relations quickly. Its discipline was avowedly aimed at encouraging its members and their families to maintain high standards of personal and social behavior and at preserving group unity. Anthropologists often define these explicit functions as manifest functions and the various unstated or implicit (and often unnoticed) services as latent functions. We have considered how the local members upheld the discipline by watching over one another, probing regularly into each person's conduct and feelings, and testifying on their spiritual condition. In conjunction with their beliefs and attitudes toward each other and toward the outside world, such practices could reduce certain anxieties and promote friendships, if not always unite the local church as a whole. Even when quarreling factions formed within a congregation, as among the Baptists during their great controversy, the members within the cliques were brought close together. Present-day stories about the frontier usually overlook this significant latent social function of the Dissenting organizations and discipline. This potentiality for fostering fellowship was perhaps another reason why the members accepted what to us may seem an onerous discipline. Together with the fellowship, we should mention other potential values many Dissenters found in their membership, such

as the encouragement of devotion to their calling and the opportunities to improve such personal and social skills as speaking
(both in public and in groups), reading, conducting meetings and
committee sessions, and even some social etiquette. Perhaps these
benefits might also be classified under informal adult education.

Besides fulfilling latent functions for individual migrants, Dissent also carried out many latent group functions. Settlers in
early frontier society, lacking many traditional informal and
formal legal agencies of control, had to take deliberate steps to
maintain order and unity. The Dissenting fellowship, discipline,
and church courts were well-suited to confront such a situation.
The community could count on a solid core of disciplined citizens
organized for religious purposes, it is true, but also latently able
to wield collective as well as individual influence for peace and
order. The popular denominations thus had a direct impact on
the larger society and also exerted additional pressure as reference
groups for many others in the community. Social scientists often
define as reference groups those whose approval other individuals
and groups seek. Obviously, reference groups may also set the
standards which others follow on a single interest or over a wide
range of behavior. Since non-members regularly attending western
Presbyterian and Dissenting churches outnumbered the members
severalfold, the Dissenting influence as reference groups was apparently greater than it seemed on the surface. The rapid rise of
many members to economic and political prominence in the West
would also have enhanced their prestige as reference groups.

The second main thesis of this study involves the more specific
institutional and cultural traits of Dissent and their impact on
western society: the popular denominations strengthened or were
the source of many institutions and qualities, secular as well as
religious, regarded as typically western and sometimes as characteristically American. In addition to its voluntary organizational
features, equalitarianism, and faith in the common man, Dissent
popularized the once peculiarly aristocratic Calvinistic system
of calling, a heritage which the larger society later secularized
into the idealization of the successful self-made man and his
worldly achievements. The more controversial attitude of earlier

Dissent included its suspicion of scholarship and art and its opposition to professionalism. With some notable exceptions, western popular denominations accepted or were ambivalent toward racism and slavery and, partly under revivalistic influence, long retained what some churchmen regarded as sectarian provincialism.

For western society, these Dissenting qualities had many consequences, among which this study was able to discuss only a few illustrative cases. The voluntary and equalitarian emphases which we found at the outset among the early Virginia Baptists became fundamental traits in western popular denominational life. Within their organization, Dissenting denominations eliminated nearly all invidious distinctions, other than race, arising from accidents of birth and condition. They sought members among the humbler people and encouraged leadership from their ranks. Long before the Jacksonian movement, they opened all denominational offices to the many and infused their organizational life with new vigor. This democratic faith was an important reason for their strong opposition toward professional prerequisites to ordination. At the same time, it is evident that western popular denominations had learned to value formal organization, rules, and offices with definite responsibilities, though the Baptists had to go through a bitter struggle before the main movement could convince the antagonistic sectarians on the necessity for organization. The Baptist anti-mission controversy turned on the distinction between one form of sectarianism and the rising denominationalism more functionally attuned to the complex secular society. Dissenting procedures were democratic and often flexible but orderly, and they encouraged members to assume organizational responsibilities to enhance their rights. It is worth noting that Tocqueville, who was investigating among other things how American society with its individualism and equalitarianism could maintain order and avoid new despotism, stressed the role of voluntary associations. Such associations linked the citizens' private interests to their social responsibilities. Conversely, many members learned through participating in organizations how to be more effective in their personal lives.

Dissenters did not object to formal titles and offices which served functional purposes and did not exclude natural talent from any office it could hold. American Methodism created a formal episcopacy, which the British movement never did, and gave the bishops great authority but it fought attempts to require theological training for ordination. We may again reflect on that amusing interlude when some western circuit riders strongly opposed to theological seminaries wanted D.D. degrees automatically conferred on the itinerants when they became full elders. Here too, we see that under these circumstances the degrees would not have symbolized any barrier to unschooled but able men attaining office. In contrast to some Continental churches, for Dissent the officers and clergy did not constitute a privileged elite or separate order, but were basically fellow laymen entrusted with certain responsibilities for the common welfare. Their spiritual leadership determined their fitness to hold office, and holding office was not a right, as the Baptists among others made amply clear by electing their ministers annually. Once elected, the ministers and officers were responsible to the members and subject to lay criticism — at least in the members' view.

Since both Calvinism and Dissent emphasized the calling, it is difficult to distinguish their respective influences in implanting this system in western life. Initially in the West, even the Presbyterians had an almost sectarian attitude toward many cultural interests and defined the calling more narrowly than did the more urbane Old World Calvinists. Dissent was even narrower in its outlook and tended to restrict the calling, aside from the ministry, to economic or political activities. This "practical" approach to the calling substantially democratized, while it restricted, this once rather aristocratic ethic which had such profound consequences for both the religious and the secular life in the United States (as shown by Max Weber, H. R. Niebuhr, Talcott Parsons, and other authorities). This simplified system of calling apparently appealed to many struggling settlers who were also encouraged to raise their aspirations. European visitors were struck by the ceaseless working of Americans, even the well to do. As expected, Bishop Asbury set an example by his untiring labor and insistence that rest was for the next world. The Methodist

Anning Owen aptly summarized the Dissenting and western Presbyterian ideal with his motto: "Work! work! work! this world is no place for rest."[1]

Devotion to this-worldly duties, we should remember, originally expressed a religious ethic for other-worldly ends and was not a mundane preoccupation with materialism. Greed as such was always sinful. Strange as it may seem to us today, sectarian Dissent feared intellectual and cultural pursuits as potentially more dangerous distractions from the path to salvation than it feared business. Within a few years, the more secularized version of the calling came to value highly both personal achievement and rational productive industry alert to its opportunities, as distinct from purely exploitive ventures. Jacksonianism, as noted before, advanced these views politically when it praised the honest toil of a productive farmer or artisan or creative businessman, as opposed to the supposedly parasitical financial oligarchy. Later in the century, this emphasis on achievement strengthened the demand for competence which in turn increasingly meant professional training and higher standards. The system of calling was an integral component of the Calvinistic social and theocratic heritage, but at the same time was individualistic in holding each person responsible for his relations with God and serving Him through this-worldly duties. Dissent based its social control on its fellowship and discipline which included the public behavior and business practices of its communicants. Dissenters understood clearly that members would stray and consequently had created disciplinary institutions — a tradition contrary to some present-day views that religion has little or nothing to do with business or practical affairs.

The western Dissenting stress on the calling would seem to contradict its persistent suspicion of scholarship and art. Opposition to cultural pursuits was originally a feature of the sectarian efforts to "withdraw" from the world, while the system of calling came from the Calvinistic ethic to enter, conquer, and transform that same world. More and more Dissenters acquired wealth and high political offices and their worldly successes were often attributed to devotion to calling. Yet, the popular denominations continue to oppose most efforts to establish professional standards, partly because they interpreted such attempts as undemocratic plots to prevent able but formally unschooled persons from realizing their potentialities. One tangible argument was that some wealthy conservatives, with no more intrinsic love for disinterested culture than the Dissenters and Jacksonians whom these conservatives disdained, tried to use criteria of excellence as weapons against the emerging democracy. The Dissenters, however, had a more basic, if perhaps unconscious, reason for fearing art and higher learning as potential distractions. Ambitious members were anxious to rise economically and politically as fast as possible and needed justification for all the labor and capital they put into their farms and businesses. Religious sanction elevated their work to a calling. If we oversimplify the complex interrelationships, we may also observe that Dissenting organization and calling helped to prepare the way for (was latently functional to) the industrialization of the Middle West later in the century. On the other hand, the suspicion of learning lingering in western popular denominations probably delayed (was latently dysfunctional to) the intellectual and theological efforts to understand this industrialization and urbanization and to reformulate their traditional practices to meet the new situation. As a result of this neglect, it is said, the popular denominations lost many working-class members.

The popular denominational outlook was essentially what we would today consider middle class and not that of a traditional peasantry or radical revolutionaries. The Dissenters soon learned to appreciate elementary education and practical training as valuable for their callings. Before 1850, however, the majority could scarcely be expected to understand the extent to which religion and practical knowledge depended upon the Western (that is, Occidental) cultural heritage and its continuing development. While criticizing scholars and artists, Dissent unconsciously assumed their existence outside its membership and pragmatically utilized their contributions whenever convenient. Early western Dissent was more apt to understand democracy as eliminating intellectual standards than as providing better educational and cultural facilities open to all to train religious and civic leadership and to enrich the common life. Yet, in becoming the largest religious organizations in the American West and in the United States as a whole, the popular denominations had achieved new status. No longer a despised minority as they had been on the eighteenth-century seaboard, they had to assume more and more responsibility for secular culture as they increasingly had for western social and political welfare.

By the 1830's it is possible to detect the first modifications in the group sentiment, as distinct from the earlier personal views of a few cultured Dissenters. Thus, the Indiana Methodist Conference petition to the state legislature asking for a change in the Calvinistic monopoly of the state university contained some appreciative comments on learning, and the conference report recommending the founding of a college referred to the intrinsic value of higher education as well as to its importance in raising the quality of elementary education. At least a growing number of denominational leaders were ceasing to regard scholarship as an aristocratic plot to subvert democracy and beginning to see it as an opportunity which should be open to the people.[2] Nevertheless, the persistent hostility to college-educated ministers shows how deeply imbedded this suspicion was. To some extent, the ambivalence toward learning survived longer among the western Dissenters than in eastern popular denominations because the new western communities did not have an influential elite to set rival standards that others could emulate. Instead, the Dissenters themselves were among the important reference groups.

According to Dr. Mecklin and other authorities, revivalism was not integral to Dissent, but it profoundly influenced the Dissenting denominations employing it. Western popular denominations considered the camp meetings and other spectacular revivalistic features as "extracurricular" activities outside the official denominational program, even if today some popular stories erroneously equate western religious life with revivalism. The major popular denominations used revivalism as a technique to win new converts and to quicken the fervor of their members, but in the process were thoroughly permeated with the revivalistic spirit. Western revivalism, in contrast to the later Finney and eastern reformistic revivalism, strengthened and prolonged emotionalism, equalitarianism, and hostility to scholarship, learned ministry, and broad civic outlook. Without assessing the views of the authorities on revivalism, we can still conclude from the Moravian experience that a sect could enjoy many cultural interests and from Quaker history that a sect could have broad humanitarian and social ethical concerns. Perhaps significantly, neither the Quakers nor the Moravians were directly involved in western revivalism. The Friends severely criticized it. The western Presbyterians did not acquire or reacquire their more churchly attitude toward cultural pursuits until many years after they had explicitly rejected western revivalism, as distinct from Finney and eastern reformistic revivalism with its direct interest in social welfare and education. The formal definition of a sect obviously depended more on empirical experiences than on its essential inner logic. The intense emotionalism and narrow outlook attributed to western revivalism actually ran counter (was dysfunctional) to the Dissenting system of calling with its stress on the sober, disciplined, and responsible members working in the community.

The growing sectarian rivalry multiplied the number of denominations coexisting in the West. At the same time, the early West experienced a less frequently mentioned development, that of many local Dissenting churches separating into two or more meetings instead of growing into larger units. Aside from such external factors as the desire to have the church close to home, the members could more easily maintain their active fellowship and discipline in small intimate meetings than in large ones. Since the communicants supported the regional, state, and national units of their denominations, this institutionalization into small local congregations helped at first to give Dissent its vitality and warm fellowship. However, later in the century when membership and community requirements changed, many towns were found to be without a single church large enough to provide such essential services as competent parish work, pastoral counseling, and religious education. We might also ask whether this sectarian rivalry and preference for small, like-minded groups would discourage the acceptance of persons with different interests. Each meeting could easily insist upon appreciably uniform views while it tolerated divergent opinions in other sects. If a member did not agree with his fellow communicants, he was likely to join another congregation of his denomination or possibly even another denomination. However vital the earlier fellowships, adherents would have had less experience in their church with "diversity within unity" than they might have had. Fortunately for western society, interdenominational and other organizations, among them political parties and civic associations, brought together the members of the various churches. The congenial, likeminded Dissenting fellowships may have been an important source of the conformity which some profess to find in many middle western communities.

Early nineteenth-century popular denominations institutionalized the prevailing racist patterns and subordinated the Negroes (and other non-Caucasians), to whom Dissent did not extend its equalitarianism. Race was an obvious basis for barring talent from high denominational offices when the Dissenters had eliminated almost all other invidious distinctions. So respectable was racism that no one attempted to conceal his prejudice. Except for groups like the Quakers, early western Dissent found it convenient to assert that pure religion had almost nothing to do with slavery or racism. In practice, the Dissenters had a double standard — the free Negroes and slaves were to accept the dualistic ethic that as long as the "Africans" could worship, they should not be concerned about their personal and social condition, while the Dissenters reserved for themselves the ethic of calling with its emphasis on worldly success and duty to change conditions. Western revivalism did not create the ancient dualistic view but did strengthen it by regarding conversion as a "spiritual" experience and the social environment, including discrimination and slavery under which members had to live, as belonging to the "material" or "sensual" realm with which religion was little concerned. In contrast to their eighteenth-century forbears who fought for religious principles, the early nineteenth-century Dissenters — again with such exceptions as the Quakers — did not seriously oppose secular laws infringing on the religious rights of the slaves. The British Baptist delegates in the 1830's felt impelled to remind their American hosts that the state laws against teaching slaves to read conflicted with the Baptist religious duty to study the Scriptures and that in denying offices to Negroes, American Baptists were contradicting their professed principles.

The Dissenting organization of small congenial meetings combined conveniently with sectarianism to justify the institutionalization of their prejudices against Negroes: the Negroes could form their own churches (under white control in the South) instead of worshiping with others. The still rankling troubles over race began when the Dissenters accepted the "white superiority" thesis. While we may wonder about southerners like Bishop Capers who pioneered in the missions to the slaves and regarded Negroes as lacking some rational faculties, similar views prevailed widely among western Dissenters. Such well-meaning leaders as Peter Cartwright regularly referred to Negroes in terms which would be shocking today. These practices reveal how general was the often unconscious refusal to grant to the Negroes (and other non-Caucasians) even elementary consideration for their personal feelings and dignity. Many Dissenters who were opposed to slavery were at the same time prejudiced against its victims. Racism enabled them temporarily to blur the contradiction between Dissenting equalitarianism and their discrimination against Negroes — at the cost of further spreading this belief so highly dysfunctional to American democracy and corrosive to Dissenting ideals.

Finally, to return to the more general features of Dissenting control, we might ask about its discipline by peers, and not by authoritative officials. The experience was surely conducive to the development of voluntary associations and feeling of equality, but under some circumstances could it have also strengthened the conformistic rather than the individualistic heritage of the popular denominations? In Dissenting faith each member was directly responsible to God, and Dissent also expected each member to be responsible in his calling, both strongly individualistic emphases. On the other hand, the control by peer groups had conformistic tendencies by encouraging members to heed the views of their equals, especially in the smaller settlements during the period when the popular denominations were still suspicious of serious intellectual and artistic pursuits which might have provided alternative means of individual self-expression.

David Riesman and his associates have suggested in *The Lonely Crowd* that in the nineteenth century the dominant personality type was what they define as "inner directed," but in the twentieth century the proportion of "outer directed" characters is increasing. As a child, the inner directed person is trained to become a relatively self-disciplined adult and above all to have "generalized but nevertheless inescapably destined goals." Yet, we have seen that the popular denominations maintained group discipline over members throughout adult life, while denomination teaching encouraged the Dissenters (presumably good examplars of inner direction) to strive strenuously in a calling toward group-approved goals. Their inner direction, in short, was partly (and only partly) conformity to peer control. Possibly, the proportion of outer directed personality was greater or the proportion of inner directed personality was less in the nineteenth century than it might appear in retrospect.[3]

IMPLICATIONS FOR FRONTIER STUDIES

At this point, perhaps we should consider briefly some implications that our findings may have for studies in American history and its frontier heritage. The present inquiry did not attempt to survey the pioneer West as such or to analyze the various frontier theories, but examining Dissenting life has raised some questions concerning the Frederick Jackson Turner thesis and other accounts of the frontier. For convenience, we shall first summarize several typical Turner views and then relate the Dissenting experience to them.[4]

For Turner, the frontier was the most significant single force shaping the West directly and America generally. The western frontier was instrumental in fragmenting society into discrete families and indeed into its constituent individuals who became like free-circulating atoms, each seeking his rightful place on his own initiative. The backwoodsmen sought to develop themselves

and to achieve their goals without social and governmental restraints, Turner believed. They were opposed to any leveling, especially by law, and were antagonistic to government. Confident and
aggressive, these ambitious climbers wanted only an equal chance
to master the environment. Each felt able to pit his personal
strength against nature and against traditions. Free land enabled
the settlers to be at once fiercely competitive and ardently equalitarian (a basic Turner concept) . The successful were never to act
superior or to assume special privileges, but were always to behave
as equals and leave the way open for others striving to rise. According to Turner, the pioneers rejected formal training, professionalism, and standards of excellence — to a degree because such
qualifications smacked of past injustices and seemed to reduce the
mobility and equality that they felt and wanted.

This frontier individualism, Turner declared, had from the
first promoted democracy, a democracy permeated by strong feelings of good fellowship. Mobility and ease of western interior
communications minimized distance, and Saint Louis and New
Orleans were neighbors. If a settler wanted to know something
about any person in the country, Turner remarked, all he had
to do was to ask his neighbor who likely as not until just the
other day had lived next door to that person. Men were free and
felt free. In Turner's lyric description, they stepped more jauntily,
held their heads higher, and thought more broadly than elsewhere. These backwoodsmen were impatient of restraints and
of men who "split hairs, or scrupled over the method of reaching
the right." That is, the frontier sharply modified, where it did
not eliminate, the old order with its ancient ruling classes, special
privileges, and traditional norms or modes of behavior. The frontiersmen had faith in themselves and in the destiny of their West;
they dreamed grandly of creating a new world. American democracy, then, was no theory. It did not cross the Atlantic in the
Susan Constant to Virginia or in the *Mayflower* to Massachusetts,
Turner continued, but rather, democracy came "stark and strong
and full of life from the American forests" and gathered new
strength "each time it touched a new frontier."

This view of the frontier influence also suggests a related and

perhaps more romantic conception of the frontier West as a return to the primitive, a regression to an earlier stage in human
evolution. To an extent Turner shared this idea:

The wilderness masters the colonist. . . . It strips off the garments of
civilization and arrays him in the hunting shirt and the moccasin. . . .
Before long he has gone to planting Indian corn and plowing with a
sharp stick; he shouts the war cry and takes the scalp in orthodox Indian
fashion.[5]

To reach civilization again, this primitive section had to go
through what Turner agreed might be the universal course of
human evolution from the crude hunting to the herding stage,
from cattle raising to subsistence clearing, from simple to intensive agriculture, and thence to manufacturing, each period profoundly affecting western and national institutions.

Turner also emphasized strongly the nationalizing influence
of the frontier. As the most effective force for Americanization,
the frontier made settlers from all sections of the country and
from Europe national and democratic in outlook. "The growth
of nationalism and the evolution of American political institutions were dependent on the advance of the frontier," Turner
said. It consolidated the nation. The Indian problems and western
demands for improvements compelled the federal government to
broaden more and more its legislative scope and administrative functions. Extending governmental responsibilities in turn
strengthened the centralizing tendencies: "Loose construction increased as the nation marched westward." Jeffersonianism gave
way to Jacksonianism with its more positive leadership and westerners increasingly wanted to use governmental agencies to provide various services. In Turner's opinion, this national outlook
and western mobility helped to check provincialism and narrow
sectionalism. The settlers actively participated in politics and
enthusiastically supported trusted leaders. Rapid rotation of offices and emotionalism characterized western politics, Turner
concluded.

This frontier, Turner also felt, either drastically altered or
rejected the older cultural traditions. Across the Alleghenies, the

past and its precedents lost their power. The West was "free of European ideas and institutions." The settlers turned their backs on the seaboard culture and vigorously and self-reliantly "began to build up a society free from dominance of ancient forms." In discarding these old restrictions and advancing equality and democracy, the frontier promoted courage, practicality, and exuberant vitality. "Buoyant, optimistic, and sometimes reckless and extravagant spirit of innovation was the very life of the West," Turner insisted. These backwoodsmen disdained legal niceties and strict fiscal practices and upheld the spoils system against trained professionalism. "Art, literature, refinement, scientific administration," and other cultural heritages had to give way to the gigantic task of creating a new world. This cultural elimination and simplification were destructive to intellectualism and art and also made religion more emotional. Gradually, however, the creative power inherent in pioneer ideals took root and grew into such notable institutions as the great middle western state universities, which Turner saw as peculiarly combining frontier practicality with ancient intellectual traditions. The West eventually began to accept the cultural contributions of the settlers, including those who came directly from the Old World. It became, as it were, a "mixing bowl," if not a part of the American melting pot.

These brief summaries of several representative views from Turner and from popular accounts fail to do justice to his insights and work. Nevertheless, they should suffice to enable us to relate popular denominational experience and several questions raised by the present study to these concepts. Since this inquiry is not a critique of the frontier theories, the various arguments advanced by others for and against these concepts will not be repeated here. It should be noted, however, that these controversies arise partly over the changing meanings given to the word "frontier." Even Turner had treated the frontier variously as a place, nature, process, stage of economy or evolution, or psycho-social force — quite diverse, if not conflicting, interpretations. At the outset, it is perhaps appropriate to observe that the individualistic interpretations of the pioneer West pay little attention to popular denominational organization, discipline, life, and attitudes — for which there is a significant volume of empirical data; or, if they mention these factors, they do not fully incorporate them into their views on western life. Yet the records surveyed in the present study indicate that it is precisely these institutional features and attitudes which are crucial for analyzing the Dissenting roles and influence on the wider community.

Actually, the more observant even among the early nineteenth-century European visitors, including Tocqueville, clearly sensed the strong religious impact on American secular life, although they generally did not investigate the specific social mechanisms which the various denominations used to exert power. Michel Chevalier concluded that contrary to the situation in his native France, in America the government minimized its public responsibilities while strong religious forces brought pressure to regulate secular society and culture. Organized religion, Harriet Martineau insisted, seriously circumscribed American thinking and behavior — all the more effectively since many Americans conditioned by their religion from childhood were not even aware of these controls.[6]

The bitter controversy in Kentucky between the religiously liberal (non-orthodox and non-Presbyterian) elite and the Presbyterian orthodoxy (many of whom also belonged to the upper classes) centered on Transylvania University, but it also involved the Presbyterian efforts to direct Kentucky society as a whole. The non-orthodox upper-class Kentuckians objected to any denomination strait-jacketing their lives. Similarly, Indiana Methodism took root earlier in rural areas than in those towns where hostile residents were antagonistic to its moralistic discipline over their activities. To an extent, such denominational regimentation may be regarded as systematically extending the traditional group controls found in many small communities. Mrs. Kirkland refers to this unofficial but effective regulation as forcibly experienced, among others, by some English families who had settled near her home under an illusion that unlimited freedom and individualism prevailed on the frontier. Soon they felt the heavy restraint on their lives, since the principle of live and let live was decidedly alien to the pioneer society:

Whoever exhibits any desire for privacy is set down as "praoud," or something worse; no matter how inoffensive, or even how benevolent he may be; and of all places in the world in which to live on the shady side of public opinion, an American back-woods settlement is the very worst.[7]

Mrs. Kirkland gives many other instances of a frontier community typically refusing to allow individual leeway and privacy and exerting collective pressure on its residents. This social control could on occasions even extend to sleeping hours, as discovered by one schoolteacher who had seen no reason for rising at dawn with others in the village when his classes did not begin until later. A self-appointed "committee" under a local exhorter questioned him about his "irregularities" and also compelled him to open his personal trunk for their inspection. These citizens finally decided to expel him from the settlement for not conforming sufficiently to the group standards.

The virtually communal use of private possessions, even personal belongings, also reflected this closely knit social life. The pioneers depended on each other for survival and "all things were common," James Finley recorded.[8] The people freely availed themselves of each other's articles and "lent" them to third and fourth parties without notifying the owner. Many items were never returned. The Kirklands found this custom costly, since their neighbors were constantly "borrowing" even sugar, tea, kitchen utensils, combs, shoes, shaving sets, paper and pen (one borrower complained about its poor point), and blankets which were ruined. In short, a settler had access to many tools and necessities almost as a right or as if they were communal property. The backwoodsmen helped each other to do things which individuals could not do alone or which a group could do more effectively or more pleasantly.

Turner himself spoke with enthusiasm about this western "capacity for extra-legal, voluntary association," but he apparently did not have the opportunity to investigate its sources or development, aside from the rapid rotation of local political offices which in turn probably had some Dissenting inspiration:

This power of the newly arrived pioneers to join together for a common end without the intervention of governmental institutions was one of their marked characteristics. . . . America does through informal association and understandings on the part of the people many of the things which in the Old World are and can be done only by governmental intervention and compulsion.[9]

Here, Turner is discussing what he apparently regarded as a strong feature of an atomistic society. Yet pioneer familiarity with voluntary organizations was a social, a collectivistic capacity or skill gained in many instances through participation in popular denominational activities. Isolated individuals or mere aggregations of discrete persons could not have acquired the "know-how" to organize and sustain associations for promoting collective goals. "Grass-roots" social experience did not grow on western trees. The ability to resort to voluntary group action presupposes a society already accustomed to organizational activities. What is more, if in reality the government had as insignificant a role in several western states as some frontier enthusiasts apparently believed (though this view runs counter to the one on nationalizing role), then the voluntary associations had to assume more than the usual range of social responsibilities. We have seen how popular denominations accepted broad social and quasi-judicial functions, manifestly for religious and moral needs of their members and latently for the general welfare.

As suggested by Mrs. Kirkland and others, reliance on voluntary associations in itself does not guarantee individualism unless the system respects personal differences and privacy and perhaps unless groups representing real alternatives exist. The frontier society had less varied choices than modern America. Moreover, organizations originally founded to promote interests of their members can become instruments of conformity, partly by demanding so much time and energy that members have less leisure and free time. In recent years, dictatorships have used so-called voluntary (but in reality regimented by state or official party) agencies to control their people by forcing them to devote nearly all their time not at work to organizational projects. Thus, these agencies effectively curtail the privacy and freedom of the "volunteers." If, as Ralph Barton Perry contends, privacy is both a luxury and a prerequisite for individualism, then the relatively equalitarian, ever watchful frontier community suspicious of privacy and influenced by the popular denominations to keep an eye on every member and to check deviations was hardly the ideal nursery for modern individualism.[10]

Theoretical analyses raise further doubts about the more extreme interpretations of frontier individualism. Among others, Robert M. MacIver reminds us in his studies on the modern state that notwithstanding its very great importance and its legal coercive power the state is never identical with the community or society. Ultimately, the state is only an agency or an association of the community. Voluntary organizations with overlapping memberships in a society may link their members to each other in a variety of ways. Consequently, a democratic nation with many free associations may be more closely integrated than a totalitarian dictatorship which abolishes voluntary organizations and attempts to monopolize many functions performed by private groups among democratic peoples.[11] A society, then, has not been fragmented into its constituent individuals, as at times Turner apparently believed, merely because voluntary organizations instead of another type of association, the state, carried out certain social functions. Some frontier concepts have confused the state with the community or society or both and assumed that in the early West society had dissolved because the state was supposedly less active than in the East.

If we turn from Turner's broad generalizations about the unbounded individualism to consider his more specific observations on frontier individualism, equality, and democracy, we find them generally applicable to pioneer Dissenters. The individualistic qualities which he finds in the backwoodsmen have obvious associations with the Dissenters resolutely engaged in their calling. To a degree, the buoyant frontier optimism and the restless energy reflected the drive idealized for the faithful in their call-ing, confident of ultimate success even as they were overcoming obstacles. It is not necessary here to discuss again the Dissenting role in promoting that good fellowship which Turner attributed to the frontier. Whether in the raw settlements or in urban Cin-cinnati, Saint Louis, or even New Orleans the Dissenters were neighbors in sentiment and attitudes, sharing many similar ideals, aspirations, and experiences. The fierce equalitarianism, the faith in the common man, and the impatience with the niceties and professionalism which Turner admired, we have already noted in the Dissenters, even to the Methodist bishops in their shirt-sleeves and the Baptists calling a fellow farmer or artisan or shopkeeper to the ministry. Dissenters expected those entrusted with office to behave as equals and they rejected professionalism, formal training, and official standards of excellence for much the same reason that Turner gives. After all, many settlers whom Turner was describing were Dissenters!

The romantic conception of the frontier as a temporary return to a primitive stage in human or social evolution has been re-jected by modern evolutionary theories with other unilinear hypotheses — that is, empirically discredited assumptions that all social groups go through parallel evolutionary stages. More sig-nificantly, the extensive anthropological research on non-literate peoples (the popular term "primitive peoples" is not always appropriate) reveals them as living mainly in traditional societies with far fewer institutional forms of individualism, as the frontier theorists understood individualism, than in the western settle-ments. Religion may permeate the entire life of a non-literate people and serve as a focus of their individual integration and social unity. In contrast, though religious organizations (the de-nominational plurality was itself a relevant difference from non-literate tribes with a single religion) had a highly significant role in the pioneer West, which may have seemed primitive, the fron-tiersmen came from a more differentiated society with a more complex technology. Though illiterates in a modern civilization may know less about survival in the wilderness than non-literates, the distinction is in outlooks and objectives.

Frontier society was far removed from the primitive or traditional kinship societies in both structure and cultural traits. Its people were extremely mobile; relative strangers from all over the country lived and worked together in new communities to improve their material well-being. The West already possessed several basic attributes (derived in some cases from Dissent) essentrial for rapidly growing into a modern impersonal industrial society. The more perceptive foreign travelers, among them Tocqueville, saw how different the frontiersmen were from feudal peasants, let alone "primitives." Unlike the Old World peasant or non-literate, the settler could readily acquire property and could sell it and move whenever he chose. As we might expect among people who had accepted the system of calling, regardless of their agrarian life, the westerners were essentially achievement-minded and economically oriented. They were closer in many ways to the European commercial classes than they were to the peasantry. After all, many settlers were, as often noted, expectant capitalists. Their improvisation of tools and techniques was a mere convenience, not primitiveness. The very inability of the back-woodsmen to sympathize with the Indians (after making allowances for their rivalry for land), even as compared with the French traders, reflected their completely different cultural outlook. Indeed, if the frontier had actually been a primitive stage of evolution, the condition would have seriously undermined the individualistic interpretations which the theorists who advanced this primitive frontier thesis tried to support. The basic sociological findings, including those of Emile Durkheim and Ferdinand Toennies earlier and Robert MacIver today, show that modern individualism depends appreciably upon extensive division of labor, institutional differentiation, and cultural diversity, which are qualities better found in modern cosmopolitan societies than among simple non-literate peoples.[12]

Turner, departing from his previous stress on individualism, strongly emphasized the nationalizing influence of the frontier. This view combined some previously mentioned concepts concerning the West with assumptions which were essentially sociological, economic, and political in nature. Two observations should be made. The first is that numerous empirical studies have long since discredited geographical determinism as a viable theory. That is, according to these findings, geographical conditions do not determine the nature of a society, though they may set limits to its possibilities. The second is that the Jacksonian relationship to a more positive government is apparently still an open question among historians. On the other hand, as far as the western Dissenters were concerned, we have already noticed their enthusiastic participation in the Jacksonian movement and the importance that they and other settlers attached to democratizing and extending governmental functions. The very rapidity with which Jacksonianism spread in the West suggests that the federal government was not always the remote abstraction to the backwoodsmen sometimes assumed today but rather a tangible agency for promoting desirable aims. Least of all should the pioneer activities in their state and local governments be overlooked. The Dissenters were experienced in relating their local church activities to the denominational regional and national programs, and they applied their religious group training to civic and political movements. This familiarity with regional and national organizations in conjunction with the historical development of the Old Northwest under federal auspices could have indicated to the Dissenters the implications of these centralizing functions (whether Jacksonian or not) mentioned by Turner. He did not fully reconcile his views on the pioneer pressure for state and national action with his views on the fragmentation of frontier society, since, for one thing, he classified voluntary associations with an atomistic society instead of with Dissenting and other social heritages, of which political interests were a vital part.

The previous comments on the collectivistic and co-operative features of the frontier society did not negate its individualistic aspects. In this period, the settlers had access to vast tracts of relatively cheap land. Most westerners lived on clearings and farms which provided subsistence and were rising in value or were engaged in small-scale, often individual, business and professional ventures in the growing towns. In such a society, ambitious individuals could often acquire substance. Yet, we should emphasize that it was often the system of calling which spurred this ambition and which was the moral and ideological wellspring of this individualism. To reiterate, then, while frontier life had strongly individualistic qualities, both historical data and theoretical analyses would broaden the individualistic interpretations to include the pioneer society, its voluntary associations, and its religious and cultural heritage. In any case, the issue was not individual versus society. Man as a social being cannot realize his potentialities outside society, and society does not exist outside its constituent individuals. While the relation of any particular individual to society is never entirely harmonious, some societies encourage initiative and in them individuals and private groups do many things without governmental intervention.[13] The frontier society probably had this voluntarism to a high degree. It was strongly equalitarian in its earlier stages, but it could well have had less individualism and cultural freedom than some contemporary European societies had at least for their more privileged classes.

Turner felt that the West rejected much of the seaboard and Old World culture. To survive under new conditions, people have always modified their ways, and in addition the frontiersmen adopted certain useful Indian techniques. Adaptation to new environment, however, is not a deliberate scuttling of cherished traditions. Instead of discarding their seaboard heritage, the Dissenters and other settlers clung to whatever cultural background they esteemed or their religion encouraged them to value, even to their prejudices, as again illustrated by the differences between ex-New England and ex-Virginia Baptists in the West in their approach to education and missions. To take a quite different example, we might consider the architectural designs chosen by the more prosperous pioneers for their residences and public buildings once they had passed the log cabin stage. The architectural history of the Old Northwest reflects their attachment to the styles prevailing earlier in the more eastern states and Europe. Many wanted to reproduce the architecture they liked in their former home communities as they remembered it. The log cabin, often regarded as the pre-eminent symbol of the frontier, was itself an Old World heritage, probably Scandinavian in origin.

Similar remarks may be made about nearly all frontier cultural and social traits.[14]

In its beginnings in the colonies, Dissent appealed primarily to the humbler, less-educated classes. Consequently, when the first Dissenters moved westward, they carried with them the early sectarian hostility to scholarly and artistic activities rather than the culture of the eastern elite or of the total seaboard society. That is, the Dissenting migrants had rejected or had been opposed to many cultural interests for religious reasons while they were still living on the seaboard and before they thought of migrating. Thus, the poorer early Virginia Baptists who settled in Kentucky, Ohio, Indiana, and Illinois carried with them their strong antagonism to the plantation aristocracy culture and to the class-conscious Virginia society. Many non-Dissenters may have temporarily given up their favorite cultural activities because the proper facilities were at first not available in the West, but they were not deliberating throwing away their heritage. In the West, the popular denominations exerted a far greater influence than they did on the seaboard where the educated classes had their own standards and the Dissenting suspicion of learning persisted longer, particularly in the rural areas, than on the coast. In many early western communities, no cultural elite existed to challenge them. In mid-nineteenth century, for example, Peter Cartwright was still denouncing organ and choral music which the eastern Methodist churches had accepted several decades earlier and was voicing sentiments which the eastern Methodists of 1800 might have better appreciated. Again, many Indiana Baptists were disturbed when the Indianapolis Baptist church introduced instrumental music in 1858. Several eastern Baptist churches had instrumental music in the eighteenth century. Western sectarian hostility to many aspects of the seaboard heritage seems to have led some frontier theorists to conclude that it was the frontier rather than the Dissenting sectarianism which had induced many westerners to turn away from the old culture.

Cincinnati, the largest western city in the 1830's, illustrated certain features of this development. The attacks on intellectual and artistic activities in the city revealed the sentiments held by many residents, among them the Dissenters who retained this attitude for some years after eastern Dissent had begun to change. The hero lore of Cincinnati fitted this pattern. Many admired Benjamin Franklin, but looked with a receptive eye particularly at the hard-working, thrifty, shrewd young man with his gospel of getting ahead. Franklin, the statesman and diplomat, was less directly emphasized. The generous contributor unable to practice frugality, who at the age of forty-two retired permanently from active business to enjoy life and to think "uninterrupted by the little cares and fatigues of business," was almost a stranger to his Queen City followers. They knew Franklin of the *Autobiography* and the "Poor Richard" maxims. The Cincinnatians appreciated his friendships with the intellectual giants in Europe more as evidence that a poor boy with little schooling could by his diligence rise to move among the great than as an indication of his urbane cosmopolitanism and his active intellectual curiosity. The unpuritanical Franklin was scarcely known. His Cincinnati admirers understood still less that he would have disagreed with those who classified artists with robbers and beggars, and authors with pickpockets and liars, and with those who regarded scholarship as a step toward an aristocratic subversion of democracy.[15]

The cultured elements in Cincinnati — mainly Unitarians and other non-Dissenters — were interested in literature and published literary magazines. Still, a non-Dissenting Yankee like Timothy Flint who traveled widely in the West seemed unusual because he was familiar with the leading Continental and British authors. The western Dissenters would have condemned many books that Flint most admired, if they had known about them, as well as the novels he wrote. While western society in general for the first few years could not provide many amenities of cultured life, these differences in the attitudes between western Dissenters and non-Dissenters again suggest that the migrants were inclined to retain the cultural outlook they had in the East or acquired from their religious heritage.[16]

Turner attributed to the New England elements the priority in seeking to create an adequate educational system in the West. He meant the non-Dissenting Yankee stock which on the whole had better education and broader outlook as well as the New England Dissenters with their greater appreciation for education than their Highland South fellow members. In this connection, we may ask whether the combination of the practical with the older intellectual traditions which Turner saw in the great middle western state universities in some degree incorporated the later pragmatic popular denominational attitude toward education, granted that the older cultural influences, among them the Continental technical schools, were probably more significant.

European settlers contributed greatly to the development of music, pageantry, and similar arts, often against Dissenting hostility. Local histories and popular denominational records mention the misunderstandings arising between the Dissenters and the Continental settlers with their Sunday recreation, music, drama, dances, and beer. Later in the century, of course, popular denominations began to broaden their outlook. During the process, Dissenters showed such curious inconsistencies as introducing music and painting and other "ornamental" subjects in Baptist and Methodist colleges, while many local churches were still denouncing such interests as sinful or lures to perdition. The situation obviously reflected the differential rates of change in attitudes, which depended in part on the background of the members and congregations.

Only briefly did Turner discuss western religions, including their sectarian rivalries, revivalism, and emotionalism — by-and-large Dissenting traits. The westerners, he said, felt their religion. While he mentioned the need for research on frontier denominations, he apparently did not have the time to analyze the actual role that religious institutions had in shaping his beloved West and its democracy. Some western historians have commented on this apparent neglect, and we can also understand George W. Pierson's concern that Turner had not noticed the great contribution that American Protestantism — what Tocqueville categorized as republican religion — made to democracy and to the West.[17] Here again, we might ask if Turner was led to attribute to the frontier the causal stimulus for many pioneer traits since he had no real opportunity to trace the impact that Dissenting and other religious and cultural heritages had on the backwoodsmen. Furthermore, during the early years, the children of western Dissenters would probably have had far less opportunity to attend schools and to compare their parental outlook with the views of people with different cultural traditions than they would have had on the seaboard. In some places, this trend could have temporarily accentuated the Dissenting influence.

The data reviewed in the present study would suggest that in advancing his more sweeping generalizations, Turner was at times on shaky ground. He did not fully utilize certain historical material and sociological principles known in his day, which would have strengthened his basic data and might have modified his conclusions. Thus, he did not theoretically reconcile his frontier individualism, nationalism, sectionalism, and innovating power. Each concept had supporting data, but partly because he misunderstood the sociological and anthropological approaches, these emphases were not subsumed under a more inclusive interpretation. On the other hand, his vivid description of the pioneers often fit the Dissenters. His colorful comments on their activism and equalitarianism bring them to life and are consistent with the independent data on the Dissenters and other settlers. Obviously, many backwoodsmen whom Turner was discussing were Dissenters or were influenced by Dissent, and, conversely, Dissenters shared many traits with other frontiersmen.

More fundamentally, it is apparent that actual experience, social background, and traditions of the settlers, among whom the Dissenters were both numerous and influential, were among the major forces shaping western society. Dissenting democracy, equalitarianism, system of calling, and organization did not spring from the wilderness. Instead, they moved in the opposite direction: Pioneer Dissenters carried these qualities into the forests and propagated them among their neighbors — "stark and strong and full of life." The frontier provided the physical setting and the limits but did not determine the pioneer social organization and culture. The frontier West was the stage, as it were, but the settlers under the influence of their cultural heritage selected the plays and their roles. Siberian wilderness, South American forests, and even French Quebec woods did not create those dynamic, aggressive, and buoyant qualities and that democracy and equalitarianism which stirred Turner's imagination. The very traits which he admired indicate the great part the Dissenting denominations had in the West, a role roughly similar to, even if more limited than, that of Puritanism in New England. They helped to mold our cherished institutions and our ways of feeling, thinking, and acting. The Dissenters left a permanent impress on the West and on modern American life as a whole.

References

References

The references begin with the main sources for each chapter as a whole. The numbered notes following these references cite the sources for specific quotations in the text. The Bibliography lists the author's full name and publications mentioned in these pages.

CHAPTER I — *Introduction*

The major references for the chapter: Buley, *The Old Northwest*; Hall, *The Religious Background of American Culture*; Leyburn, *Frontier Folkways*; Mecklin, *The Story of American Dissent*; H. R. Niebuhr, *The Social Sources of Denominationalism*; Paxson, *History of the American Frontier*; Sweet, *Religion on the American Frontier* (4 vols.; *The Baptists, The Presbyterians, The Congregationalists,* and *The Methodists,* hereafter mentioned separately by their denominational subtitles), *Religion in Colonial America, Religion in the Development of American Culture*; Troeltsch, *The Social Teaching of the Christian Churches*; Turner, *The Frontier in American History, Rise of the New West, The Significance of Sections in American History,* and *The United States*; and Weber, *The Protestant Ethic and the Spirit of Capitalism* and *The Sociology of Religion*.

The Frontier in American History by Frederick Jackson Turner is one of the best-known accounts of frontier individualism and its possible impact on modern American society. Daniel B. Aaron, "Cincinnati, 1818–1838"; Dixon Ryan Fox (ed.), *Sources of Culture in the Middle West*; and G. R. Taylor (ed.), *The Turner Thesis Concerning the Role of the Frontier in American History* contain some critical comments on the Turner thesis. James G. Leyburn has compared the American frontier with several others in *Frontier Folkways*. In addition to the journals and autobiographies of pioneer religious leaders, studies on western religious life include P. G. Mode, *The Frontier Spirit in American Christianity* and W. W. Sweet's documentary collections and commentaries, especially his *Religion on the American Frontier*.

Troeltsch discusses his sect and church typologies in *The Social Teaching of the Christian Churches* (particularly I, 331 ff.; II, 461 ff., 688–712, 993–97). In *The Sociology of Religion* and to a degree in *The Protestant Ethic and the Spirit of Capitalism*, Max Weber examines the traits of religious organizations. Many scholars have recently begun to re-examine these sociological concepts, among them P. L. Berger, Russell Dynes, G. Benton Johnson, D. A. Martin, Elizabeth K. Nottingham, Talcott Parsons, B. R. Wilson, and J. M. Yinger. Chapter vii below will refer in more detail to the analytical distinctions among sects, denominations, and churches. R. M. MacIver and C. H. Page in *Society* and Elizabeth Nottingham in *Religion and Society* define many of the terms used in the present study.

T. C. Hall, *The Religious Background of American Culture*; F. H. Littell, *The Anabaptist View of the Church*; and R. J. Smithson, *The Anabaptists* review certain influences of the sectarian Protestantism of the Reformation era (and earlier) on American Dissenting denominations. Many recent publications discuss the role of the Dissenting denominations in Great Britain, among them H. F. L. Cocks, *The Nonconformist Conscience*; S. G. Dimond, *The Psychology of the Methodist Revival*; H. M. Lynd, *England in the Eighteen Eighties*; H. E. Mathews, *Methodism and the Education of the People*; and W. J. Warner, *The Wesleyan Movement in the Industrial Revolution*.

NOTES

1. "The Puritan Tradition," in *Wellsprings of the American Spirit*, ed. F. E. Johnson (New York: Institute for Religious and Social Studies, 1948), p. 2.

2. Among those who prefer the term "Dissent" in classifying the Baptists, Methodists, and other once sectarian denominations in America are Thomas C. Hall, J. M. Mecklin, and J. T. McNeill in "The Dissenting Tradation," F. E. Johnson (ed.), *op. cit.* They use it partly to avoid the popular confusion with Puritanism, an important historical and analytical distinction.

3. James Graham Leyburn, *Frontier Folkways* (New Haven: Yale University Press, 1935), pp. 1, 192 ff. He is referring to: R. S. and H. M. Lynd, *Middletown* (New York: Harcourt, Brace & Co, 1929); Sherwood Anderson, *Winesburg, Ohio* (New York: Penguin Books, 1946); and Sinclair Lewis, *Babbitt* (New York: Grossett, 1922). The subsequent community studies are: W. L. Warner, *Democracy in Jonesville* (New York: Harper & Bros., 1949) and A. B. Hollingshead, *Elmtown's Youth* (New York: John Wiley & Sons, 1949).

4. *The Frontier in American History*, (New York: Henry Holt & Co., 1931) pp. 4–7, 18, 22–23, 30, 206–7, 212, 253–54, *et passim*.

5. "Cincinnati, 1818–1838: A Study of Attitudes in the Urban West" (Ph.D. dissertation, Harvard University, 1942), pp. ii–x.

6. J. G. Leyburn, *loc. cit.*

7. *Circuit Riders Days Along the Ohio* (New York & Cincinnati: The Methodist Book Concern, 1923), p. 11 *et passim* and *Religion on the American Frontier* (Chicago: University of Chicago Press, 1946), IV, 3 *et passim*.

CHAPTER II — *The Background of Western Popular Denominations*

The main references for the Virginia background: Asbury, *Journal*; Bangs, *A History of the Methodist Episcopal Church*; Cobb, *The Rise of Religious Liberty in America*; Fithian, *Journal & Letters*; Gewehr, *The Great Awakening in Virginia*; C. F. James, *Documentary History of the Struggle for Religious Liberty in Virginia*; Leland, *The Writings* (especially *The Virginia Chronicle*); Little, *Imprisoned Preachers and Religious Liberty in Virginia*; Mecklin, *The Story of American Dissent*; Morton, *Robert Carter of Nomini Hall*; Semple, *A History of the Rise and Progress of the Baptists in Virginia*; and Sweet, *Religion in Colonial America, Religion in the Development of American Culture*, and *The Baptists* (Vol. I, *Religion on the American Frontier*).

For Connecticut: Asbury, *Journal*; Baker, *An Introduction to the History of Early New England Methodism*; Bangs, *A History of the Methodist Episcopal Church*; Greene, *The Development of Religious Liberty in Connecticut*; Keller, *The Second Great Awakening in Connecticut*; Koch, *Republican Religion*; Leland, *The Writings*; Mecklin, *The Story of American Dissent*; Morse, *A Neglected Period of Connecticut's History*; Newman, *A History of the Baptist Churches in the United States*; and Purcell, *Connecticut in Transition*.

On early Western developments: Aaron, "Cincinnati"; Asbury, *Journal*; Babcock, *Forty Years of Pioneer Life: Memoir of John Mason Peck*; Bangs, *A History of the Methodist Episcopal Church*; Barclay, *Early American Methodism*; Bishop, *An Outline of the History of the Church in the State of Kentucky*; Bond, *The Civilization of the Old Northwest*; Buley, *The Old Northwest*; Cartwright, *Autobiography*; Cleveland, *The Great Revival in the West*; Finley, *Autobiography* and *Sketches of Western Methodism*; Flint, *Recollections of the Last Ten Years*; Kirkland, *The Evening Book, Forest Life, A New Home — Who'll Follow?*, and *Western Clearings*; Leyburn, *Frontier Folkways;* Lindley (ed), *Indiana as Seen by Early Travelers*; Mills and Smith, *Report of a Missionary Tour*; Mode, *The Frontier Spirit in American Christianity;* Nottingham, *Methodism and the Frontier*; Paxson, *History of the American Frontier*; Rusk, *The Literature of the Middle Western Frontier*; Schermerhorn and Mills, *A Correct View*; Sonne, *Liberal Kentucky*; Spencer, *A History of Kentucky Baptists*; Sweet, *Religion on the American Frontier, Religion in the Development of American Culture*, and *The Rise of Methodism in the West*; John Taylor, *A History of Ten Baptist Churches*; Toulmin, *The Western Country in 1793*; Turner, *The Frontier in American History, Rise of the New West, The Significance of Sections*, and *The United States*; Wright, *Culture on the Moving Frontier*; and various state histories, among them: Alvord, *The Illinois*

Country; Buck, *Illinois in 1818*; Chaddock, *Ohio before 1850*; Clark, *A History of Kentucky*; Esarey, *A History of Indiana*; Pease, *The Frontier State*; and Roseboom and Weisenburger, *A History of Ohio* (hereafter collectively designated as "state histories").

Gewehr summarizes the impact of the Great Awakening and the Virginia developments in *The Great Awakening in Virginia*. C. F. James, John Leland, L. P. Little, and Robert Semple present vivid accounts of the Baptist campaign. Semple reflects the attitudes of his day and also includes biographical sketches of Baptist leaders. The various Virginia Baptist churches adopted the Philadelphia Confession with varying reservations. *The Creeds of Christendom*, ed. Philip Schaff, III, 738–41, contains the text of the Confession. Asbury, *Journal* and Bangs, *A History of the Methodist Episcopal Church*, refer at some length to the rise of Methodism in Virginia as they saw it.

John Leland, the outstanding leader of the Virginia Baptists, moved to Connecticut and became the spokesman for the Connecticut Baptists. His *Writings* and Newman's *History* describe his activities. See also Greene, *The Development of Religious Liberty in Connecticut*; Koch, *Republican Religion*; and Purcell, *Connecticut in Transition*.

NOTES

1. R. H. Pitt, "Introduction," Lewis Peyton Little, *Imprisoned Preachers and Religious Liberty in Virginia* (Lynchburg, Va.: J. P. Bell Co., 1938), presents a brief summary of the Baptist position. Further statements are in Charles Fenton James, *Documentary History of the Struggle for Religious Liberty in America* (Lynchburg, Va.: J. P. Bell Co., 1900), and S. H. Cobb, *The Rise of Religious Liberty in America* (New York: Macmillan Co., 1902).

2. Francis Asbury, *Journal, 1771–1815* (3 vols.; New York: Lane & Scott, 1852), I, 208–30, includes communications from Jarratt. Wesley Marsh Gewehr, *The Great Awakening in Virginia, 1740–1790* (Durham, N. C.: Duke University Press, 1930) also quotes from Jarratt, pp. 23, 140–51, *et passim*. W. W. Sweet, *Methodism in American History* (New York: Methodist Book Concern, 1933) has a brief background account of early American Methodism.

3. As quoted in Gewehr, *op. cit.*, p. 260.

4. As quoted in J. M. Mecklin, *The Story of American Dissent* (New York, Harcourt, Brace & Co., 1934), pp. 255–56.

5. Gustav Adolf Koch, *Republican Religion: The American Revolution and the Cult of Reason* (New York: Henry Holt & Co., 1933), p. 10, n. 14, *et passim*; R. J. Purcell, *Connecticut in Transition* (Washington, D.C.: American Historical Association, 1918), pp. 72–73.

6. Charles Roy Keller, *The Second Great Awakening in Connecticut* (New Haven: Yale University Press, 1942), pp. 195–96.

7. Elizabeth K. Nottingham, *Methodism and the Frontier: Indiana Proving Ground* (New York: Columbia University Press, 1941), p. 27 *et passim*.

8. Ralph Henry Gabriel, *The Course of American Democratic Thought: An Intellectual History Since 1815* (New York: Ronald Press Co., 1940), p. 13.

9. Figures on membership and attendance at services are scattered in various references: The Wiley estimate for the Crawfordsville District, W. W. Sweet,

Circuit Rider Days in Indiana (Indianapolis: W. K. Stewart Co., 1916), p. 74; on the Baptists, John Newton Brown, *History of the American Baptist Publication Society* (Philadelphia: American Baptist Publication Society, n.d.), p. 126; on the Lexington, Kentucky, churches, Andrew Reed and James Matheson, *A Narrative of the Visit to the American Churches by the Deputation from the Congregational Union of England and Wales* (2 vols.; New York: Harper & Bros., 1835), I, 132.

CHAPTER III – *The Presbyterians*

The major reference: Sweet, *The Presbyterians*, Vol. II of *Religion on the American Frontier*, especially the records of the Synod of Kentucky, the Cumberland and Transylvania Presbyteries, and the church sessions. Other main sources: Bishop, *An Outline of the History of the Church* (including the David Rice *Memoirs*); Bond, *The Civilization of the Old Northwest*; Briggs, *American Presbyterianism*; Buley, *The Old Northwest*; Cleveland, *The Great Revival*; Flint, *Recollections*; Foster, *A Sketch of the History of the Cumberland Presbyterian Church*; Lindley (ed.), *Indiana as Seen by Early Travelers*; Mills and Smith, *Report of a Missionary Tour*; Mode, *The Frontier Spirit in American Christianity*; Muelder, *Church History in a Puritan Colony* and "Jacksonian Democracy in Religious Organizations"; Niebuhr, *The Social Sources of Denominationalism*; Paxson, *History of the American Frontier*; The Presbyterian Church in the U. S. A., *The Form of Government and Forms of Process*; Schermerhorn and Mills, *A Correct View*; Sonne, *Liberal Kentucky*; Sweet, *Religion in the Development of American Culture*; Thompson, *A History of the Presbyterian Churches*; Toulmin, *The Western Country*; Troeltsch, *Protestantism and Progress* and *The Social Teaching*; Turner, *The Frontier in American History, Rise of the New West*, and *The Significance of Sections*; and Wright, *Culture on the Moving Frontier*.

In the introductory section of *The Presbyterians*, W. W. Sweet has summarized the initial history of the Presbyterian expansion to the West. In *The Frontier in American History, The Significance of Sections*, and *The United States*, F. J. Turner discusses the broader features of the American movements westward. The present study has primarily followed the presentation of Charles A. Briggs, *American Presbyterianism*, Robert E. Thompson, *A History of the Presbyterian Churches in the United States*, and Sweet. The readers may find the texts of the Westminster Confession and the American modifications in Philip Schaff, *The Creeds of Christendom*, III, 600–673, and the formal rules for the session procedures in the Presbyterian Church's *The Form of Government and Forms of Process*. Hall, in *The Religious Background of American Culture*, emphasizes the more churchly background of Presbyterianism, as distinct from Dissent.

The latter part of this chapter has also used, among others, Aaron, "Cincinnati"; Lindley (ed.), *Indiana as Seen by Early Travelers*; Hermann Muelder, "Jacksonian Democracy in Religious Organizations" and *Church History in a Puritan Colony of the Middle West*; and H. N. Sonne, *Liberal Kentucky*.

On the various controversies within Presbyterianism, including the separation of the Cumberland Presbyterians, the immediate sources in Sweet, *The Presbyterians*, include the minutes of the Synod of Kentucky, beginning p. 327; the minutes of the Cumberland Presbytery, pp. 282–305; extracts from the minutes of the Transylvania Presbytery, pp. 186–90. In "Jacksonian Democracy in Religious Organizations," Muelder traces the background of the major conflicts. Jacob Young, a Methodist, has some personal observations in his *Autobiography*.

NOTES

1. "The Sessional Records of the First Presbyterian Church, Murfreesboro, Tennessee," April 11 to May 26, 1829, W. W. Sweet, *Religion on the American Frontier*, Vol. II (Chicago: University of Chicago Press 1936), 453–58. Sections of the records not relevant to the case have been omitted.

2. "Sessional Record," Duck Creek Church, Ohio, Sweet, *op. cit.*, pp. 407–11.

3. Andrew Reed and James Matheson, *A Narrative of the Visit to the American Churches* (2 vols.; New York: Harper & Bros., 1835), I, 120.

4. Isaac Reed, "The Christian Traveler," in *Indiana as Seen by Early Travelers*, ed. Harlow Lindley (Indianapolis: Indiana Historical Commission, 1916), pp. 473–89, *et passim*. Sweet, *op. cit.*, pp. 394–401, contains the "Register" of the United Congregations of Cincinnati and Columbia.

5. Catharine Caroline Cleveland, *The Great Revival in the West, 1797–1805* (Chicago: University of Chicago Press, 1916), pp. 48–49.

6. As quoted in N. Henry Sonne, *Liberal Kentucky, 1780–1828* (New York: Columbia University Press, 1939), pp. 119–124, *et passim*.

7. N. H. Sonne, *op. cit., passim*; Daniel B. Aaron, "Cincinnati" (Ph.D. dissertation, Harvard University, 1942), chap. vi; Fernandez C. Holliday, *Indiana Methodism* (Cincinnati: Hitchcock & Walden, 1873), pp. 317–318. Chapter ix below discusses in further detail the Presbyterian efforts to assume special prerogatives in higher education.

CHAPTER IV – *The Baptists*

Leading sources: Babcock (ed.), *Forty Years of Pioneer Life: Memoir of John Mason Peck*; Cady, *The Baptist Church in Indiana*; Carroll, *The Genesis of American Anti-Missionism*; Newman, *A History of the Baptist Churches*; J. A. Smith, *A History of the Baptists in the Western States*; Spencer, *A History of Kentucky Baptists*; Stott, *Indiana Baptist History*; Sweet, *The Baptists*; John Taylor, *A History of Ten Baptist Churches*; Torbet, *A Social History of the Philadelphia Baptist Association*; and Turner, *The Frontier in American History* and *Rise of the New West*.

Cady and Sweet in particular provide excellent details of the organization and discipline, as well as the history of the early Baptists. Babcock, Stott, and Taylor give many examples of licensing, ordination, and difficulties of frontier ministers and formation of churches and associations as well as sketches of leaders.

NOTES

1. For these and many other illustrative cases, readers may refer to: Rufus Babcock (ed.), *Forty Years of Pioneer Life: Memoir of John Mason Peck* (Philadelphia: American Baptist Publication Society, 1864), pp. 27–29, *et passim*; W. W. Sweet, *Religion on the American Frontier* (Chicago: University of Chicago Press, 1931), Vol. I, chap. iii; and John Taylor, *A History of Ten Baptist Churches* (Frankfort, Ky.: J. H. Holeman, 1823), *passim*.

2. Babcock, *loc. cit.*

3. Jacob Bower, "Autobiography," in W. W. Sweet, *op. cit.*, p. 202.

4. Timothy Flint, *Recollections of the Last Ten Years* (New York: Alfred Knopf, 1932), pp. 36, 64, 112–13, *et passim*.

5. John Taylor, *op. cit.*, pp. 49–50 (also Sweet, *op. cit.*, pp. 151–53).

6. *Ibid*, pp. 137–42 (also in Sweet, *op. cit.*, pp. 177–182).

7. John Frank Cady, *The Baptist Church in Indiana* (Berne, Ind.: Berne Witness Co., 1942), gives numerous examples illustrating the variations.

8. Babcock, *op. cit.*, pp. 95, 157, *et passim*. Peck discusses the various quarrels and controversies among the Baptists, often arising from the influence of the anti-mission movement. Sweet, *op. cit.*, contains documents of churches appealing to neighboring churches for experienced members to help settle disputes, pp. 246–47, 262–65, 299–300, *et passim*.

9. Sweet *op. cit.*, pp. 263–65.

10. Babcock, *op. cit.*, pp. 24–25.

11. F. A. Cox and J. Hoby, *The Baptists in America* (London: T. Ward & Co., 1836), p. 261.

12. John Taylor, *op. cit.*, pp. 75–76.

13. "The Records of the Forks of Elkhorn Baptist Church," September, 1801 to June 13, 1812, W. W. Sweet, *op. cit.*, pp. 283–370. The quoted excerpts do not contain the full minutes for any single session, since parts were selected to illustrate the range of the discipline. For the full records, the reader may refer to Sweet, *loc. cit.* John H. Spencer, *A History of Kentucky Baptists* (Cincinnati, 1886), I, 152 ff., contains a brief biography of William Hickman, pastor of the Forks of Elkhorn Church for many years and an outstanding leader of his denomination.

14. William T. Stott, *Indiana Baptist History, 1798–1908* (Franklin, Ind.: Franklin College, 1908), p. 55 *et passim*. Stott has recorded many interesting events from early Indiana Baptist history.

15. John Taylor, *op. cit.*, pp. 137 ff. (The Covenant of the Buck Run Church).

CHAPTER V – *The Methodists*

The major references: Anderson, *Methodism*; Asbury, *Journal*; Bangs, *A History of the Methodist Episcopal Church*; Barclay, *Early American Methodism*; Boehm, *Reminiscences, Historical and Biographical*; Buckley, *A History of Methodists*; Cartwright, *Autobiography*; Dimond, *The Psychology of the Methodist Revival*; Finley, *Autobiography* and *Sketches of Western Methodism* (including the Burke "Autobiography"); Grant, *Peter Cartwright*; Holliday, *Indiana Methodism*; Mathews, *Methodism and the Education*; Methodist Episcopal Church, *A Form of Discipline*, *The Doctrines and Discipline*, *Journals of the General Conference*, and *Minutes of the Annual Conferences*; Muelder, "Jacksonian Democracy in Religious Organizations"; Nottingham, *Methodism and the Frontier*; Phoebus, *Beams of Light*; Posey, *The Development of Methodism in the Old Southwest*; Sherman, *History of the Revisions of the Discipline*; Stevens, *A Compendious History of American Methodism*; Sweet, *Circuit-Rider Days Along the Ohio*, *Circuit-Rider Days in Indiana*, *Methodism in American History*, *The Methodists*, and *The Rise of Methodism*; Tigert, *A Constitutional History of American Episcopal Methodism*; Tipple, *Francis Asbury The Prophet of the Long Road*; Watters, *Peter Cartwright*; Wiley, "Methodism in Southeastern Indiana"; and Young, *Autobiography of a Pioneer*.

A large volume of sources is available on Methodism, among them conference and organizational records, journals and autobiographies of leaders, histories, and analyses. Sweet has published the minutes of several pioneer western conferences — Western, Ohio, Indiana, and Illinois — which with the General Conference and Annual Conference records have provided some basic data for the present chapter, as have the personal journals of Asbury, Boehm, Cartwright, Finley, Holliday, Wiley, Young, and others. The official denominational book of regulations and doctrines, the *Discipline* (the 1784 and 1808 editions were used), is an essential source on disciplinary requirements of Methodism, while the journals of the itinerants contain vivid accounts of their efforts to apply the rules in the West. *The Methodists* (Vol. IV of the *Religion on the American Frontier*) by Sweet includes substantial selections from various organizational papers and from personal documents of frontier Methodists. This chapter, of course, has made extensive use of histories and analyses, including those of Bangs, Barclay, Buckley, Dimond, Muelder, Nottingham, Posey, Sherman, Stevens, Sweet, and Tigert.

NOTES

1. In addition to Asbury's *Journal* (New York: Lane & Scott, 1852) and biographies, such as E. S. Tipple, *Francis Asbury The Prophet of the Long Road* (New York: Methodist Book Concern, 1916), journals of his contemporaries often mention Asbury at length. The General Conference, for example, asked Henry Boehm to accompany Asbury for a time. Boehm has included his observations of Asbury in his *Reminiscences, Historical and Biographical, of Sixty-Four Years in the Ministry* (New York: Carlton & Porter, 1866).

2. Asbury, *op. cit.*, I, 38, 48, 111, 136, 448; II, 18, 37, 156–60 (an autobiographical note), *et passim*.

3. Nathan Bangs, *A History of the Methodist Episcopal Church*, Vols. I–III

(New York: T. Mason & G. Lane, 1840), Vol. IV (New York: G. Lane & P. P. Sandford, 1841), II, 413–18 *et passim*; and E. K. Nottingham, *Methodism and the Frontier* (New York: Columbia University Press, 1941), chaps. i, v, *et passim*.

4. Asbury, *op. cit.*, I, 375; III, 158, 196, 200, 339, 365; Bangs, *loc. cit.* See also, James Burke, "Autobiography," in J. B. Finley, *Sketches of Western Methodism* (Cincinnati: Methodist Book Concern, 1854), p. 91, *et passim*.

5. Asbury, *op. cit.*, III, 465.

6. Of the various historical references to the tension over Methodist centralization of authority, one of the more thoughtful examinations is H. R. Muelder, "Jacksonian Democracy in Religious Organizations" (Ph.D. dissertation, University of Minnesota, 1933), chaps. iii, ix, x, xi. James Gilruth's journal entry, August 23, 1834, on certain "Monarkal Views" (Sweet, *The Methodists*, p. 381) is an example of the reaction even loyal members apparently had on occasions toward this control.

7. John Atkinson, *Centennial History of American Methodism* (New York, 1889), pp. 164–65; Cleveland, *The Great Revival in the West* (Chicago: University of Chicago Press, 1916), pp. 23–26; Sweet, *The Rise of Methodism in the West* (New York: Methodist Book Concern, 1920), chaps. i–iv.

8. Abel Stevens, *A Compendious History of American Methodism* (New York: Carlton & Porter, 1867), p. 267.

9. Sweet, *The Rise of Methodism*, pp. 45–49, *et passim*; W. W. Sweet, *Circuit-Rider Days Along the Ohio* (New York: Methodist Book Concern, 1923), p. 39 (on Bascom's $12.10); Peter Cartwright, *Autobiography of Peter Cartwright* (New York: Carlton & Porter, 1856), pp. 96–97, 102–7, *et passim*; Burke, Finley, Holliday, Wiley, Young, and others mention the financial difficulties which itinerants faced.

10. Boehm, *op. cit.*, p. 492 *et passim*; Burke, "Autobiography," in Finley, *Sketches*, *passim*; Cartwright, *op. cit.*, pp. 74–78, 93–95, 182–86, *et passim*; James B. Finley, *Autobiography* (Cincinnati: Cranston & Curts, 1853), pp. 272, 276, *et passim*.

11. *The Doctrines and Discipline of the Methodist Episcopal Church* (New York: John Wilson & Daniel Hitt, 1808), pp. 48–49.

12. Finley, *Autobiography*, p. 178.

13. Even after 1804, the marriage of itinerants remained under disciplinary control. According to the September 6, 1821, minutes, the Ohio Conference ordered a presiding elder to reprimand a circuit-rider allegedly for saying he would as soon marry a non-Methodist as he would a member. The itinerant had not said it, and the matter was dropped. The October 15, 1825, minutes records that a candidate for eldership was not elected, though otherwise eligible, because of his marriage to a non-Methodist. — Sweet, *Circuit-Rider Days Along the Ohio*, pp. 199, 217, 265–68, 279, n. 2; 288.

14. As quoted from the Bradburn collection of Wesley letters, pp. 80–81, in Sidney G. Dimond, *The Psychology of the Methodist Revival* (London: Humphrey Milford Oxford University Press, 1926), p. 58.

15. Sweet has summarized the procedures for trials in *Religion on the American Frontier* (Chicago: University of Chicago Press, 1946), IV, 643–46.

16. Finley, *Sketches of Western Methodism*, p. 109.

CHAPTER VI – *The Friends*

The main sources: Bond, *The Civilization of the Old Northwest*; Braithwaite, *The Beginnings of Quakerism*; Brinton, *Children of Light*,

Guide to Quaker Practice, and *Quaker Education in Theory and Practice*; Buley, *The Old Northwest*; Drake, *Quakers and Slavery in America*; Jones, *The Later Periods of Quakerism*; Kelsey, *Friends and the Indians*; Lindley (ed.), *Indiana as Seen by Early Travelers*, "The Quaker Contribution to the Old Northwest," and "The Quakers in the Old Northwest"; Russell, *The History of Quakerism*; A. C. Thomas, *A History of the Friends in America*; Woolman, *The Journal of John Woolman*; Society of Friends, Indiana Yearly Meeting, *Address to the People of the United States* (the appeal for Indians), *Address of the Yearly Meeting . . . to All in the United States* (the appeal for abolition), *The Discipline*, and *Minutes of the Indiana Yearly Meeting of Friends, 1821–1845*; Ohio Yearly Meeting, *The Discipline*; "The Minutes of the Whitewater (Men's) Monthly Meeting, 1809–1830," "The Record of the Whitewater Monthly Meeting of Women Friends, 1809–1836," and "Records of the Minutes of Whitewater Quarterly Meeting, 1817–1849."

This chapter has relied extensively on the documents and the *Discipline* of the Indiana Yearly Meeting and to less extent on the records of the Whitewater Monthly and Quarterly Meetings. The details of its activities on behalf of the Indians and abolitionism are in the minutes and reports of the Indiana Yearly Meeting for the years indicated. For interpretation and further data, Brinton, Drake, Jones, Kelsey, Lindley, and Russell have been most directly helpful, especially Jones and Russell.

NOTES

1. Rufus Jones, *The Later Periods of Quakerism* (London: Macmillan & Co., 1921) , provides an over-all history of the Quakers during the period under consideration. For migration to the Old Northwest, readers may also refer to Harlow Lindley, "The Quaker Contribution to the Old Northwest," in *Children of Light*, ed. Howard H. Brinton (New York: Macmillan Co., 1938), pp. 307–30; and Elbert Russell, *The History of Quakerism* (New York: Macmillan Co., 1942), chap. xxi.

2. *The Discipline of the Society of Friends of Indiana Yearly Meeting* (Cincinnati: A. Pugh, Printer, 1839). This *Discipline* differs slightly from the 1819 Ohio Yearly Meeting *Discipline* which the Indiana Meeting had previously been using. The changes are recorded in the 1838 minutes of the Indiana Yearly Meeting. Jones, *op. cit.*, chap. iv, contains a history of development of printed *Disciplines*, as does Russell, more briefly, *op. cit.*, chap. xvii.

3. A visiting English Quaker, William Forster, writes that after sinking all their capital and making improvements, many pioneer Friends gave up their land purchased in anticipation of other Quakers coming to the same neighborhood. They had to move to a Quaker settlement, often at a considerable loss, and start over again, but Forster remarks, such sacrifices were preferable to bringing up children "secluded from good society, and remote from meeting." — William Forster, "Memoirs of William Forster," in *Indiana as Seen by Early Travelers*, ed. Harlow Lindley (Indianapolis: Indiana Historical Commission, 1916), pp. 263–64.

4. The Indiana Yearly Meeting work among the Indians is recorded in the minutes of the Meeting for the indicated years. Further information on

the Society's interest appears in R. W. Kelsey, *Friends and the Indians, 1655–1917* (Philadelphia: Associated Executive Committee of Friends on Indian Affairs, 1917), especially chapter vii. Jones and Russell have many references.

5. In 1838, the Indiana Yearly Meeting circulated the *Address to the People of the United States and to the Members of Congress in Particular. On the Civilization and Christian Instruction of the Aborigines of Our Country* (Cincinnati: A. Pugh, Pr., 1838) to appeal to American conscience for Indian rights and for drastic changes in American relations with the Indians.

6. Thomas E. Drake, *Quakers and Slavery in America* (New Haven: Yale University Press, 1950) contains an over-all summary of the Quaker interest. The Indiana Yearly Meeting minutes have provided the basic data for this chapter on its committee on "People of Color," supplemented by Jones, *op. cit.*, pp. 375–423, *et passim*; and Russell, *op. cit.*, chap. xxvii. *The Journal of John Woolman* (Philadelphia: Friends' Book Store, 1914) shows the growth of his concern for Negro freedom which led to his campaign for the Quaker anti-slavery position. As Russell has observed (pp. 364–68), American Quakers and especially Indiana Friends were conservative and on the whole opposed to "political" abolitionism, although they were expected to petition, make public appeals, and even lobby. The English Friends criticized the American Society for not being more active.

7. In 1837, the Indiana Yearly Meeting circulated an *Address of the Yearly Meeting of the Religious Society of Friends, Commonly Called Quakers, in Indiana, Illinois, the Western Part of Ohio &c.* to appeal to the public for Negro freedom and rights of citizenship.

8. W. C. Braithwaite, *The Beginnings of Quakerism* (Cambridge: Cambridge University Press, 1955); Jones, *op. cit.*; and Russell, *op. cit.* were the main historical sources for this section, supplemented by Howard H. Brinton, *Guide to Quaker Practice* (Wallingford, Pa.: Pendle Hill, n.d.), and *Quaker Education in Theory and Practice* (Wallingford, Pa.: Pendle Hill, 1940); and Lindley, "The Quaker Contribution to the Old Northwest." Jones, I, 120–45, reviews the development of the various Quaker offices, and the Indiana *Discipline* describes the duties of their officers.

CHAPTER VII – *The Historical Background*

Main references on the historical background: Atkins and Fagley, *History of American Congregationalism*; Barclay, *Early American Methodism*; Braithwaite, *The Beginnings of Quakerism*; Briggs, *American Presbyterianism*; Cocks, *The Noncomformist Conscience*; Dimond, *The Psychology of the Methodist Revival*; Gerth and Mills, *From Max Weber*; Hall, *The Religious Background of American Culture*; Harkness, *John Calvin*; Jones, *The Later Periods of Quakerism*; Lindsay, *A History of the Reformation*; Littell, *The Anabaptist View of the Church*; Mathews, *Methodism and the Education of the People*; Mecklin, *The Story of American Dissent*; Newman, *A History of the Baptist Churches*; H. R. Niebuhr, *The Social Sources of Denominationalism*; Schaff, *The Creeds of Christendom*; Preserved Smith, *The Age of the Reformation*; Smithson, *The Anabaptists*; Sweet, *Religion in Colonial America* and *The Story of Religion in America*; Tawney, *Religion and the Rise of Capitalism*; Thompson, *A History of the Presbyterian Churches*; Torbet, *A Social*

History of the Philadelphia Baptist Association; Troeltsch, *Protestantism and Progress* and *The Social Teaching of the Christian Churckes*; Walton, "English Nonconformity and the Idea of Community"; and Weber, *The Protestant Ethic and the Spirit of Capitalism* and *The Sociology of Religion*.

This chapter has relied mainly on Hall, *The Religious Background*; Harkness, *John Calvin*; Lindsay, *A History of the Reformation*; H. R. Niebuhr, *The Social Sources*; Preserved Smith, *The Age of the Reformation*; Tawney, *Religion and the Rise of Capitalism*; Thompson, *A History of the Presbyterian Churches*; Troeltsch, *The Social Teaching*; and Weber, *The Protestant Ethic*. Other sources include Georg Jellinek, *The Declaration of the Rights of Man and of Citizens* (New York: Henry Holt & Co., 1901); M. M. Knappen, *Tudor Puritanism* (Chicago: University of Chicago Press, 1939); Troeltsch, *Protestantism and Progress*; Esme Winfield-Stratford, *The History of British Civilization* (New York: Harcourt, Brace & Co., 1938).

NOTES

1. Ernst Troeltsch, *The Social Teaching of the Christian Churches* (New York: Macmillan Co., 1931), II, 576 ff. (the quotation from Calvin is on p. 882, n. 313) ; T. C. Hall, *The Religious Background of American Culture* (Boston: Little, Brown, & Co., 1930), chaps. v, vii, viii, ix, *et passim*; Georgia Harkness, *John Calvin: Man and His Ethics* (New York: Henry Holt & Co., 1931) , *passim*; T. M. Lindsay, *A History of the Reformation* (New York: Charles Scribner's Sons, 1906, 1907) , II, 59, 108–10, *et passim*; H. R. Niebuhr, *The Social Sources of Denominationalism* (New York: Henry Holt & Co., 1929) , chaps. ii, iii and iv.

2. Max Weber, *The Protestant Ethic and the Spirit of Capitalism* (London: Allen & Unwin, Ltd., 1930) , chaps. ii, iv, *et passim*; R. H. Tawney, *Religion and the Rise of Capitalism* (New York: Harcourt, Brace & Co., 1926) , *passim*; Troeltsch, *op. cit.*, II, 604–11, 641–55, 808, 812–20.

3. Lindsay, *op. cit.*, II, 134–35; Troeltsch, *op. cit.*, II, 641–50.

4. Troeltsch, *op. cit.*, II, 580–92, 620–21, 628–30, *et passim*.

5. Lindsay, *op. cit.*, II, 92–102, 133, 154; Harkness, *op. cit.*, *passim*.

6. H. R. Niebuhr, *op. cit.*, 80–105, 154–64; R. E. Thompson, *A History of the Presbyterian Churches* (New York: Christian Literature Co., 1895) , pp. 1–12, 24–25, 29, 34–38, 70–71, 87–89, 96, 232–33, 248, 299, *et passim*; C. A. Briggs, *American Presbyterianism* (New York: Charles Scribner's Sons, 1885) , *passim*.

7. Hall, *op. cit.*, chaps. i–xi; H. R. Niebuhr, *op. cit.*, chaps. ii, iii; Troeltsch, *op. cit.*, II, 656–714, 807–20.

8. Troeltsch, *op. cit.*, II, 703–14, 721–24, 780–87, 802–20, *et passim*; Ernst Troeltsch, *Protestantism and Progress* (London: Williams & Norgate, 1912), 121–27; Hall, *op. cit.*, *passim*. Additional background on the Baptists in the United States may be found in Albert H. Newman, *A History of the Baptist Churches* (New York: Christian Literature Co., 1894). F. H. Littell, *The Anabaptist View of the Church* (Hartford: American Society of Church History, 1952) and R. J. Smithson, *The Anabaptists* (London: James Clarke & Co., 1935) discuss the development, role, and subsequent impact of sectarian Protestantism which had significant influence on American popular denominations.

9. The references are the same as Note 8, with the addition of S. H. Cobb, *The Rise of Religious Liberty in America* (New York: Macmillan Co., 1902), 8–18, 63–68, 148 ff., 422–40, *et passim*; C. F. James, *Documentary History of the Struggle for Religious Liberty in Virginia* (Lynchburg, Va.: J. P. Bell, Co., 1900), pp. 9, 201–8; and John Leland, *The Writings of the Late Elder John Leland* (New York: Printed by G. W. Wood, 1845), *passim*; and A. H. Newman, *op. cit., passim*.

10. Among the recent studies on sect and church concepts are: Peter L. Berger, "Sectarianism and Religious Sociation," *American Journal of Sociology*, LXIV, No. 1 (July, 1958), 41–44; Berger, "The Sociological Study of Sectarianism," *Social Research*, XXI, No. 4 (Winter, 1954), 467–85; Russell Dynes, "Church-Sect Typology and Socio-Economic Status," *American Sociological Review*, XX, No. 5 (October, 1955), 555–60; G. Benton Johnson, "On Church and Sect," *American Sociological Review*, XXVIII, No. 4 (August, 1963), 539–49; Johnson, "A Critical Appraisal of the Church-Sect Typology," *American Sociological Review*, XXII, No. 1 (February, 1957), 88–92; D. A. Martin, "The Denomination," *British Journal of Sociology*, XIII, No. 1 (March, 1962), 1–14; Elizabeth K. Nottingham, *Religion and Society* (Garden City, N. Y.: Doubleday, 1954); Bryan R. Wilson, "An Analysis of Sect Development," *American Sociological Review*, XXIV, No. 1 (February, 1959), 4–15; and J. Milton Yinger, *Religion, Society and the Individual* (New York: Macmillan Co., 1957). Max Weber also commented on American sectarian denominations and their concepts of the calling in "The Protestant Sects and the Spirit of Capitalism," *From Max Weber*, ed. H. H. Gerth and C. W. Mills (New York: Oxford University Press, 1946), chap. xii.

CHAPTER VIII — *Attitudes Toward Ministerial Education*

The main references: Aaron, "Cincinnati"; Asbury, *Journal*; Atkins and Fagley, *History of American Congregationalism*; Babcock (ed.), *Forty Years of Pioneer Life*; Baird, *Religion in America*; Baker, *An Introduction to the History of Early New England Methodism*; Bangs, *A History of the M. E. Church*; Barclay, *Early American Methodism*; Beecher, *Plea for the West*; Bishop, *An Outline of the History of the Church*; Bond, *The Civilization of the Old Northwest*; Briggs, *American Presbyterianism*; Buley, *The Old Northwest*; Cady, *The Baptist Church in Indiana*; Carroll, *The Genesis of American Anti-Missionism*; Cartwright, *Autobiography*; Cox and Hoby, *The Baptists in America*; Duvall, *The Methodist Episcopal Church and Education*; Finley, *Autobiography* and *Sketches of Western Methodism*; Flint, *Recollections*; Foster, *A Sketch of the History of the Cumberland Presbyterian Church*; Gross, "Religious Work on Methodist College Campuses"; Hall, *The Religious Background of American Culture*; Holliday, *Indiana Methodism*; Jones, *The Later Periods of Quakerism*; Kirkland, *The Evening Book, Forest Life, A New Home — Who'll Follow?*, and *Western Clearings*; Koch, *Republican Religion*; Lindley (ed.), *Indiana as Seen by Early Travelers*; Mathews, *Methodism and the Education of the People*; Mecklin, *The Story of American Dissent*; B. E. Meland, *America's Spiritual Culture* (New

York: Harper & Bros., 1948); Mills and Smith, *Report of a Missionary Tour*; Mode, *The Frontier Spirit in American Christianity*; Muelder, *Church History in a Puritan Colony* and "Jacksonian Democracy in Religious Organizations"; Newman, *A History of the Baptist Churches*; Nottingham, *Methodism and the Frontier*; Paxson, *History of the American Frontier*; Perry, *Puritanism and Democracy*; Posey, *The Development of Methodism in the Old Southwest*; Reed and Matheson, *A Narrative of the Visit*; Rusk, *The Literature of the Middle Western Frontier*; Schermerhorn and Mills, *A Correct View*; Scouller, *History of the United Presbyterian Church*; J. A. Smith, *A History of the Baptists in the Western States*; Sonne, *Liberal Kentucky*; Spencer, *A History of Kentucky Baptists*; Stevens, *A Compendious History*; Stott, *Indiana Baptist History*; Sweet, *Circuit-Rider Days Along the Ohio, Circuit-Rider Days in Indiana, Religion on the American Frontier* (4 vols.), and *The Rise of Methodism in the West*; John Taylor, *A History of Ten Baptist Churches* and *Thoughts on Missions*; Tewksbury, *The Founding of American Colleges and Universities*; Ward, *Andrew Jackson*; and Young, *Autobiography*.

NOTES

1. W. W. Sweet, *Religion on the American Frontier* (Chicago: University of Chicago Press, 1936), II, 7–8, 26–27; R. H. Bishop, *An Outline of the History of the Church in the State of Kentucky* (Lexington, Ky.: T. T. Skillman, 1824), pp. 52–56, 259–80, *et passim*; Robert E. Thompson, *A History of the Presbyterian Churches in the United States* (New York: Christian Literature Co., 1895), *passim*.

2. Sweet, *op. cit.*, II, 249–50 and also 44–45, 70–73, 77–78.

3. Sweet, *op. cit.*, II, 44–45, *et passim*.

4. Ralph Barton Perry, *Puritanism and Democracy* (New York: Vanguard Press, 1944), pp. 656–57, n. 36, *et passim*.

5. Samuel Miller, *A Brief Retrospect of the Eighteenth Century* (London: J. Johnson, 1805), I, 11; R. H. Gabriel, "The Enlightenment Tradition," in *Wellsprings of the American Spirit*, ed. F. E. Johnson (New York: Institute for Religious and Social Studies, 1948), p. 40.

6. J. B. Finley, *Autobiography of James Bradley Finley* (Cincinnati: Cranston & Curts, 1853), pp. 309–20.

7. Lyman Beecher, *Plea for the West* (Cincinnati: Truman & Smith, 1835), *passim*; Robert V. Foster, *A Sketch of the History of the Cumberland Presbyterian Church* (New York: Christian Literature Co., 1894), chaps. ii–v, viii, *et passim*; Samuel J. Mills and Daniel Smith, *Report of a Missionary Tour* (Andover, Mass.: Flagg & Gould, 1815), *passim*; J. F. Schermerhorn and Samuel J. Mills, *A Correct View* (Hartford: Peter P. Gleason & Co., 1814), *passim*; D. G. Tewksbury, *The Founding of American Colleges and Universities* (New York: Teachers College, Columbia University, 1932), pp. 55, 73–74, 79, 89–103, *et passim*.

8. *The Baptist Almanac*, 1853 (Philadelphia: American Baptist Publication and Sunday School Society, 1852), p. 26; F. A. Cox and James Hoby, *The Baptists in America* (London: T. Ward & Co., 1836), pp. 33–35, *et passim*.

9. A. H. Newman, *A History of the Baptist Churches in the United States*

(New York: Christian Literature Co, 1894), pp. 336–340, 408, *et passim*; Jacob Bower, "Autobiography," W. W. Sweet, *op. cit.*, I, 203–4. Dr. Newman states that only three Baptist ministers west of the Hudson had college education at the turn of the century

10. As quoted in B. H. Carroll, Jr., *The Genesis of American Anti-Missionism* (Louisville: Baptist Book Concern, 1902), pp. 115–17.

11. As quoted in Carroll, *op. cit.*, pp. 131–34.

12. J. F. Cady, *The Baptist Church in Indiana* (Berne, Ind.: Berne Witness Co., 1942), pp. 119–21, *et passim*.

13. Rufus Babcock (ed.), *Forty Years of Pioneer Life: Memoir of John Mason Peck* (Philadelphia: American Baptist Publication Society, 1864), pp. 39, 111, 157, 225–29, *et passim*; Cady, *op. cit.*, pp. 25–26, 42–43, 45–59, 66–81, 119–21, *et passim*; Sweet, *op. cit.*, I, chap. iv.

14. Francis Asbury, *Journal* (New York: Lane & Scott, 1852), I, 514; III, 155, 211, *et passim*.

15. *A Form of Discipline for the Ministers, Preachers, and Members of the Methodist Episcopal Church* (Elizabeth-Town: Shepard Kollack, 1788), Sections XVIII and XXV.

16. W. W. Sweet, *The Rise of Methodism in the West* (New York: Methodist Book Concern, 1920), pp. 93–95.

17. Peter Cartwright, *Autobiography* (New York: Carlton & Porter, 1856), scattered references to education for the ministry, pp. 4–7, 78–82, 197, 405, 408–9, 486, *et passim*.

18. W. W. Sweet, *Methodism in American History* (New York: Methodist Book Concern, 1933) pp. 221–27.

19. J. B. Finley, *Sketches of Western Methodism* (Cincinnati: Methodist Book Concern, 1854), p. 334.

20. *Journals of the General Conference of the Methodist Episcopal Church* (New York: Carlton & Phillips, 1855, 1856), I, 399, 412, and the records for 1816, 1820, 1840, 1844, *passim*; Sweet, *Religion on the American Frontier*, IV, 66–68, 302–4 (including n. 6), 391; Allen Wiley, "Methodism in Southeastern Indiana," *Indiana Magazine of History*, XXIII (September, 1927), 240–41; Jacob Young, *Autobiography of a Pioneer* (Cincinnati: Cranston & Curts, 1857), pp. 51–58, 75–77 (Young valued education for itinerants).

21. Cartwright, *loc. cit.*; Sweet, *op. cit.*, IV, 67–68.

22. W. W. Sweet, *Circuit-Rider Days in Indiana* (Indianapolis: W. K. Stewart Co., 1916), pp. 39–41, 62, 76–77, 101–3, 107–8, 213; Sweet, *Methodism in American History*, *passim*; J. B. Finley, *Autobiography* (Cincinnati: Cranston & Curts, 1853), pp. 15, 39–42.

23. Finley, *op. cit.*, pp. 172 and 15, 113–14, 179–80, 340, *et passim*.

24. As quoted in S. M. Duvall, *The Methodist Episcopal Church and Education Up To 1869* (New York: Teachers College, Columbia University Bureau of Publications, 1928), p. 47.

25. Duvall, *op. cit.*, pp. 17–26, 41–61.

26. Cartwright, *loc. cit.*; Young, *loc. cit.*; W. B. Posey, *The Development of Methodism in the Old Southwest* (Tuscaloosa, Ala.: Weatherford Printing Co., 1933), pp. 64–65, 72 (including n. 55). Nathan Bangs discusses the over-all development in detail in *A History of the Methodist Episcopal Church* (New York: T. Mason & G. Lane, 1840), I, 195–96, 201–3; II, 390 ff., 413–18, III, 45–58, 303–4. See also Abel Stevens, *A Compendious History of American Methodism* (New York: Carlton & Porter, 1867), pp. 336, 447, 458–60, 509, *et passim*.

27. W. C. Howells, *Recollections of Life in Ohio* (Cincinnati: Robert Clarke Co., 1895), p. 104.

CHAPTER IX – *Attitudes Toward Education*

The same main references as chapters vii and viii, and in addition: the various state histories and Bernhard, *Travels Through North America*; Boehm, *Reminiscences, Historical and Biographical*; Boone, *A History of Education in Indiana*; Bremer, *The Homes of the New World*; Brinton, *Children of Light* and *Quaker Education in Theory and Practice*; Brown, *History of the American Baptist Publication Society*; Butts and Cremin, *A History of Education in American Culture*; Chevalier, *Society, Manners and Politics in the United States*; Cleveland, *The Great Revival in the West*; Faust, *The German Element in the United States*; I. J. Finley and Rufus Putnam, *Pioneer Record and Reminiscences . . . of Ross County, Ohio*; Fish, *The Rise of the Common Man*; Fox (ed.), *Sources of Culture in the Middle West*; Goodykoontz, *Home Missions on the American Frontier*; Grant, *Peter Cartwright: Pioneer*; Hamilton, *Men and Manners in America*; Hintz, *Quaker Influence in American Literature*; Howells, *Recollections of Life in Ohio*; Hubbart, *The Older Middle West*; Kirkpatrick, *Timothy Flint*; Leyburn, *Frontier Folkways*; Lindley, "The Quaker Contribution to the Old Northwest" and "The Quakers in the Old Northwest"; Martineau, *Retrospect of Western Travel* and *Society in America*; Nevins, *American Social History as Recorded by British Travellers*; Newcomb, *Architecture of the Old Northwest Territory*; Russell, *The History of Quakerism*; Schlesinger, *The Age of Jackson*; Henry Nash Smith, *Virgin Land*; Sweet, *The American Churches, American Culture and Religion, Religion in the Development of American Culture*, and *Revivalism in America*; G. R. Taylor (ed.), *The Turner Thesis*; Tipple, *Francis Asbury*; Tocqueville, *Democracy in America*; Toulmin, *The Western Country*; Trollope, *Domestic Manners of the Americans*; Turner, *The Frontier in American History, Rise of the New West, The Significance of Sections in American History*, and *The United States*; Tyler, *Freedom's Ferment*; Unonius, *A Pioneer in Northwest America*; Venable, *Beginnings of Literary Culture in the Ohio Valley*; Watters, *Peter Cartwright*; and Wright, *Culture on the Moving Frontier*.

On Presbyterianism and education in the West, Aaron, "Cincinnati"; Beecher, *Plea for the West*; Bremer, *The Homes of the New World* (especially for over-all observations of Western life); M. B. Clark, "The Old Log College at Livonia"; Sonne, *Liberal Kentucky*; Sweet, *The Presbyterians*; and Tewksbury, *The Founding of American Colleges and Universities*. Sonne discusses the controversy between the Presbyterians and the religious liberals over Transylvania University and its educational policies. The Presbyterian influence on the cultural life of Cincinnati is discussed by Aaron. See also Allen, "Patterns of Thought in American Periodical Criticism"; Chevalier, *Society, Manners and Politics in the*

United States; Flint, *Recollections of the Last Ten Years*; and Trollope, *Domestic Manners of the Americans*. Thompson, *A History of the Presbyterian Churches* has many scattered references on the historical development of Presbyterian attitudes.

For information on the Baptist attitudes, most useful were Babcock (ed.), *Forty Years of Pioneer Life*; Brown, *History of the American Baptist Publication Society*; Cady, *The Baptist Church in Indiana*; Carroll, *The Genesis of American Anti-Missionism*; Cox and Hoby, *The Baptists in America*; Newman, *A History of the Baptist Churches*; J. A. Smith, *A History of the Baptists in the Western States East of the Mississippi*; Spencer, *A History of Kentucky Baptists;* Stott, *Indiana Baptist History*; Sweet, *The Baptists*; and Taylor, *A History of Ten Baptist Churches*.

Among the many references on the Methodist attitudes, are: Anderson (ed.), *Methodism*; Asbury, *Journal*; Bangs, *A History of the Methodist Episcopal Church*; Barclay, *Early American Methodism*; Boehm, *Reminiscences*; Dimond, *The Psychology of the Methodist Revival*; Duvall, *The Methodist Episcopal Church and Education Up To 1869*; Finley, *Autobiography* and *Sketches of Western Methodism*; Holliday, *Indiana Methodism; Journals of the General Conference of the Methodist Episcopal Church*; Mills and Smith, *Report of a Missionary Tour*; Nottingham, *Methodism and the Frontier*; Posey, *The Development of Methodism in the Old Southwest*; Schermerhorn and Mills, *A Correct View*; Stevens, *A Compendious History of American Methodism*; Sweet, *Circuit-Rider Days Along the Ohio, Circuit-Rider Days in Indiana, Methodism in American History*, and *The Methodists*; Wiley, "Methodism in Southeastern Indiana"; and Young, *Autobiography*.

For the Friends, the main sources were Brinton, *Quaker Education*; the minutes of the Indiana Yearly Meeting; Hintz, *Quaker Influence in American Literature*; Jones, *The Later Periods of Quakerism*; Lindley, "The Quaker Contribution to the Old Northwest"; and Russell, *The History of Quakerism*.

NOTES

1. W. W. Sweet, *Religion on the American Frontier* (Chicago: University of Chicago Press, 1936), II, 7–9, 25–28, 70–81; D. G. Tewksbury, *The Founding of American Colleges and Universities Before the Civil War* (New York: Bureau of Publications, Teachers College, Columbia University, 1932), pp. 91–103. N. H. Sonne, *Liberal Kentucky* (New York: Columbia University Press, 1939) deals with the Presbyterian efforts to control higher education.

2. D. G. Tewksbury, *op cit.*, pp. 1, 3–5, 63, 91–103. G. H. Barnes, *The Antislavery Impulse* (New York: D. Appleton-Century Co., 1933) describes Weld and others at Lane Seminary.

3. Lyman Beecher, *Plea for the West* (Cincinnati: Truman & Smith, 1835), 10–15, 19–20, 23, 30–31, *et passim*. See also S. J. Mills and Daniel Smith, *Report of a Missionary Tour . . . West of the Allegany Mountains* (Andover, Mass.:

Flagg & Gould, 1815) and J. F. Schermerhorn and S. J. Mills, *A Correct View . . . with Regard to Religion and Morals* (Hartford: P. P. Gleason & Co., 1814). Sweet, *op. cit.*, II, 41–43, 99–101, *et passim*, contains an account of the Plan of Union.

4. On Presbyterian relations with Transylvania University, see N. H. Sonne, *op. cit., passim.*

5. Sonne, *op. cit.*, pp. 210 ff.

6. D. B. Aaron, "Cincinnati, 1818–1838" (Ph. D. dissertation, Harvard University, 1942), pp. 61, 140–41, 336–49, 354, 376–81, 395, 448–61, *et passim*; Michel Chevalier, *Society, Manners and Politics in the United States* (Boston: Weeks, Jordan & Co., 1839), pp. 205–8, *et passim.*

7. For examples see: Fredrika Bremer, *The Homes of the New World* (London: Arthur Hall, Virtue & Co., 1853), II, 223–33, 239–43, 350, 426, *et passim.*

8. Sweet, *op. cit.*, I, 480. J. F Cady, *The Baptist Church in Indiana* (Berne, Ind.: Berne Witness Co., 1942) provides the best background of the Baptist attitudes, together with Rufus Babcock (ed.), *Forty Years of Pioneer Life* (Philadelphia: American Baptist Publication Society, 1864); B. H. Carroll, Jr., *The Genesis of American Anti-Missionism* (Louisville: Baptist Book Concern, 1902); and W. T. Stott, *Indiana Baptist History* (Franklin, Ind.: Franklin College, 1908).

9. Cady, *op. cit.*, chaps. ii, iii, iv, and pp. 25–28, 70–73, 75, 94–97, 103–123, *et passim*; Carroll, *op. cit.*, chaps. vii, viii, pp. 188–99, *et passim*; H. R. Muelder, "Jacksonian Democracy in Religious Organizations" (Ph.D. dissertation, University of Minnesota, 1933), pp. 74 ff., 117, n. 4, *et passim.*

10. *The Baptist Almanac, 1843* (Philadelphia: American Baptist Publication Society, 1842), p. 35.

11. F. A. Cox and James Hoby, *The Baptists in America* (London: T. Ward & Co., 1836), pp. 370–77, 487–88, 506–7, *et passim.*

12. J. N. Brown, *History of the American Baptist Publication Society* (Philadelphia: American Baptist Publication Society, n.d.), pp. 108, 124–28, 206, *et passim.*

13. S. G. Dimond, *The Psychology of the Methodist Revival* (London: Humphrey Milford Oxford University Press, 1926), pp. 33–34 and chap. iii on Wesley's reading.

14. Francis Asbury, *Journal* (New York: Lane & Scott, 1852), in various places, including I, 55, 193; II, 249; S. M. Duvall, *The Methodist Episcopal Church and Education* (New York: Bureau of Publications, Teachers College, Columbia University, 1928), pp. 20–36.

15. For the account of the Methodist activities in education, this section has relied on Duvall, *op. cit.*; Nathan Bangs, *A History of the Methodist Episcopal Church* (New York: T. Mason & G. Lane, 1840); *Journals of the General Conference of the Methodist Episcopal Church* (New York: Carlton & Phillips, 1855, 1856); W. B. Posey, *The Development of Methodism in the Old Southwest* (Tuscaloosa, Ala.: Weatherford Printing Co., 1933); W. W. Sweet, *op. cit.*, Vol. IV, and also *Methodism in American History* (New York: Methodist Book Concern, 1933). Bangs and the General Conference journals contain many scattered references, usually grouped according to the General Conference dates, especially 1816, 1820, and 1840. Among Bangs' comments on education and on Methodist publications, periodicals, and hymnals are I, 72, 336; II, 4–5, 104–8, 317–21, 349–51; III, 19–26, 43–47, 104–8, 133–39; IV, 21–43 (an example of Methodist rejoinders to criticisms of Methodist education), 70–84, *et passim*. For Duvall, see especially chap. iv and pp. 15–17, 20–36, 62–67, 70–84, 100–103, 110–15, 123.

16. F. C. Holliday, *Indiana Methodism* (Cincinnati: Hitchcock & Walden, 1873), pp. 317–19, and also pp. 134–35, 281–97, and chap. xv generally; W. W. Sweet, *Circuit-Rider Days in Indiana* (Indianapolis: W. K. Stewart Co., 1916), 91 ff. (especially pp. 101–3, 132–34 for petitions to the Indiana Legislature).

17. W. W. Sweet, *Circuit-Rider Days Along the Ohio* (New York: Methodist Book Concern, 1923), p. 200; Posey, *op. cit.*, pp. 76–77.

18. W. W. Sweet, *Religion on the American Frontier*, IV, chap. xiv; J. B. Finley, *Sketches of Western Methodism* (Cincinnati: Methodist Book Concern, 1854), chap. xxi. See also Bangs, *op. cit., passim*; Sweet, *Methodism in American History, passim*.

19. Sweet, *Circuit-Rider Days in Indiana*, pp. 82–83.

20. J. B. Finley, *Autobiography* (Cincinnati: Cranston & Curts, 1853), p. 276.

21. J. B. Finley, *Sketches of Western Methodism*, pp. 341–42.

22. Allen Wiley, "Methodism in Southeastern Indiana," *Indiana Magazine of History*, XXIII (June, 1927), 181.

23. W. K. Anderson (ed.), *Methodism* (New York: Methodist Publishing House, 1947), pp. 148–64; Dimond, *op. cit.*, p. 218; Finley, *op. cit.*, chap. xx; E. K. Nottingham, *Methodism and the Frontier* (New York: Columbia University Press, 1941), pp. 25–26, 40, 50, 63 ff., 81–84. Bangs, *op. cit.*, has a number of scattered references. See also B. F. Crawford, *Our Methodist Hymnody* (Carnegie, Pa.: Carnegie Church Press, 1940) and C. F. Price, *The Music and Hymnody of the Methodist Hymnal* (New York: Methodist Book Concern, 1911).

24. *Doctrines and Discipline of the Methodist Episcopal Church* (New York: John Wilson & Daniel Hitt, 1808), p. 49.

25. W. W. Sweet, *Religion on the American Frontier*, IV, 728–30; Finley, *op. cit.*, chap. xvi.

26. Posey, *op. cit.*, p. 110.

27. Holliday, *op. cit.*, pp. 134–35.

28. R. G. Boone, *A History of Education in Indiana* (New York: D. Appleton & Co., 1892), pp. 88–90, and also 68–69, 237–40, 407–10, *et passim*; H. H. Brinton, *Quaker Education in Theory and Practice* (Wallingford, Pa.: Pendle Hill, 1940), chap. iii and pp. 54–57, 60–62, 68–93, *et passim*; Rufus Jones, *The Later Periods of Quakerism* (London: Macmillan & Co., 1921), II, chaps. xv, xvii; Tewksbury, *op. cit.*, pp. 169–171, 173, 193–206.

29. Indiana Yearly Meeting, *Minutes*, 1839.

30. Jones, *op. cit.*, II, p. 689–90.

31. Logan Esarey, *A History of Indiana*, Vol. I (Indianapolis: W. K. Stewart Co., 1915); Vol. II (Indianapolis: B. F. Bowen & Co., 1918), I, 289–95; II, 679 ff.; and Willis Frederick Dunbar, "The Influence of the Protestant Denominations on Higher Education in Michigan" (Ph.D. dissertation, University of Michigan, 1939).

CHAPTER X – *Sectarianism*

The major sources are essentially the same as for chapter viii and ix. Among the more useful references were: Aaron, "Cincinnati"; Bernhard, *Travels Through North America*; Bremer, *The Homes of the New World*; Cady, *The Baptist Church in Indiana*; Gabriel, *The Course of American Democratic Thought*; Kirkland, *The Evening Book, Forest Life, A New Home — Who'll Follow?*, and *Western Clearings*; Lindley (ed.), *Indiana as Seen by Early Travelers*; Martineau, *Retrospect of*

Western Travel and *Society in America*; Nottingham, *Methodism and the Frontier*; Rusk, *The Literature of the Middle Western Frontier*; Tryon (ed.), *A Mirror for Americans*; Tyler, *Freedom's Ferment*; and Venable, *Beginnings of Literary Culture in the Ohio Valley*.

NOTES

1. Ernst Troeltsch, *The Social Teaching of the Christian Churches* (New York: Macmillan Co., 1931), II, 994, *et passim*.

2. Troeltsch, *op. cit.*, II, 657 and also I, 51–54; II, 461 ff., 656 ff., 675 ff., 807–20.

3. S. G. Dimond, *The Psychology of the Methodist Revival* (London: Humphrey Milford Oxford University Press, 1926), chaps. iii and iv.

4. Francis Asbury, *Journal* (New York: Lane & Scott, 1852), I, 112, 136; II, 156–60, 297, 460; III, 6, 144, 261–63, 360, *et passim*; Francis J. McConnell, "Francis Asbury," *Religion in Life*, XV, No. 1 (Winter, 1945–46), 23–36; E. S. Tipple, *Francis Asbury The Prophet of the Long Road* (New York: Methodist Book Concern, 1916), *passim*.

5. Peter Cartwright, *Autobiography of Peter Cartwright* (New York: Carlton & Porter, 1856); H. H. Grant, *Peter Cartwright: Pioneer* (New York: Abingdon Press, 1931); P. M. Watters, *Peter Cartwright* (New York: Eaton & Mains, 1910). Carl Sandburg, *Abraham Lincoln: The Prairie Years* (New York: Harcourt, Brace & Co., 1926), I, 335–37, discusses the Cartwright-Lincoln election campaign.

6. Jacob Young, *Autobiography of a Pioneer* (Cincinnati: Cranston & Curts, 1857), p. 98, *et passim*; for background, A. F. Tyler, *Freedom's Ferment* (Minneapolis: University of Minnesota Press, 1944), chaps. iv, v, vi, vii, and viii.

7. Allen Wiley, "Methodism in Southeastern Indiana," *Indiana Magazine of History*, XXIII (March, 1927), 62; James Burke, "Autobiography," J. B. Finley, *Sketches of Western Methodism* (Cincinnati: Methodist Book Concern, 1854), p. 54; J. B. Finley, *Autobiography* (Cincinnati: Cranston & Curts, 1853), pp. 287–88, *et passim*; Jacob Young, *op. cit.*, 80–81, 138, 146–157, 187–92, 284–85, *et passim*.

8. Cartwright, *op. cit.*, 64–72, 99, 117, 177, 285, 341–47, 370–72, 393; Philip Watters, *op. cit.*, p. 75.

9. E. K. Nottingham, *Methodism and the Frontier* (New York: Columbia University Press, 1941), pp. 25–26, 50, 153.

10. Allen Wiley, *op. cit.*, p. 134.

11. Nathan Bangs, *A History of the Methodist Episcopal Church* (New York: G. Lane & P. P. Sandford, 1841), IV, 86; J. F. Cady, *The Baptist Church in Indiana* (Berne, Ind.: Berne Witness Co., 1942), pp. 9, 238–42, 279, and also 176–77, *et passim*; F. A. Cox and James Hoby, *The Baptists in America* (London: T. Ward & Co., 1836), p. 482.

12. Cady, *op. cit.*, pp. 176–77.

13. W. S. Davison, "The Plight of Rural Protestantism," *Religion in Life*, XV, No. 3 (Summer, 1946), 377–90.

14. Frederick J. Turner, *The Significance of Sections* (New York: Henry Holt & Co., 1932), p. 24.

15. Cady, *op. cit.*, pp. 11–14 *et passim*; Timothy Flint, *Recollections* (New York: Knopf, 1932), pp. 75–76; "Minutes of the Whitewater (Men's) Monthly Meeting, 1809–1830," *passim*; C. M. Kirkland, *Forest Life* (New York: C. S. Francis & Co., 1844), I, 27–28, 37–38; Allen Wiley, *op. cit.*, p. 175.

16. Robin M. Williams, *American Society* (New York: Alfred A. Knopf, 1951), pp. 464–65, 532–36.

17. H. H. Gerth and C. W. Mills (eds.), *From Max Weber* (New York: Oxford University Press, 1946), chap. xii, esp. pp. 304–6.

18. R. L. Rusk, *The Literature of the Middle Western Frontier* (New York: Columbia University Press, 1926), I, 51–57 (Notes 153 and 154 on the low educational level and the Kentucky data on schooling). A survey of Kentucky as a whole gave approximately 31,834 children in school and 107,328 without any educational facilities. — T. D. Clark, *A History of Kentucky* (New York: Prentice-Hall, Inc., 1937), p. 316.

19. R. G. Boone, *A History of Education in Indiana* (New York: D. Appleton & Co., 1892), pp. 3–31, 79, 87, 89–91, 103–4, *et passim*; Rusk, *op. cit.*, I, 46, 51–57, 65, *et passim*.

20. C. M. Kirkland, *Western Clearings* (New York: Wiley & Putnam, 1845), pp. 155–57.

21. Kirkland, *Forest Life*, I, 215, 233–35; Flint, *op. cit.*, p. 181; Rusk, *op. cit.*, I, 65–66.

22. Kirkland, *Western Clearings*, p. 54; C. M. Kirkland, *A New Home — Who'll Follow* (New York: C. S. Francis, 1840), pp. 320–22.

23. R. G. Boone, *op. cit.*, pp. 41 ff., 89, 103–7.

24. Boone, *op. cit.*, pp. 238–39.

25. C. M. Kirkland, *The Evening Book* (New York: Charles Scribner, 1852), *passim*; Kirkland, *Forest Life*, I, 38–47, 197, 215–25; Kirkland, *New Home*, pp. 145–49 *et passim*; Kirkland, *Western Clearings, passim*; Rusk, *op. cit.*, I, 76, 209–10, *et passim*.

26. R. B. Perry, *Puritanism and Democracy* (New York: Vanguard Press, 1944), pp. 12–15, 591–93; R. H. Gabriel, *The Course of American Democratic Thought* (New York: Ronald Press Co., 1940), pp. 12–38 *et passim*.

27. Kirkland, *Forest Life*, I, 215–16 *et passim*; Rusk, *op. cit.*, I, 46 *et passim*; Gabriel, *op. cit.*, *passim*; W. C. Howells, *Recollections of Life in Ohio* (Cincinnati: Robert Clarke Co., 1895), p. 104.

28. Flavel Bascom, "Autobiography," W. W. Sweet, *Religion on the American Frontier*, Vol. III (Chicago: University of Chicago Press, 1939), 258; Flint, *op. cit.*, 45–49, 62, 179, *et passim*; Kirkland, *Evening Book*, pp. 182–83.

29. Kirkland, *Forest Life*, I, 38–47, 50, 197, 216; II, 51; Kirkland, *New Home*, pp. 145–49. J. A. Smith, *A History of the Baptists in the Western States East of the Mississippi* (Philadelphia: American Baptist Publication Society, 1896), p. 57, mentions the interest of Judge Holman, Baptist leader, in gardening.

30. Karl Bernhard, *Travels Through North America* (Philadelphia: Carey, Lea & Carey, 1828), II, 162–65.

31. Sweet, *op. cit.*, I, 508.

32. Bernhard, *op. cit.*, I, 150–55; II, 192–193.

33. For an example of slightly earlier Methodist attitude: Asbury, *op. cit.*, I, 112; II, 297; III, 261–63. C. B. Goodykoontz, *Home Missions on the American Frontier* (Caldwell, Idaho: Caxton Printers, Ltd., 1939) discusses the home missions activities of various denominations.

34. Fredrika Bremer, *The Homes of the New World* (London: Arthur Hall, Virtue & Co., 1853), II, 223–24, 226–33, 350, 426.

35. Bremer, *op. cit.*, II, 226–33; but also see, Gustaf Unonius, *A Pioneer in Northwest America* (Minneapolis: University of Minnesota Press, 1950), pp. 311 ff.

36. Bremer, *op. cit.*, II, 239–43.

37. F. L. Paxson, *History of the American Frontier* (Boston: Houghton Mifflin Co., 1924), pp. 114–17, *et passim*; E. K. Nottingham, *op. cit.*, p. 31.

38. Among the many observers: Morris Birkbeck, "Notes on a Journey in

America from the Coast of Virginia to the Territory of Illinois," in *Indiana as Seen by Early Travelers*, ed. Harlow Lindley (Indianapolis: Indiana Historical Commission, 1916), p. 178 and Richard Lee Mason, "Narrative of Richard Lee Mason in the Pioneer West," *ibid.*, pp. 235–36; and Flint, *op. cit.*, p. 62.

39. G. G. Atkins and F. L. Fagley, *History of American Congregationalism* (Boston: Pilgrim Press, 1942), pp. 87, 100; J. M. Morse, *A Neglected Period of Connecticut's History* (New Haven: Yale University Press, 1933), pp. 142–43. W. C. Howell, *op. cit.*, refers to the differences in attitudes of several Western denominations toward recreation.

40. Avery Craven, "The Advance of Civilization into the Middle West in the Period of Settlement," *Sources of Culture in the Middle West*, ed. Dixon Ryan Fox (New York: D. Appleton-Century Co., 1934), p. 65; Bremer, *op. cit.*, I, 297; III, 2–3, 436–39, *et passim*.

CHAPTER XI – *The Baptist Anti-Mission Movement*

The major references: Babcock (ed.), *Forty Years of Pioneer Life;* Cady, *The Baptist Church in Indiana*; Carroll, *The Genesis of American Anti-Missionism*; Cox and Hoby, *The Baptists in America*; Goodykoontz, *Home Missions on the American Frontier*; Mills and Smith, *Report of a Missionary Tour*; Muelder, "Jacksonian Democracy in Religious Organizations"; Newman, *A History of the Baptist Churches in the United States*; Schermerhorn and Mills, *A Correct View*; A. M. Schlesinger, Jr., *The Age of Jackson*; J. A. Smith, *A History of the Baptists in the Western States East of the Mississippi*; Spencer, *A History of Kentucky Baptists from 1769 to 1885*; Stott, *Indiana Baptist History*; Sweet, *Religion on the American Frontier*, Vol. I: *The Baptists*; and John Taylor, *A History of Ten Baptist Churches* and *Thoughts on Missions*.

John Mason Peck was an outstanding missionary in the West during the height of the anti-mission movement. This chapter has found his *Memoir* (ed. Rufus Babcock) together with the Carroll volume with its extensive quotations from the leaders of the anti-mission movements useful sources. Cady has also dealt extensively with the movement in Indiana.

NOTES

1. Rufus Babcock (ed.), *Forty Years of Pioneer Life* (Philadelphia: American Baptist Publication Society, 1864), *passim*; J. F. Cady, *The Baptist Church in Indiana* (Berne, Ind.: Berne Witness Co., 1942), pp. 25–28, 31–52, 54–60, 67–77, *et passim*; B. H. Carroll, Jr., *The Genesis of American Anti-Missionism* (Louisville: Baptist Book Concern, 1902), especially chaps. i–vii; R. H. Muelder, "Jacksonian Democracy in Religious Organizations" (Ph.D. dissertation, University of Minnesota, 1933), chaps. v and vi; W. T. Stott, *Indiana Baptist History* (Franklin: Franklin College, 1908), pp. 55–71, 88–90, *et passim*; W. W. Sweet, *Religion on the American Frontier*, Vol. I (New York: Henry Holt & Co., 1931), chap. iv.

2. Allen Wiley, "Methodism in Southeastern Indiana," *Indiana Magazine of History*, XXIII (March, 1927), 18–19.

3. This and subsequent pages on the Indiana development depend primarily on Babcock, *op. cit.*; Cady, *loc. cit.*; Muelder, *loc cit.*; J. A. Smith, *A History of the Baptists in Western States East of the Mississippi* (Philadelphia: American Baptist Publication Society, 1896), pp. 122–30, *et passim*; and John Taylor, *Thoughts on Missions* (Franklin County, Ky., 1820).

4. Babcock (ed.), *op. cit.*, 110–11; Cady, *op. cit.*, p. 44 *et passim*.

5. J. A. Smith, *op. cit.*, pp. 122–27; Cady, *op. cit.*, pp. 45–49.

6. Carroll, *op. cit.*, contains extensive quotations from Parker's writings and addresses, pp. 87–92, 108–23, *et passim* and Cady, *op. cit.*, deals at length with the anti-mission movements and their leaders.

7. Carroll, *op. cit.*, chap. vi, *et passim*; Cady, *op. cit.*, pp. 56–76, 119–21.

8. J. A. Smith, *op. cit.*, *passim*; Cady, *op. cit.*, *passim*.

9. Carroll, *op. cit.*, pp. 7–8 *et passim*.

10. John Taylor, *op. cit.*, pp. 5–7, 9–10, 12, 21–22, 27, *et passim*.

CHAPTER XII – *Revivalism*

The leading sources for Western revivals: Asbury, *Journal*; Babcock (ed.), *Forty Years of Pioneer Life*; Bangs, *A History of the Methodist Episcopal Church*; Boehm, *Reminiscences, Historical and Biographical*; Cartwright, *Autobiography*; Cleveland, *The Great Revival in the West*; Cox and Hoby, *The Baptists in America*; Davenport, *Primitive Traits in Religious Revivals*; Dimond, *The Psychology of the Methodist Revival*; Finley, *Autobiography* and *Sketches of Western Methodism*; Gewehr, *The Great Awakening in Virginia*; Mecklin, *The Story of American Dissent*; Mode, *The Frontier Spirit in American Christianity*; Nottingham, *Methodism and the Frontier*; Spencer, *A History of Kentucky Baptists*; Sweet, *Religion in Colonial America* and *Revivalism in America*; John Taylor, *A History of Ten Baptist Churches*; Thompson, *A History of the Presbyterian Churches in the United States*; Wiley, "Methodism in Southeastern Indiana"; and Young, *Autobiography of a Pioneer*.

For the New England, Finney, and eastern reformistic revivals: Baker, *An Introduction to the History of Early New England Methodism*; Barnes, *The Antislavery Impulse*; Cole, *The Social Ideas of the Northern Evangelists*; Cross, *The Burned-Over District*; Finney, *Lectures on Revivals of Religion*; Keller, *The Second Great Awakening in Connecticut*; T. L. Smith, *Revivalism and Social Reform*; and B. P. Thomas, *Theodore Weld: Crusader for Freedom*.

NOTES

1. W. W. Sweet, *Revivalism in America* (New York: Charles Scribner's Sons, 1944), pp. 44–70.

2. P. G. Mode, *Sourcebook and Bibliographical Guide for American Church History* (Menasha, Wis.: Collegiate Press, George Banta Publishing Co., 1921), pp. 271–72.

3. Nathan Bangs, *A History of the Methodist Episcopal Church* (New York:

T. Mason & G. Lane, 1840), II, 101–18 (revival excitement as heavenly visitation); Peter Cartwright, *Autobiography* (New York: Carlton & Porter, 1856), pp. 30, 45–52, *et passim*; C. C. Cleveland, *The Great Revival in the West* (Chicago: University of Chicago Press, 1916), pp. 90–101, *et passim*; J. H. Spencer, *A History of Kentucky Baptists* (Cincinnati: By the author, 1886), I, 507–21; Allen Wiley, "Methodism in Southeastern Indiana," *Indiana Magazine of History*, XXIII (December, 1927), 423–24.

4. Leonard Woolsey Bacon, *A History of American Christianity* (New York: Charles Scribner's Sons, 1898), pp. 176–77.

5. Robert Ellis Thompson, *A History of the Presbyterian Churches in the United States* (New York: Christian Literature Co., 1895), p. 37; also see pp. 5–38 and chaps. iv and v.

6. F. M. Davenport, *Primitive Traits in Religious Revivals* (New York: Macmillan Co., 1905), pp. 284–85.

7. For Mecklin's comments on the impact of revivalism on Dissent and related issues: J. M. Mecklin, *The Story of American Dissent* (New York: Harcourt, Brace & Co., 1934), pp. 36–38, 207, 219–21, 229–30, 359, *et passim*; for John Mason Peck's experiences: Rufus Babcock (ed.), *Forty Years of Pioneer Life* (Philadelphia: American Baptist Publication Society, 1864), pp. 151, 157, 162–63, 206, 225, 230.

8. W. K. Anderson (ed.), *Methodism* (New York: Methodist Publishing House, 1947), pp. 229–32; James Burke, "Autobiography," J. B. Finley, *Sketches of Western Methodism* (Cincinnati: Methodist Book Concern, 1854), p. 24; Finley, *ibid.*, chap. xx.

9. Peter Manniche, *Living Democracy in Denmark* (Copenhagen: G. E. C. Gad Publisher, 1952), *passim*. Marquis Childs, *Sweden the Middle Way* (New Haven: Yale University Press, 1947) also has a chapter on Grundtvig and the Danish development.

10. As quoted in Cleveland, *op. cit.*, pp. 57, 90, 96, *et passim*.

11. R. F. Butts and L. A. Cremin, *A History of Education in American Culture* (New York: Henry Holt & Co., 1953), pp. 66–73.

12. Davenport, *op. cit.*, pp. 301–4.

13. Peter Cartwright, *Autobiography of Peter Cartwright* (New York: Carlton & Porter, 1856), pp. 45–46, 48–52, 141–47, 236 ff., *et passim*.

14. As quoted in Dixon Wecter, *The Hero in America* (New York: Charles Scribner's Sons, 1941), p. 164.

15. John Lyle, MS, as quoted in W. W. Sweet, *Religion on the American Frontier*, Vol. II (Chicago: University of Chicago Press, 1936), 89; J. G. Leyburn, *Frontier Folkways* (New Haven: Yale University Press, 1935), p. 199 *et passim*.

16. F. C. Holliday, *Indiana Methodism* (Cincinnati: Hitchcock & Walden, 1873), pp. 182–83.

17. F. J. Turner, *The Frontier in American History* (New York: Henry Holt & Co., 1920), pp. 351–52; Allen Wiley, *op. cit.*, pp. 31–38, 140, *et passim*.

18. Timothy Flint, *Recollections of the Last Ten Years* (New York: A. A. Knopf, 1932), p. 36.

19. Dr. Alexander, as quoted in Cleveland, *op. cit.*, pp. 146–47; Andrew Reed and James Matheson, *A Narrative of the Visit to the American Churches* (New York: Harper & Bros., 1835), II, 10–16, 30, 41–45, *et passim*; W. W. Sweet, *Religion in Colonial America* (New York: Charles Scribner's Sons, 1942), pp. 335–37; Sweet, *Revivalism in America*, pp. 14–19, 131–34.

20. F. A. Cox and James Hoby, *The Baptists in America* (London: T. Ward & Co., 1836), pp. 181, 274, 459–61, 507–10; Allen Wiley, *op. cit.*, p. 261 *et passim*.

21. A. I. Abell, *The Urban Impact on American Protestantism* (Cambridge, Mass.: Harvard University Press, 1943) examines the changes in the Protestant churches resulting from urbanization and industrialization.

22. G. H. Barnes, *Antislavery Impulse* (D. Appleton-Century, Co., Inc., 1933), chaps. ii, vi, vii, and viii; C. R. Keller, *The Second Great Awakening in Connecticut* (New Haven: Yale University Press, 1942), pp. 42, 50–56, 89–91.

23. C. G. Finney, *Lectures on Revivals of Religion* (New York: Fleming H. Revell Co., 1868), pp. 10–12, 386, *et passim*; Barnes, *loc. cit.*

24. Barnes, *op. cit.*, chap. viii; B. P. Thomas, *Theodore Weld: Crusader for Freedom* (New Brunswick, N.J.: Rutgers University Press, 1950), pp. 11–26, 30–33, 38–42, chap. iii.

25. T. L. Smith, *Revivalism and Social Reform* (New York: Abingdon Press, 1957), summarizes this phase.

CHAPTER XIII – *Attitudes toward Slavery*

The main background references: Alexander, *History of the Methodist Episcopal Church, South*; Alvord, *Governor Edward Coles*; Asbury, *Journal*; Bangs, *A History of the Methodist Episcopal Church*; Barclay, *Early American Methodism*; Barnes, *The Antislavery Impulse*; Bishop, *An Outline of the History of the Church in The State of Kentucky*; Boehm, *Reminiscences*; Bremer, *The Homes of the New World*; Buckley, *A History of Methodists in the United States*; Buley, *The Old Northwest*; Cady, *The Baptist Church in Indiana*; Cartwright, *Autobiography*; Chevalier, *Society, Manners and Politics in the United States*; Cole, *The Social Ideas of the Northern Evangelists*; Cox and Hoby, *The Baptists in America*; Culver, *Negro Segregation in the Methodist Church*; Drake, *Quakers and Slavery in America*; Elkins, *Slavery*; Flint, *Recollections*; Friends, *Address of the Yearly Meeting of the Religious Society of Friends . . . to All in the United States*; Indiana Yearly Meeting, *Minutes*; Harris, *The History of Negro Servitude in Illinois*; Hart, *Slavery and Abolition*; Hubbart, *The Older Middle West*; Johnson, *History of the Southern Presbyterian Church*; Jones, *The Later Periods of Quakerism*; Kelsey, *Friends and the Indians*; Loescher, *The Protestant Churches and the Negro*; MacDonald, *Jacksonian Democracy*; Martineau, *Retrospect of Western Travel* and *Society in America*; Matlack, *The Antislavery Struggle and Triumph in the Methodist Episcopal Church*; H. R. Niebuhr, *The Social Sources of Denominationalism*; Phoebus, *Beams of Light on Early Methodism in America*; Pierson, *Tocqueville and Beaumont in America*; Posey, *The Development of Methodism in the Old Southwest*; Putnam, *The Baptists and Slavery*; Russell, *The History of Quakerism*; Sweet, *Religion on the American Frontier*; John Taylor, *A History of Ten Baptist Churches*; B. P. Thomas, *Theodore Weld: Crusader for Freedom*; Tigert, *A Constitutional History of American Episcopal Methodism*; Tryon (ed.), *A Mirror for Americans*; Tyler, *Freedom's Ferment*; Ward, *Andrew Jackson: Symbol for an Age*; Woolman, *The Journal of John Woolman*; and the various state histories.

For the Presbyterian developments, this chapter has relied basically on Barnes, *The Antislavery Impulse*; Bishop, *An Outline of the History of the Church in the State of Kentucky*, including David Rice's "Memoirs"; T. C. Johnson, *History of the Southern Presbyterian Church*; H. R. Niebuhr, *The Social Sources of Denominationalism*; Scouller, *History of the United Presbyterian Church*; Sweet, *Religion on the American Frontier*, Vol. II; B. P. Thomas, *Theodore Weld: Crusader for Freedom*; and Tyler, *Freedom's Ferment*.

The Baptist sources include: Alvord, *Governor Edward Coles*; Cady, *The Baptist Church in Indiana*; Cox and Hoby, *The Baptists in America*; Harris, *The History of Negro Servitude in Illinois*; Putnam, *The Baptists and Slavery*; Spencer, *A History of Kentucky Baptists*; and Sweet, *Religion on the American Frontier*, Vol. I.

For the Methodists, among the more useful references were: Aaron, "Cincinnati"; Alexander, *History of the Methodist Episcopal Church, South*; Bangs, *A History of the Methodist Episcopal Church*; Cartwright, *Autobiography*; Culver, *Negro Segregation in the Methodist Church*; *Journals of the General Conference of the Methodist Episcopal Church*; Stevens, *A Compendious History of American Methodism*; Sweet, *Methodism in American History* and *Religion on the American Frontier*, Vol. IV; and Tigert, *A Constitutional History of American Episcopal Methodism*.

The main sources on the Friends are the same as chapter vi.

NOTES

1. H. R. Niebuhr, *The Social Sources of Denominationalism* (New York: Henry Holt & Co., 1929), chap. ix, and pp. 3–11, 188–99, 236. Thomas Hamilton, *Men and Manners in America* (Edinburgh: William Blackwood, 1833), I, 91–100, 324–25; II, 210–11, 217–28, *et passim*, strongly criticizes the American prejudice against Negroes. Harriet Martineau refers frequently to the situation in her writings. For comments by religious observers, an example is: F. A. Cox and James Hoby, *The Baptists in America* (London: T. Ward & Co., 1836), pp. 275–78 *et passim*. See also Alexis C. de Tocqueville, *Democracy in America* (New York: A. A. Knopf, 1945), I, chap. xviii.

2. B. F. Wright, "Political Institutions and the Frontier," in *Sources of Culture in the Middle West*, ed. D. R. Fox (New York: D. Appleton-Century Co., 1934), pp. 19–28. Timothy Flint has many comments in *Recollections of the Last Ten Years* (New York: A A. Knopf, 1932), pp. 128–49, 154–59, *et passim*.

3. R. H. Bishop, *An Outline of the History of the Church in the State of Kentucky* (Lexington, Ky.: T. T. Skillman, 1824), Parts I and III, *passim* (including the David Rice "Memoirs"); W. W. Sweet, *Religion on the American Frontier*, Vol. II (Chicago: University of Chicago Press, 1936), 111–19, 121–25.

4. G. H. Barnes, *The Antislavery Impulse* (New York: D. Appleton-Century Co., Inc., 1933), 7–15, 38–46, 64–87, *et passim*; Sweet, *op. cit.*, II, 111–19, 121–25, 744–48; B. P. Thomas, *Theodore Weld: Crusader for Freedom* (New Brunswick, N. J.: Rutgers University Press, 1950), 6–8, 11–24, 27–31, 37–48, 70–78, 81–121 and chaps. iii, v, vii, viii; A. F. Tyler, *Freedom's Ferment* (Minne-

apolis: University of Minnesota Press, 1944), pp. 257–58, 463–512, 529–30, *et passim.*

5. W. M. Gewehr, *The Great Awakening in Virginia* (Durham, N.C.: Duke University Press, 1930), pp. 236–38.

6. J. H. Spencer, *A History of Kentucky Baptists* (Cincinnati: By the Author, 1886), I, 183 ff., 186 ff.; II, 120, *et passim*; Sweet, *op. cit.*, I, 77–101, 338, 508.

7. C. W. Alvord, *Governor Edward Coles* (Springfield, Ill.: Trustees of the Illinois State Historical Library, 1920), *passim*; J. F. Cady, *The Baptist Church in Indiana* (Berne, Ind.: Berne Witness Co., 1942), pp. 40, 81, 86, 194–202; N. D. Harris, *The History of the Negro Servitude in Illinois* (Chicago: A. C. McClurg & Co., 1904), *passim*; J. A. Smith, *A History of the Baptists in the Western States East of the Mississippi* (Philadelphia: American Baptist Publication Society, 1896), pp. 39–47, 137–39; Sweet, *op. cit.*, I, 77–101.

8. F. A. Cox and James Hoby, *op. cit.*, pp. 41, 86–87, 103, 275–78, 317–20, 326–28, 415–20, 507.

9. As quoted in J. N. Brown, *History of the American Baptist Publication Society* (Philadelphia: American Baptist Publication Society, n.d. — 1856?), p. 76.

10. M. B. Putnam, *The Baptists and Slavery* (Ann Arbor, Mich.: George Wahr, 1913), *passim.*

11. Nathan Bangs, *A History of the Methodist Episcopal Church* (New York: T. Mason & G. Lane, 1840), I, 133–35, 216–18; II, 97–98, 154, *et passim*; W. C. Barclay, *Early American Methodism* (New York: Board of Missions and Church Extension of the Methodist Church, 1949, 1950), I, chap. iv; II, chap. i, 61 ff.; J. M. Buckley, *A History of Methodists in the United States* (New York: Charles Scribner's Sons, 1907), pp. 308–312, 335–48, 351, 378, 385, 394–95, 464–76; D. W. Culver, *Negro Segregation in the Methodist Church* (New Haven: Yale University Press, 1953), *passim*; L. C. Matlack, *The Antislavery Struggle and Triumph in the Methodist Episcopal Church* (New York: Phillips & Hunt, 1881), *passim*; Abel Stevens, *A Compendious History of American Methodism* (New York: Carlton & Porter, 1867), pp. 125–26, 163, 168, 189, 202–3, 417, *et passim*; W. W. Sweet, *Methodism in American History* (New York: Methodist Book Concern, 1933), pp. 111, 120, 187–191, 231–53, *et passim*; Sweet, *Religion on the American Frontier*, IV, 123–201, 336; J. J. Tigert, *A Constitutional History of American Episcopal Methodism* (Nashville: Publishing House of the Methodist Episcopal Church, South; Barbee & Smith, Agents, 1894), 216–24, 291–95, 323, *et passim.*

12. Peter Cartwright, *Autobiography of Peter Cartwright* (New York: Carlton & Porter, 1856), pp. 192, 245; Harriet Martineau, *Society in America* (London: Saunders & Otley, 1837), II, 335–36, *et passim.*

13. Sweet, *Religion on the American Frontier*, IV, 336, Note 11.

14. Tigert, *loc. cit.* See also Buckley, *op. cit.*, p. 385.

15. Francis Asbury, *Journal* (New York: Lane & Scott, 1852), III, 298.

16. For these and other conferences: *Journals of the General Conference of the Methodist Episcopal Church* (New York: Carlton & Phillips, 1855, 1856), for the years indicated; Bangs, *op. cit.*, for the conferences; Stevens, *op. cit.*, *passim*; Tigert, *op, cit., passim.*

17. Cartwright, *op. cit.*, pp. 128–29, 164, 195–96, 245, 361–64, 414–33, 503; H. H. Grant, *Peter Cartwright: Pioneer* (New York: Abingdon Press, 1931), pp. 155–83.

18. W. B. Posey, *The Development of Methodism in the Old Southwest* (Tuscaloosa, Ala.: Weatherford Printing Co., 1933), 91–92, 94–98, 100, *et*

passim. In addition to the General Conference Journals, Bangs, *op. cit.,* IV, 378–80; Buckley, *op. cit.,* Stevens, *op. cit.,* and Tigert, *op. cit.,* discuss the major issues.

19. Gross Alexander, *History of the Methodist Episcopal Church, South* (New York: Christian Literature Co., 1894), pp. 2–10, 15–37, 66–67, 114–120, *et passim;* W. C. Barclay, *op. cit.,* I, chap. iv; II, 61 ff.

20. Cartwright, *op cit.,* pp. 170–72.

21. W. W. Wightman, *Life of William Capers, D. D.* (Nashville: Southern Methodist Publishing House, 1859), pp. 292–96.

22. F. C. Holliday, *Indiana Methodism* (Cincinnati: Hitchcock & Walden, 1873), pp. 35, 54–57; Allen Wiley, "Methodism in Southeastern Indiana," *Indiana Magazine of History,* XXIII (September, 1927), p. 257.

23. Indiana Yearly Meeting, *Minutes,* 1839, pp. 24–26; 1840, p. 4; Indiana Yearly Meeting reprint of the London Yearly Meeting special Epistle on slavery, 1840; F. L. Paxson, *History of the American Frontier* (Boston: Houghton Mifflin Co., 1924), pp. 163–64.

24. For a concise summary of some of the differences between slavery in the United States and slavery elsewhere, see S. M. Elkins, *Slavery* (Chicago: University of Chicago Press, 1959). For Brazil, Donald Pierson, *Negroes in Brazil* (Chicago: University of Chicago Press, 1942).

CHAPTER XIV – *Popular Denominations and Jacksonianism*

Major references: Aaron, "Cincinnati"; Alvord, *Governor Edward Coles;* Babcock (ed.), *Forty Years of Pioneer Life;* Bond, *The Civilization of the Old Northwest;* Buley, *The Old Northwest;* Cady, *The Baptist Church in Indiana;* Cartwright, *Autobiography;* Fish, *The Rise of the Common Man;* Fox (ed.), *Sources of Culture in the Middle West;* Gabriel, *The Course of American Democratic Thought;* Grant, *Peter Cartwright: Pioneer;* Harris, *The History of Negro Servitude in Illinois;* Koch, *Republican Religion;* MacDonald, *Jacksonian Democracy;* Meyers, *The Jacksonian Persuasion;* Muelder, "Jacksonian Democracy in Religious Organizations"; Nottingham, *Methodism and the Frontier;* Paxson, *History of the American Frontier;* Perry, *Puritanism and Democracy;* Schlesinger, *The Age of Jackson;* Sonne, *Liberal Kentucky;* Syrett, *Andrew Jackson;* Turner, *The Frontier in American History, Rise of the New West, The Significance of Sections in American History,* and *The United States;* Tyler, *Freedom's Ferment;* Ward, *Andrew Jackson: Symbol for an Age;* Webster, *History of the Democratic Party Organization in the Northwest;* and the various state histories.

NOTES

1. Francis Asbury, *Journal* (New York: Lane & Scott, 1852), I, 136; II, 460; III, 6, 144, 360, *et passim.*

2. Alfred Brunson, *A Western Pioneer* (Cincinnati: Hitchcock & Walden, 1872), I, 43 *et passim.* See also references for chapter ii above.

3. N. H. Sonne, *Liberal Kentucky* (New York: Columbia University Press, 1939), pp. 110–11.

4. C. Dale Johnson, "Sectarian Protestantism and Vertical Mobility: Another Dimension" (an unpublished essay presented at the Pacific Sociological Society, San Diego, March 6, 1964). Many other studies indicate similar processes, as noted by G. Benton Johnson, "On Church and Sect," *American Sociological Review*, XXVIII, No. 4 (August, 1963), 539–49, and chapter ii above.

5. H. H. Grant, *Peter Cartwright: Pioneer* (New York: Abingdon Press, 1931), p. 165; J. F. Cady, *The Baptist Church in Indiana* (Berne, Ind.: Berne Witness Co., 1942), pp. 41 ff., *et passim*. Homer J. Webster examines the rapid organizational growth of Jacksonianism in the West in *History of the Democratic Party Organization in the Northwest, 1824–1840* (Columbus, Ohio: F. J. Heer Printing Co., 1915).

6. On the development of Jacksonian views the following pages used among others: R. H. Gabriel, *The Course of American Democratic Thought* (New York: Ronald Press Co., 1940); Marvin Meyers, *The Jacksonian Persuasion* (New York: Vintage Books, 1960); H. R. Muelder, "Jacksonian Democracy in Religious Organizations" (Ph.D. dissertation, University of Minnesota, 1933); R. B. Perry, *Puritanism and Democracy* (New York: Vanguard Press, 1944); A. M. Schlesinger, Jr., *The Age of Jackson* (Boston: Little, Brown & Co., 1945); H. C. Syrett, *Andrew Jackson* (Indianapolis: Bobbs-Merrill Co., 1953); A. F. Tyler, *Freedom's Ferment* (Minneapolis: University of Minnesota Press, 1944; J. W. Ward, *Andrew Jackson: Symbol for an Age* (New York: Oxford University Press, 1955); H. J. Webster, *op. cit.*

7. An example of European views on the relative freedom of America from utopian and quasi-religious political dogmas is: R. L. Bruckberger, *Image of America* (New York: Viking Press, 1959), chaps. viii and xx.

8. Perry, *op. cit.*, p. 139 *et passim*.

9. F. C. Holliday, *Indiana Methodism* (Cincinnati: Hitchcock & Walden, 1873), *passim*; William Dean Howells, "Introduction," W. C. Howells, *Recollections of Life in Ohio* (Cincinnati: Robert Clarke Co., 1895), p. v; C. M. S. Kirkland, *Forest Life* (New York: C. S. Francis & Co., 1844), II, 79, *et passim*.

CHAPTER XV – *The Heritage of the*
Popular Denominations

1. Abel Stevens, *A Compendious History of American Methodism* (New York: Carlton & Porter, 1867), p. 218.

2. W. W. Sweet, *Circuit-Rider Days in Indiana* (Indianapolis: W. K. Stewart Co., 1916), pp. 31, 101–3, *et passim*.

3. David Riesman, Nathan Glazer, and Reuel Denney, *The Lonely Crowd* (Garden City, N. Y.: Doubleday & Co., 1955), pp. 18–42 *et passim*.

4. The summaries are based especially on Frederick Jackson Turner, *The Frontier in American History* (New York: Henry Holt & Co., 1920), and also *Rise of the New West, 1819–1829* (New York: Harper & Bros., 1906), *The Significance of Sections in American History* (New York: Henry Holt & Co., 1932), and *The United States, 1830–1850: The Nation and Its Sections* (New York: Henry Holt & Co., 1935).

5. Turner, *The Frontier in American History*, pp. 3–4.

6. Alexis C. de Tocqueville, *Democracy in America* (New York: A. A. Knopf, 1945), I, 71, 191, 263–70, 300 ff.; II, 20–28, 102–10; Michel Chevalier, *Society, Manners and Politics in the United States* (Boston: Weeks, Jordan & Co., 1839), pp. 142–43; Harriet Martineau, *Society in America* (London: Saunders & Otley, 1837), III, 7–8, 11–15, 21, 225–43, 249–69.

7. C. M. Kirkland, *A New Home — Who'll Follow?* (New York: C. S. Francis, 1840), pp. 250–51 and also 124–136, 328–29. Mrs. Kirkland was a perceptive observer of the frontier society. Additional comments on frontier life and control appear in: *The Evening Book* (New York: Charles Scribner, 1852), pp. 282–86; *Forest Life* (New York: C. S. Francis & Co., 1844), I, *passim*; II, 151–58.

8. J. B. Finley, *Autobiography of James Bradley Finley* (Cincinnati: Cranston & Curts, 1853), pp. 70–71.

9. Turner, *The Frontier in American History*, pp. 343–44. See also Kirkland, Forest Life, I, 212–15, 227–30, on effects of the rotation of offices.

10. R. B. Perry, *Puritanism and Democracy* (New York: Vanguard Press, 1944), pp. 210–12, 464.

11. R. M. MacIver, *The Web of Government* (New York: Macmillan Co., 1949), *passim*; R. M. MacIver and C. H. Page, *Society: An Introductory Analysis* (New York: Rinehart & Co., 1949), pp. 5–22, chaps. iii, vii–x, xii, xvii, xviii.

12. MacIver and Page, *op. cit.*, chaps. iii, vii, viii, and ix; Emile Durkheim, *The Division of Labor in Society* (New York: Macmillan Co., 1933); Charles P. Loomis, *Fundamental Concepts of Sociology* (New York: American Book Co., 1940), a translation with adaptations of Ferdinand Toennies, *Gemeinschaft und Gesellschaft*.

13. For a critical discussion of the relation of the individual and his society: C. H. Cooley, *Human Nature and the Social Order* (New York: Charles Scribner's Sons, 1922); and G. H. Mead, *Mind, Self and Society* (Chicago: University of Chicago Press, 1934).

14. Rexford Newcomb, *Architecture of the Old Northwest Territory* (Chicago: University of Chicago Press, 1950), pp. 31 ff., 65, *et passim*; H. R. Shurtleff, *The Log Cabin Myth* (Cambridge, Mass.: Harvard University Press, 1939), *passim*.

15. D. B. Aaron, "Cincinnati, 1818–1838" (Ph.D. dissertation, Harvard University, 1942), chap. vi, and pp. 58–61, 85–89, 147–51; Chevalier, *op. cit.*, chaps. xviii and xix.

16. Aaron, *loc. cit.*, M. A. Allen, "Patterns of Thought in American Periodical Criticism from 1835 to 1840" (M.A. thesis, University of Texas, 1944).

17. G. W. Pierson, "The Frontier and American Institutions," in *The Turner Thesis Concerning the Role of the Frontier in American History*, ed. G. R. Taylor (Boston: D. C. Heath & Co., 1949).

Bibliography

Selected Bibliography

AARON, DANIEL BARUCH. "Cincinnati, 1818–1838: A Study of Attitudes in the Urban West." Unpublished Ph.D. dissertation, Harvard University, 1942. Pp. xxx + 491 + xxxviii. Chart and Appendix.

ABELL, AARON IGNATIUS. *The Urban Impact on American Protestantism, 1865–1900.* "Harvard Historical Studies," Vol. LIV. Cambridge, Mass.: Harvard University Press, 1943. Pp. x + 275.

ALEXANDER, GROSS. *History of the Methodist Episcopal Church, South.* "American Church History Series," Vol. XI. New York: Christian Literature Co., 1894. Pp. xii + 142.

ALLEN, MARJORIE ARVILLA. "Patterns of Thought in American Periodical Criticism from 1835 to 1840: A Study of Eight Magazines." Unpublished Master's thesis. University of Texas, 1944. Pp. iv + 114.

ALVORD, CLARENCE WALWORTH. *Governor Edward Coles.* Edited with an Introduction and Notes by Clarence Walworth Alvord (and Containing ELIHU B. WASHBURNE, *Sketch of Edward Coles, Second Governor of Illinois, and of the Slavery Struggle of 1823–4.* Prepared for the Chicago Historical Society. Chicago: Jansen, McClurg & Co., 1882). "Collections of the Illinois State Historical Library," Vol. XV; "Biographical Series," Vol. I. Springfield, Ill.: Trustees of the Illinois State Historical Library, 1920. Pp. viii + 435.

————. *The Illinois Country, 1673–1818.* "The Centennial History of Illinois," Vol. I. Chicago: A. C. McClurg & Co., 1922. Pp. xvi + 524.

ANDERSON, WILLIAM K. (ed.). *Methodism.* New York: Methodist Publishing House, 1947. Pp. 317.

ASBURY, FRANCIS. *Journal, 1771–1815.* 3 vols. New York: Lane & Scott, 1852. Pp. 524, 492, 500.

ATKINS, GAIUS GLENN, and FAGLEY, FREDERICK L. *History of American Congregationalism.* Boston & Chicago: Pilgrim Press, 1942. Pp. xii + 432.

BABCOCK, RUFUS (ed.). *Forty Years of Pioneer Life: Memoir of John Mason Peck.* Philadelphia: American Baptist Publication Society, 1864. Pp. 360.

BACON, LEONARD WOOLSEY. *A History of American Christianity.* "American Church History Series," Vol. XIII. New York: Charles Scribner's Sons, 1898. Pp. x + 429.

BAIRD, ROBERT. *Religion in America; or, An Account of the Origin, Progress, Relation to the State, and Present Condition of the Evangelical Churches in the United States. With Notices of the Unevangelical Denominations.* New York: Harper & Bros. 1844. Pp. xii + 343.

BAKER, GEORGE CLAUDE, JR. *An Introduction to the History of Early New England Methodism, 1789–1839.* Durham, N. C.: Duke University Press, 1941. Pp. viii + 145.

BANGS, NATHAN. *A History of the Methodist Episcopal Church.* 3d. rev. ed. Vols. I–III. New York: T. Mason & G. Lane, 1840. Vol. IV. New York: G. Lane & P. P. Sandford, 1841. Pp. ii + 371, 430, 471, 505.

The Baptist Almanac, 1841–1853. Philadelphia: American Baptist Publication and Sunday School Society, 1840–52. (The titles, 1841–46: *The Almanac and Baptist Register*; 1847–50: *The Baptist Almanac and Annual Register*; 1851–53: *The Baptist Almanac*).

BARCLAY, WADE CRAWFORD. *Early American Methodism, 1769–1844.* "History of Methodist Missions," Part I. 2 vols. New York: Board of Missions and Church Extension of the Methodist Church, 1949, 1950. Pp. xliv + 449, xiv + 562.

BARNES, GILBERT HOBBS. *The Antislavery Impulse, 1830–1844.* New York: D. Appleton-Century Co., Inc., 1933. Pp. x + 298.

BEECHER, LYMAN. *Plea for the West.* Cincinnati: Truman & Smith, 1835. Pp. 172.

BERGER, PETER L. "Sectarianism and Religious Sociation," *American Journal of Sociology,* LXIV, No. 1 (July, 1958), 41–44.

———. "The Sociological Study of Sectarianism," *Social Research,* XXI, No. 4 (Winter, 1954), 467–85.

BERNHARD, KARL, Duke of Saxe-Weimar Eisenach. *Travels Through North America, During the Years 1825 and 1826.* 2 vols. Philadelphia: Carey, Lea & Carey, 1828. Pp. iv + 212, 238.

BISHOP, ROBERT HAMILTON. *An Outline of the History of the Church in the State of Kentucky, During a Period of Forty Years: Containing the Memoirs of Rev. David Rice, and Sketches of the Origin and Present State of Particular Churches, and of the Lives and Labours of a Number of Men Who Were Eminent and Useful in Their Day.* Lexington, Ky.: Thomas T. Skillman, 1824. Pp. xii + 420.

BOEHM, HENRY. *Reminiscences, Historical and Biographical, of Sixty-Four Years in the Ministry,* ed. JOSEPH B. WAKELEY. New York: Carlton & Porter, 1866. Copyrighted 1865, Pp. 493.

BOND, BEVERLEY WAUGH, JR. *The Civilization of the Old Northwest: A Study of Political, Social, and Economic Development, 1788–1812.* New York: Macmillan Co., 1934. Pp. xiv + 543.

Boone, Richard Gause. *A History of Education in Indiana*. New York: D. Appleton & Co., 1892. Pp. xi + 454.

Bowers, David F. (ed.). *Foreign Influences in American Life*. "Princeton Studies in American Civilization." Princeton, N. J.: Princeton University Press, 1944. Pp. x + 254.

Braithwaite, William Charles. *The Beginnings of Quakerism*. 2d. rev. ed. by Henry Joel Cadbury. Cambridge, England: Cambridge University Press, 1955. Pp. xxviii + 607.

Bremer, Fredrika. *The Homes of the New World; Impressions of America*. Translated from the Swedish by Mary Howitt. 3 vols. London: Arthur Hall, Virtue & Co., 1853. Pp. xv + 407, 460, 463.

―――. *America of the Fifties: Letters of Fredrika Bremer*. Selected and Edited by Adolph B. Benson. New York: American-Scandinavian Foundation; London: Humphrey Milford Oxford University Press, 1924. Pp. xx + 344.

Brewer, Earl D. C. "Sect and Church in Methodism," *Social Forces*, XXX, No. 4 (May, 1952), 400–408.

Briggs, Charles Augustus. *American Presbyterianism: Its Origins and Early History*. New York: Charles Scribner's Sons, 1885. Pp. xviii + 373 + cxlii.

Brinton, Howard H. (ed.). *Children of Light. In Honor of Rufus M. Jones*. New York: Macmillan Co., 1938. Pp. xii + 416.

―――. *Guide to Quaker Practice*. "Pendle Hill Pamphlet," No. 20. Wallingford, Pa.: Pendle Hill, n.d. Pp. 70.

―――. *Quaker Education in Theory and Practice*. "Pendle Hill Pamphlet," No. 9. Wallingford, Pa.: Pendle Hill, 1940. Pp. 136.

Brown, John Newton. *History of the American Baptist Publication Society, From Its Origin in 1824, to Its Thirty-Second Anniversary in 1856*. Philadelphia: American Baptist Publication Society, n.d. (1856?). Pp. 275.

Buck, Solon Justus. *Illinois in 1818*. "The Centennial History of Illinois," Introductory Vol. 2d rev. ed. Chicago: A. C. McClurg & Co., 1918. Pp. xxviii + 362.

Buckley, James M. *A History of Methodists in the United States*. "American Church History Series." 6th ed. New York: Charles Scribner's Sons, 1907. Pp. xx + 714.

Buley, Roscoe Carlyle. *The Old Northwest: Pioneer Period, 1815–1840*. 2 vols. Indianapolis: Indiana Historical Society, 1950. Pp. xvi + 632, x + 686.

Butts, R. Freeman, and Cremin, Lawrence A. *A History of Education in American Culture*. New York: Henry Holt & Co., 1953. Pp. xii + 628.

Cady, John Frank. *The Origin and Development of the Missionary Baptist Church in Indiana*. (Abbreviated Title: *The Baptist Church in Indiana*). Berne, Ind.: Berne Witness Co., Printers (Copyrighted by the Author), 1942. Pp. 354.

CARROLL, B. H., JR. *The Genesis of American Anti-Missionism*. Louisville, Ky.: Baptist Book Concern, 1902. Pp. 229.

CARTWRIGHT, PETER. *Autobiography of Peter Cartwright, The Backwoods Preacher*, ed. W. P. STRICKLAND. New York: Carlton & Porter, 1856. Pp. 525.

CHADDOCK, ROBERT E. *Ohio Before 1850: A Study of the Early Influence of Pennsylvania and Southern Populations in Ohio.* "Studies in History, Economics and Public Law," ed. FACULTY OF POLITICAL SCIENCE OF COLUMBIA UNIVERSITY, Vol. XXXI, No. 2. New York: Columbia University (Longmans, Green & Co., Agents), 1908. Pp. 155.

CHEVALIER, MICHEL. *Society, Manners and Politics in the United States: Being a Series of Letters on North America.* Translated from the Third Paris Edition by T. G. BRADFORD. Boston: Weeks, Jordan & Co., 1839. Pp. iv + 467.

CLARK, MINNIE B. "The Old Log College at Livonia," *Indiana Magazine of History*, XXIII (March, 1927), 73–81.

CLARK, THOMAS D. *A History of Kentucky*. New York: Prentice-Hall, Inc., 1937. Pp. xvi + 702.

CLEVELAND, CATHARINE CAROLINE. *The Great Revival in the West, 1797–1805*. Chicago: University of Chicago Press, 1916. Pp. xiv + 215.

COBB, SANFORD HOADLEY. *The Rise of Religious Liberty in America: A History*. New York: Macmillan Co., 1902. Pp. xxii + 541.

COCKS, HARRY FRANCIS LOVELL. *The Noncomformist Conscience.* "The Forward Books," No. 6. London: Independent Press, Ltd., 1943. Pp. 94.

———. "The Social Thought of 19th Century English Nonconformity," *Christianity and Society*, X (Summer, 1945), 16–24.

COLE, CHARLES C., JR. *The Social Ideas of the Northern Evangelists, 1826–1860.* "Columbia Studies in the Social Sciences," No. 580. New York: Columbia University Press, 1954. Pp. vi + 268.

COX, FRANCIS AUGUSTUS, and HOBY, JAMES. *The Baptists in America; A Narrative of the Deputation from the Baptist Union in England to the United States and Canada.* London: T. Ward & Co., 1836. Pp. x + 516.

CRAWFORD, BENJAMIN FRANKLIN. *Our Methodist Hymnody*. 4th printing. Carnegie, Pa.: Carnegie Church Press, 1940. Pp. 245.

CROSS, WHITNEY R. *The Burned-Over District: The Social and Intellectual History of Enthusiastic Religion in Western New York, 1800–1850.* Ithaca, N. Y.: Cornell University Press, 1950. Pp. xvi + 383.

CULVER, DWIGHT W. *Negro Segregation in the Methodist Church.* "Yale Studies in Religious Education," No. 22. New Haven: Yale University Press, 1953. Pp. xii + 218.

CURTI, MERLE. *The Making of an American Community: A Case Study of Democracy in a Frontier County.* With the assistance of ROBERT DANIEL, SHAW LIVERMORE, JR., JOSEPH VAN HISE, and MARGARET W. CURTI. Stanford, Calif.: Stanford University Press, 1959. Pp. xii + 483.

DAVENPORT, FREDERICK MORGAN. *Primitive Traits in Religious Revivals: A Study in Mental and Social Evolution.* New York: Macmillan Co., 1905. Pp. xiv + 323.

DAVISON, WALTER S. "The Plight of Rural Protestantism," *Religion in Life,* XV, No. 3 (Summer, 1946), 377–90.

DIMOND, SIDNEY GEORGE. *The Psychology of the Methodist Revival: An Empirical and Descriptive Study.* London: Humphrey Milford Oxford University Press, 1926. Pp. xvi + 296.

DRAKE, THOMAS E. *Quakers and Slavery in America.* "Yale Historical Publications," Miscellany, LI. New Haven: Yale University Press, 1950. Pp. ix + 245.

DUVALL, SYLVANUS MILNE. *The Methodist Episcopal Church and Education Up To 1869.* "Teachers College, Columbia University Contributions to Education," No. 284. New York: Bureau of Publications, Teachers College, Columbia University, 1928. Pp. x + 127.

DYNES, RUSSELL R. "Church-Sect Typology and Socio-Economic Status," *American Sociological Review,* XX, No. 5 (October, 1955), 555–60.

EGGLESTON, EDWARD. *The Hoosier School-Master.* Introduction by Vernon Loggins. "American Century Series," gen. ed. LOUIS M. HACKER. New York: Sagamore Press, Inc., 1957, Pp xiv + 176.

ELKINS, STANLEY M. *Slavery: A Problem in American Institutional and Intellectual Life.* Chicago: University of Chicago Press, 1959. Pp. viii + 248.

ESAREY, LOGAN. *A History of Indiana.* Vol. I. Indianapolis: W. K. Stewart Co., 1915. Pp. x + 515; Vol. II. Indianapolis: B. F. Bowen & Co., 1918. Pp. xiv + 573–1148.

FAUST, ALBERT BERNHARDT. *The German Element in the United States; With Special Reference to Its Political, Moral, Social, and Educational Influence.* 2 vols. Boston & New York: Houghton Mifflin Co., 1909. Pp. xxiv + 591, xvi + 605.

FINLEY, ISAAC J. and PUTNAM, RUFUS. *Pioneer Record and Reminiscences of the Early Settlers and Settlement of Ross County, Ohio.* Cincinnati: Robert Clarke & Co., 1871. Pp. 148.

FINLEY, JAMES BRADLEY. *Autobiography of James Bradley Finley; Or, Pioneer Life in the West,* ed. W. P. STRICKLAND. Cincinnati: Cranston & Curts. New York: Hunt & Eaton, 1853. Pp. 455.

———. *Sketches of Western Methodism: Biographical, Historical, and Miscellaneous,* ed. W. P. STRICKLAND. Cincinnati: Methodist Book Concern for the Author, 1854. Pp. 541.

FINNEY, CHARLES GRANDISON. *Lectures on Revivals of Religion.* New York: Fleming H. Revell Co., 1868. Pp. 445.

FISH, CARL RUSSELL. *The Rise of the Common Man, 1830–1850.* "A History of American Life Series," Vol. VI. New York: Macmillan Co., 1927. Pp. xxii + 391.

FITHIAN, PHILIP VICKERS. *Journal & Letters of Philip Vickers Fithian, 1773–1774: A Plantation Tutor of the Old Dominion.* Edited, with an Introduction, by HUNTER DICKINSON FARISH. Williamsburg, Va.: Colonial Williamsburg, Inc., 1943. Pp. xlvi + 323.

FLINT, TIMOTHY. *Recollections of the Last Ten Years.* With an Introduction and Edited by C. HARTLEY GRATTAN. From the 1826 edition unchanged even to typographical errors. Boston: Cummings, Hillard, & Co., 1826. New York: Alfred A. Knopf, 1932. Pp. xx + 382.

FOSTER, ROBERT V. *A Sketch of the History of the Cumberland Presbyterian Church.* "American Church History Series," Vol. XI. New York: Christian Literature Co., 1894. Pp. 257–309.

FOX, DIXON RYAN (ed.) *Sources of Culture in the Middle West: Backgrounds Versus Frontier.* New York & London: D. Appleton-Century Co., Inc., 1934. Pp. viii + 110.

The Friend. "Influence of Music and Objections to Its Cultivation," *The Friend,* LXVII (August 5 and 12, 1893), 12, 20.

FRIENDS, SOCIETY OF. *Epistles* (of the various Yearly Meetings, especially the Indiana and the London Yearly Meetings, 1822–1840).

———. Indiana Yearly Meeting. *Address to the People of the United States and to the Members of Congress in Particular. On the Civilization and Christian Instruction of the Aborigines of Our Country. By Indiana Yearly Meeting of Friends, Held at Whitewater, by Adjournments, from the 8th of the 10th Month, to the 13th of the Same Inclusive, 1838.* Cincinnati: A. Pugh, Printer, 1838. Pp. 16.

———. Indiana Yearly Meeting. *Address of the Yearly Meeting of the Religious Society of Friends, Commonly Called Quakers, in Indiana, Illinois, the Western Part of Ohio, &c.: to All in the United States, Who Profess the Christian Religion, and Hope for Salvation, through the Mercy and Merits of our Lord and Saviour Jesus Christ.* (1837). Pp. 7.

———. Indiana Yearly Meeting. *The Discipline of the Society of Friends of Indiana Yearly Meeting. Revised By the Meeting Held at White Water, in the Year 1838, and Printed by the Direction of the Same.* Cincinnati: A. Pugh, Printer, 1839. Pp. viii + 97.

———. Indiana Yearly Meeting. *Minutes of the Indiana Yearly Meetings of Friends, 1821–1845.*

———. Ohio Yearly Meeting. *The Discipline of the Society of Friends of Ohio Yearly Meeting; Printed By the Direction of the Meeting Held*

at Mountpleasant, in the year 1819. Mountpleasant, Ohio: Printed by
Elisha Bates, Pp. 102.

————. "The Minutes of the Whitewater (Men's) Monthly Meeting,
1809–1830." Unpublished manuscript records in the vaults of the
First Friends Meeting House, Richmond, Indiana.

————. "The Record of Whitewater Monthly Meeting of Women
Friends, 1809–1836." Unpublished manuscript records in the vaults
of the First Friends Meeting House, Richmond, Indiana.

————. "Records of the Minutes of Whitewater Quarterly Meeting,
1817–1849." Unpublished manuscript records in the vaults of the
First Friends Meeting House, Richmond, Indiana.

GABRIEL, RALPH HENRY. *The Course of American Democratic Thought:
An Intellectual History Since 1815.* New York: Ronald Press Co., 1940.
Pp. xii + 452.

GERTH, HANS HEINRICH, and MILLS, C. WRIGHT (eds.). *From Max Weber:
Essays in Sociology.* Translated, edited, with an Introduction by H. H.
Gerth and C. Wright Mills. New York: Oxford University Press, 1946.
Pp. xii + 490.

GEWEHR, WESLEY MARSH. *The Great Awakening in Virginia, 1740–1790.*
Durham, N. C.: Duke University Press, 1930. Pp. x + 292.

GOODYKOONTZ, COLIN BRUMMITT. *Home Missions on the American Frontier, With Particular Reference to the American Home Missionary
Society.* Caldwell, Idaho: Caxton Printers, Ltd. 1939. Pp. 460.

GRANT, HELEN HARDIE. *Peter Cartwright: Pioneer.* New York: Abingdon
Press, 1931. Pp. 222.

GREENE, MARIA LOUISE. *The Development of Religious Liberty in Connecticut.* Boston & New York: Houghton, Mifflin & Co., 1905. Pp. xiv
+ 552.

GROSS, JOHN O. "Religious Work on Methodist College Campuses from
Cokesbury to 1945," *Christian Education,* XXIX (March, 1946), 210–
22.

GRUND, FRANCIS J. *Aristocracy in America: From the Sketch-Book of a
German Nobleman.* With an Introduction by George E. Probst. From
the 1839 London Edition by RICHARD BENTLEY. New York: Harper
& Bros., 1959, pp. xviii + 302.

HALL, THOMAS CUMING. *The Religious Background of American Culture.* Boston: Little, Brown, & Co., 1930. Pp. xiv + 348.

HAMILTON, THOMAS. *Men and Manners in America.* 2 vols. Edinburgh:
William Blackwood; London: T. Cadell, 1833. Pp. xi + 393, iii + 402.

HARKNESS, GEORGIA. *John Calvin: Man and His Ethics.* New York: Henry
Holt & Co., 1931. Pp. xv + 266.

HARRIS, NORMAN DWIGHT. *The History of Negro Servitude in Illinois
and of the Slavery Agitation in That State, 1719–1864.* Chicago: A. C.
McClurg & Co., 1904. Pp. xi + 276.

HART, ALBERT BUSHNELL. *Slavery and Abolition, 1831–1841.* "The American Nation: A History Series," Vol. XVI, ed. ALBERT BUSHNELL HART. New York: Harper & Bros., 1906. Pp. xv + 360.

HERBERG, WILL. *Protestant-Catholic-Jew: An Essay in American Religious Sociology.* Garden City, N. Y.: Doubleday & Co., 1955. Pp. 320.

HINTZ, HOWARD WILLIAM. *The Quaker Influence in American Literature.* New York: Fleming H. Revell Co., 1940. Pp. 96.

HOLLIDAY, FERNANDEZ C. *Indiana Methodism: Being an Account of the Introduction, Progress, and Present Position of Methodism in the State; and also a History of the Literary Institutions under the Care of the Church, with Sketches of the Principal Methodist Educators in the State, down to 1872.* Cincinnati: Hitchcock & Walden, 1873. Pp. 360.

HOWELLS, WILLIAM COOPER. *Recollections of Life in Ohio, From 1813 to 1840.* With an Introduction by His Son, William Dean Howells. Cincinnati: Robert Clarke Co., 1895. Pp. xiv + 207.

HUBBART, HENRY CLYDE. *The Older Middle West 1840–1880: Its Social, Economic and Political Life and Sectional Tendencies Before, During and After the Civil War.* New York: D. Appleton-Century Co., Inc., 1936. Pp. x + 305.

HUNT, CHESTER L. "The East Needs Puritan Capital," *The Christian Century,* LXXII, No. 28 (July 13, 1955), 816–18.

HUTTON, GRAHAM. *Midwest at Noon.* Chicago: University of Chicago Press, 1946. Pp. xvi + 351.

JAMES, CHARLES FENTON. *Documentary History of the Struggle for Religious Liberty in Virginia.* Lynchburg, Virginia: J. P. Bell Co., 1900. Pp. 272.

JOHNSON, FREDERICK ERNEST (ed.). *Wellsprings of the American Spirit.* "Religion and Civilization Series." New York: Published by the Institute for Religious and Social Studies. Distributed by Harper & Bros., 1948. Pp. xii + 241.

JOHNSON, G. BENTON. "A Critical Appraisal of the Church-Sect Typology," *American Sociological Review,* XXII, No. 1 (February, 1957), 88–92.

———. "On Church and Sect," *American Sociological Review,* XXVIII, No. 4 (August, 1963), 539–49.

JOHNSON, THOMAS C. *History of the Southern Presbyterian Church.* "American Church History Series," Vol. XI. New York: Christian Literature Co., 1894. Pp. 311–487.

JONES, RUFUS MATTHEW. *The Later Periods of Quakerism.* 2 vols. London: Macmillan & Co., Ltd., 1921. Pp. xxxvi + 540, vi + 541–1020.

KELLER, CHARLES ROY. *The Second Great Awakening in Connecticut.* "Yale Historical Publications," No. XL. New Haven: Yale University Press, 1942. Pp. xii + 275.

KELSEY, RAYNER WICKERSHAM. *Friends and the Indians, 1655–1917.* Philadelphia: The Associated Executive Committee of Friends on Indian Affairs, 1917. Pp. xi + 291.

KIRKLAND, CAROLINE MATILDA STANSBURY. *The Evening Book: Or, Fireside Talk on Morals and Manners, With Sketches of Western Life.* New York: Charles Scribner, 1852, Pp. 312.

———. *Forest Life.* 2 vols. New York: C. S. Francis & Co.,; Boston: J. H. Francis, 1844. Pp. 250, 234.

———. *A New Home — Who'll Follow?: Or, Glimpses of Western Life.* 2d ed. New York: C. S. Francis; Boston: J. H. Francis, 1840. Pp. iv + 337. (Also the title of *Our New Home in the West.* New York: James Miller, 1872. Pseud. MRS. MARY CLAVERS.)

———. *Western Clearings.* New York: Wiley & Putnam, 1845. Pp. viii + 238.

KIRKPATRICK, JOHN ERVIN. *Timothy Flint, Pioneer, Missionary, Author, Editor, 1780–1840.* Cleveland: Arthur H. Clark Co., 1911. Pp. 331.

KOCH, GUSTAV ADOLF. *Republican Religion: The American Revolution and the Cult of Reason.* "Studies in Religion and Culture. American Religion Series," VII. New York: Henry Holt & Co., 1933. Pp. xvi + 334.

LELAND, JOHN. *The Writings of the Late Elder John Leland, Including Some Events in His Life, Written By Himself, With Additional Sketches, &c. By Miss L. F. Greene, Lanesboro, Mass.* New York: Printed by G. W. Wood, 1845. Pp. 744.

LEYBURN, JAMES GRAHAM. *Frontier Folkways.* New Haven: Yale University Press, 1935. Pp. x + 291.

LINDLEY, HARLOW (ed.). *Indiana as Seen by Early Travelers. A Colleclection of Reprints from Books of Travel, Letters and Diaries Prior to 1830.* Selected and edited by HARLOW LINDLEY. "Indiana Historical Collections." Indianapolis: Published by the Indiana Historical Commission, 1916. Pp. 596.

———. "The Quaker Contribution to the Old Northwest," in *Children of Light,* ed. Howard H. Brinton. Pp. 307–30.

———. "The Quakers in the Old Northwest." *Proceedings of the Mississippi Valley Historical Association,* V, 60–72.

LINDSAY, THOMAS M. *A History of the Reformation.* 2 vols. New York: Charles Scribner's Sons, 1906–7. Pp xvi + 528, xviii + 631.

LITTELL, FRANKLIN HAMLIN. *The Anabaptist View of the Church: An Introduction to Sectarian Protestantism.* "Studies in Church History," Vol. VIII, ed. JAMES H. NICHOLS and WILHELM PAUCK. Prize Essay of the Frank S. Brewer Fund. Hartford (?): American Society of Church History, 1952. Pp. xii + 148.

LITTLE, LEWIS PEYTON. *Imprisoned Preachers and Religious Liberty in Virginia: A Narrative Drawn Largely from the Official Records of*

Virginia Counties, Unpublished Manuscripts, Letters, and Other Original Sources. With an Introduction by the Rev. R. H. Pitt. Lynchburg, Va.: J. P. Bell Co., Inc., 1938. Pp. xx + 534.

LOESCHER, FRANK S. *The Protestant Churches and the Negro: A Pattern of Segregation.* With a Foreword by BISHOP WILLIAM SCARLETT. New York: Association Press, 1948. Pp. 159.

MACDONALD, WILLIAM. *Jacksonian Democracy 1829–1837.* "The American Nation: A History Series," Vol. XV, ed. ALBERT BUSHNELL HART. New York: Harper & Bros., 1906. Pp. xiv + 345.

MACIVER, ROBERT MORRISON. *Society: A Textbook of Sociology.* New York: Farrar & Rinehart, Inc., 1937. Pp. xii + 596.

———. *The Web of Government.* New York: Macmillan Co., 1949. Pp. x + 498.

———. and PAGE, CHARLES H. *Society: An Introductory Analysis.* New York: Rinehart & Co., Inc., 1949. Pp. xx + 697.

MANROSS, WILLIAM WILSON. *A History of the American Episcopal Church.* Milwaukee: Morehouse Publishing Co., 1935. Pp. xviii + 404.

MARTIN, D. A. "The Denomination," *British Journal of Sociology,* XIII, No. 1 (March, 1962), 1–14.

MARTINEAU, HARRIET. *Retrospect of Western Travel.* 3 vols. London: Saunders & Otley, 1838. Pp. viii + 318, vi +292, vi + 293.

———. *Society in America.* 3 vols. London: Saunders & Otley, 1837. Pp. xx + 364, vi + 369, vi + 365.

MATHEWS, H. F. *Methodism and the Education of the People, 1791–1851.* London: Epworth Press, 1949. Pp. 215.

MATLACK, LUCIUS C. *The Antislavery Struggle and Triumph in the Methodist Episcopal Church.* New York: Phillips & Hunt; Cincinnati: Walden & Stowe, 1881. Pp. 379.

MAY, HENRY F. *Protestant Churches and Industrial America.* New York: Harper & Bros., 1949. Pp. x + 297.

MCCONNELL, FRANCIS J. "Francis Asbury," *Religion in Life,* XV (Winter, 1945–46), 23–36.

MECKLIN, JOHN MOFFATT. *The Story of American Dissent.* New York: Harcourt, Brace & Co., 1934. Pp. vi + 381.

MERTON, ROBERT K. *Social Theory and Social Structure.* Revised and Enlarged Edition. Glencoe, Ill.: Free Press, 1957. Pp. xviii + 645.

THE METHODIST EPISCOPAL CHURCH. *A Form of Discipline for the Ministers, Preachers, and Members of the Methodist Episcopal Church in America.* Considered and Approved at a Conference Held at Baltimore, in the State of Maryland, on Monday the 27th Day of December, 1784. Elizabeth-Town: Printed by Shepard Kollock, 1788. Reprinted 1888 in Exeter, N. H.: News Letter Press. Pp. 47.

———. *The Doctrines and Discipline of the Methodist Episcopal*

Church. The Fourteenth Edition. New York: Published by John Wilson & Daniel Hitt, for the Methodist Connection, 1808. Pp. 215.

————. *Journals of the General Conference of the Methodist Episcopal Church, 1796–1844.* 2 vols. Vol. I, New York: Carlton & Phillips, 1855. Pp. 504. Vol. II, New York: Carlton & Phillips, 1856. Pp. 172 + 210 + 245. (Includes the 1844 Debates).

————. *Minutes of the Annual Conferences of the Methodist Episcopal Church,* 1773–1839. 2 vols. New York: T. Mason & G. Lane, 1840. Pp. 574, 680.

METHODIST HISTORICAL DEPOSITORY. Burton Historical Library, Detroit (incomplete unpublished manuscript records):

————. "Records of the Brooklyn Circuit (Organized at the Sixth Session, Michigan Conference at White Pigeon, September 15, 1841), First Session, Brooklyn, December 18, 1841."

————. "Records of the Dover and Medina Circuit Quarterly Conferences, November 13, 1858 to August 1, 1868."

————. "The Dundee Class Book. David Curtis, Class Leader. Michigan Conference, Anarbor District. December 20, 1836–Sept. 1859."

————. "Class Book for South Branch of Macon Class, Dundee Circuit, Monroe District, David Curtis, Class Leader."

————. "Records" of the First Three Quarterly Meetings of the Dundee Mission, October 21, 1837, January 20, 1838, and April 31, 1838.

————. "Records of the Quarterly Conferences of the Highland Circuit, October 19, 1867, to August 4, 1887."

————. "Records of the Oakville Circuit Quarterly Meetings, Detroit Conference, January 1, 1859–February 10, 1866."

————. "Quarterly Conference Records of Palmyra Circuit. November 10, 1838–February 22, 1851."

MEYERS, MARVIN. *The Jacksonian Persuasion: Politics and Belief.* New York: Vintage Books, 1960. Pp. xiv + 292 + vi.

MILLER, SAMUEL. *A Brief Retrospect of the Eighteenth Century. Part the First; in Three (?) Volumes: Containing a Sketch of the Revolutions and Improvements in Science, Arts, and Literature, during That Period.* 2 vols. London: J. Johnson, 1805. Pp. xvi + 492, iv + 420.

MILLS, SAMUEL J., and SMITH, DANIEL. *Report of a Missionary Tour through That Part of the United States Which Lies West of the Allegany Mountains; Performed under the Direction of the Massachusetts Missionary Society.* Andover, Mass.: Printed by Flagg & Gould, 1815. Pp. 64.

MODE, PETER GEORGE. *The Frontier Spirit in American Christianity.* New York: Macmillan Co., 1923. Pp. xii + 196.

————. *Sourcebook and Bibliographical Guide for American Church History.* Menasha, Wis.: Collegiate Press, George Banta Publishing Co., 1921. Pp. xxiv + 735.

MORSE, JARVIS MEANS. *A Neglected Period of Connecticut's History, 1818–1850.* "Yale Historical Publications," XXV. New Haven: Yale University Press, 1933. Pp. viii + 359.

MORTON, LOUIS. *Robert Carter of Nomini Hall: A Virginia Tobacco Planter of the Eighteenth Century.* Williamsburg, Va.: Colonial Williamsburg, Inc., 1945. Pp. xviii + 332.

MUELDER, HERMANN RICHARD. *Church History in a Puritan Colony of the Middle West.* "Centennial Lectures." Galesburg, Ill.: Published by the Central Congregational Church and the First Presbyterian Church, 1937. Pp. 79.

———. "Jacksonian Democracy in Religious Organizations." Unpublished Ph.D. dissertation, University of Minnesota, 1933. Pp. iii + xv + 457.

NEVINS, ALLAN. *American Social History as Recorded By British Travellers.* New York: Henry Holt & Co., 1923. Pp. viii + 577.

NEWCOMB, REXFORD. *Architecture of the Old Northwest Territory: A Study of Early Architecture in Ohio, Indiana, Illinois, Michigan, Wisconsin, & Part of Minnesota.* Chicago: University of Chicago Press, 1950. Pp. xvii + 176 + xcvi. Plates.

NEWMAN, ALBERT HENRY. *A History of the Baptist Churches in the United States.* "American Church History Series," Vol. II. New York: Christian Literature Co., 1894. Pp. xvi + 513.

NIEBUHR, HELMUT RICHARD. *Christ and Culture.* New York: Harper & Bros., 1951. Pp. xii + 259.

———. *The Social Sources of Denominationalism.* New York: Henry Holt & Co., 1929. Pp. x + 304.

NIEBUHR, REINHOLD. *An Interpretation of Christian Ethics.* New York: Harper & Bros. 1935. Pp. viii + 244.

NOTTINGHAM, ELIZABETH K. *Methodism and the Frontier: Indiana Proving Ground.* New York: Columbia University Press, 1941. Pp. x + 231.

———. *Religion and Society.* "Doubleday Short Studies in Sociology," ed. CHARLES H. PAGE. Garden City, N. Y.: Doubleday & Co. (now, New York: Random House), 1954. Pp. x + 84.

PARRINGTON, VERNON LOUIS. *Main Currents in American Thought: An Interpretation of American Literature from the Beginnings to 1920.* 3 vols. New York: Harcourt, Brace & Co., 1927, 1930. Pp. xviii + 413, xxii +493, xl + 429.

PARSONS, TALCOTT. *Religious Perspectives of College Teaching.* New Haven: Edward W. Hazen Foundation, n.d. Pp. 47.

———. *Structure and Process in Modern Societies.* Glencoe, Ill.: Free Press, 1960. Pp. vi + 344.

———. "The Theoretical Development of the Sociology of Religion," *The Journal of the History of Ideas,* V (April, 1944), 176–90.

PAXSON, FREDERIC LOGAN. *History of the American Frontier, 1763–1893* Boston: Houghton Mifflin Co., 1924. Pp. viii + 598.

PEASE, THEODORE CALVIN. *The Frontier State, 1818–1848.* "The Centennial History of Illinois," Vol. II. Chicago: A. C. McClurg & Co., 1922. Pp. x + 475.

PERRY, RALPH BARTON. *Puritanism and Democracy.* New York: Vanguard Press, 1944. Pp. xviii+ 688.

PFAUTZ, HAROLD W. "The Sociology of Secularization: Religious Groups," *American Journal of Sociology,* LXI, No. 2 (September, 1955), 121–28.

PHOEBUS, GEORGE A. *Beams of Light on Early Methodism in America. Chiefly Drawn from the Diary, Letters, Manuscripts, Documents, and Originals Tracts of the Rev. Ezekiel Cooper.* Compiled by GEORGE A. PHOEBUS. New York: Phillips & Hunt; Cincinnati: Cranston & Stowe. 1887. Pp. xiv + 337.

PIERSON, GEORGE WILSON.*Tocqueville and Beaumont in America.* New York: Oxford University Press, 1938. Pp. xvi + 852.

POSEY, WALTER BROWNLOW. *The Development of Methodism in the Old Southwest, 1783–1824.* Tuscaloosa, Ala.: Weatherford Printing Co., 1933. Pp. xvi + 151.

THE PRESBYTERIAN CHURCH IN THE UNITED STATES OF AMERICA. *The Form of Government and Forms of Process, of the Presbyterian Church, in the United States of America; and the Directory for the Worship of God, As Amended and Ratified by the General Assembly at Their Session in May 1821.* Elizabeth-Town, N. J.: Mervin Hale, 1822. Pp. 339–466. (Book II contains the *Discipline*).

PRICE, CARL F. *The Music and Hymnody of the Methodist Hymnal.* New York: Methodist Book Concern, 1911. Pp. 296.

PURCELL, RICHARD JOSEPH. *Connecticut in Transition, 1775–1818.* Washington, D.C.: American Historical Association; London: Humphrey Milford Oxford University Press, 1918. Pp. x + 471.

PUTNAM, MARY BURNHAM. *The Baptists and Slavery, 1840–1845.* Ann Arbor, Mich.: George Wahr, 1913. Pp. 96.

REED, ANDREW, and MATHESON, JAMES. *A Narrative of the Visit to the American Churches by the Deputation from the Congregational Union of England and Wales.* 2 vols. New York: Harper & Bros., 1835. Pp. xiv + 336, vi + 363.

RIESMAN, DAVID; GLAZER, NATHAN; and DENNY, REUEL. *The Lonely Crowd.* Garden City, N. Y.: Doubleday & Co., 1955. Pp. 359.

ROSEBOOM, EUGENE HOLLOWAY, and WEISENBURGER, FRANCIS PHELPS. *A History of Ohio.* New York: Prentice-Hall, Inc., 1934. Pp. xiv + 545.

RUSK, RALPH LESLIE. *The Literature of the Middle Western Frontier.* 2 vols. New York: Columbia University Press, 1926. Pp. xvi + 457, vi + 419.

Russell, Elbert. *The History of Quakerism.* New York: Macmillan Co., 1942. Pp. xxvi + 586.

Schaff, Philip. *The Creeds of Christendom, With a History and Critical Notes.* 3 vols. New York: Harper & Bros., 1877. Pp. xiv + 941, viii + 557, viii + 880.

Schermerhorn, John F. *Report to the Society for Propagating the Gospel among the Indians and Others in North America.* 1814 ? Pp. 48. (Bound with Schermerhorn and Mills, *Correct View.*)

————. and Mills, Samuel J. *A Correct View of That Part of the United States Which Lies West of the Allegany Mountains, with Regard to Religion and Morals.* Hartford, Ct.: Peter P. Gleason & Co., Printers, 1814. Pp. 52.

Schlesinger, Arthur Meier, Jr. *The Age of Jackson.* Boston: Little, Brown & Co., 1945. Pp. xiv + 577.

Schneider, Herbert W. *A History of American Philosophy.* "Columbia Studies in American Culture," No. 18. New York: Columbia University Press, 1946. Pp. xiv + 646.

Scouller, James Brown. *History of the United Presbyterian Church of North America.* "American Church History Series," Vol. XI. New York: Christian Literature Co., 1894. Pp. 143–256.

Seidenspinner, Clarence. *Great Protestant Festivals.* New York: Henry Schuman, Inc., 1952. Pp. 148.

Semple, Robert B. *A History of the Rise and Progress of the Baptists in Virginia.* Richmond, Va.: Published by the Author; John O'Lynch, Printer, 1810. Pp. viii + 447.

Sherman, David. *History of the Revisions of the Discipline of the Methodist Episcopal Church.* New York: Nelson & Phillips; Cincinnati: Hitchcock & Walden, 1874. Pp. 422.

Smith, Henry Nash. *Virgin Land: The American West as Symbol and Myth.* New York: Vintage Books, 1957. Pp. viii + 305 + vii.

Smith, Justin Almerin. *A History of the Baptists in the Western States East of the Mississippi.* Philadelphia: American Baptist Publication Society, 1896. Pp. 420.

Smith, Preserved. *The Age of the Reformation.* New York: Henry Holt & Co., 1920. 1938 Printing. Pp. xii + 861.

Smith, Timothy L., *Revivalism and Social Reform in Mid-Nineteenth Century America.* New York & Nashville: Abingdon Press, 1957. Pp. 253.

Smithson, Robert Jamieson. *The Anabaptists — Their Contribution to Our Protestant Heritage.* London: James Clarke & Co., Ltd., 1935. Pp. 228.

Sonne, Niels Henry. *Liberal Kentucky, 1780–1828.* "Columbia Studies in American Culture," No. 3. New York: Columbia University Press, 1939. Pp. xii + 287.

SPEER, WILLIAM. *The Great Revival of 1800*. Philadelphia: Presbyterian Board of Publication, 1872. Pp. 112.

SPENCER, JOHN H. *A History of Kentucky Baptists from 1769 to 1885, Including More than 800 Biographical Sketches*. The Manuscript Revised and Corrected by MRS. BURRILLA B. SPENCER. 2 vols. Cincinnati: Printed for the Author, 1886. (Copyright by the Author, 1885). Pp. viii + 767 + 7, 671 + 8.

STEPHENSON, GEORGE M. *The Puritan Heritage*. New York: Macmillan Co., 1952. Pp. vi + 282.

STEVENS, ABEL. *A Compendious History of American Methodism*. New York: Carlton & Porter, 1867. Pp. 608.

STOTT, WILLIAM T. *Indiana Baptist History, 1798–1908*. Franklin, Indiana: Franklin College, Published by the Author, 1908. Pp. vii + 381.

SWEET, WILLIAM WARREN. *The American Churches: An Interpretation*. New York & Nashville: Abingdon-Cokesbury Press, 1948. Pp. 153.

———. *American Culture and Religion: Six Essays*. Dallas: Southern Methodist University Press, 1951. Pp. x + 114.

———. *Circuit-Rider Days Along the Ohio: Being the Journals of the Ohio Conference from Its Organization in 1812 to 1826*. Edited with Introduction and Notes by WILLIAM WARREN SWEET. New York & Cincinnati: Methodist Book Concern, 1923. Pp. 299.

———. *Circuit-Rider Days in Indiana: The Minutes and Journal of the Indiana Conference of the Methodist Episcopal Church, 1832–1844*. Edited with an Introduction by WILLIAM WARREN SWEET. Indianapolis: W. K. Stewart Co., 1916. Pp. viii + 344.

———. *Methodism in American History*. New York: Methodist Book Concern, 1933. Pp. 434.

———. *Religion in Colonial America*. New York: Charles Scribner's Sons, 1942. Pp. xvi + 367.

———. *Religion in the Development of American Culture, 1765–1840*. "History of Religion in America," Vol. II. New York: Charles Scribner's Sons, 1952. Pp. xvi + 338.

———. *Religion on the American Frontier. A Collection of Source Materials*. General Introduction by Shirley Jackson Case. 4 vols. Vol. I: *The Baptists, 1763–1830*. New York: Henry Holt and Co., 1931 (Chicago: University of Chicago Press). Pp. x + 652. Vol. II: *The Presbyterians, 1783–1840*. Chicago: University of Chicago Press, 1936. Pp. xiv + 939. Vol. III: *The Congregationalists, 1783–1850*. Chicago: University of Chicago Press, 1939. Pp. xii + 435. Vol. IV: *The Methodists, 1783–1840*. Chicago: University of Chicago Press, 1946. Pp. x + 800.

———. *Revivalism in America — Its Origin, Growth and Decline*. New York: Charles Scribner's Sons, 1944. Pp. xviii + 192.

———. *The Rise of Methodism in the West: Being the Journal of the Western Conference, 1800–1811*. Edited, with Notes and Introduction, by WILLIAM WARREN SWEET. New York: Methodist Book Concern; Nashville: Smith & Lamar, 1920. Pp. 207.

————. *The Story of Religion in America.* Revised and Enlarged Edition. Originally Published under the Title of *The Story of Religions in America*, 1930; Enlarged, 1939. New York & London: Harper & Bros., 1950. Pp. xii + 492.

SYRETT, HAROLD C. *Andrew Jackson: His Contribution to the American Tradition.* "Makers of the American Tradition Series." Hiram Haydn and Donald Bigelow, gen. ed. Indianapolis: Bobbs-Merrill Co., Inc., 1953. Pp. 298.

TAWNEY, RICHARD HENRY. *Religion and the Rise of Capitalism.* "Holland Memorial Lectures," 1922. New York: Harcourt, Brace & Co., 1926. Pp. x + 337.

TAYLOR, GEORGE ROGERS (ed.). *The Turner Thesis Concerning the Role of the Frontier in American History.* Edited with an Introduction by GEORGE ROGERS TAYLOR. "Problems in American Civilization Series." Boston: D. C. Heath & Co., 1949. Pp. x + 106.

TAYLOR, JOHN. *A History of Ten Baptist Churches, of Which the Author Has Been Alternately a Member: In Which Will Be Seen Something of a Journal of the Author's Life, for More Than Fifty Years. Also: A Comment on Some Parts of Scripture; in Which the Author Takes the Liberty to Differ from Other Expositors.* Frankfort, Ky.: Printed by J. H. Holeman, 1823. Pp. iv + 300.

————. *Thoughts on Missions.* Franklin County, Ky., 1820. Pp. 36.

TEWKSBURY, DONALD G. *The Founding of American Colleges and Universities Before the Civil War: With Particular References to the Religious Influences Bearing upon the College Movement.* "Teachers College, Columbia University Contributions to Education," No. 543. New York: Bureau of Publications, Teachers College, Columbia University, 1932. Pp. xii + 254.

THOMAS, ALLEN CLAPP. *A History of the Friends in America.* Assisted by RICHARD HENRY THOMAS. 6th rev. ed. Philadelphia: John C. Winston Co., 1930.

THOMAS, BENJAMIN PLATT. *Theodore Weld: Crusader for Freedom.* New Brunswick, N.J.: Rutgers University Press, 1950. Pp. xii + 307.

THOMPSON, ROBERT ELLIS. *A History of the Presbyterian Churches in the United States.* "American Church History Series," Vol. VI. New York: Christian Literature Co., 1895. Pp. xxxii + 424.

TIGERT, JOHN JAMES. *A Constitutional History of American Episcopal Methodism.* Nashville, Tenn.: Publishing House of the Methodist Episcopal Church, South: Barbee & Smith, Agents, 1894. Pp. 414.

TIPPLE, EZRA SQUIER. *Francis Asbury The Prophet of the Long Road.* New York & Cincinnati: Methodist Book Concern, 1916. Pp. 333.

TOCQUEVILLE, ALEXIS CHARLES HENRI CLEREL DE. *Democracy in America.*

Translated from the French *De La Democratie en Amerique*. The Henry Reeve Text as Revised by FRANCIS BOWEN Now Further Corrected and Edited with Introduction, Editorial Notes, and Bibliographies by PHILLIPS BRADLEY. First Edition, Paris, 1835. From the Fourteenth Edition, 1864 based on the Twelfth Edition, Corrected by the Author, 1848. 2 vols. New York: Alfred A. Knopf, 1945. Pp. cxiv + 434 + xii, xiv + 401 + x.

————. *Journey to America*. Translated by GEORGE LAWRENCE. Edited by J. P. MAYER. New Haven: Yale University Press, 1960. Pp. 394.

TORBET, ROBERT GEORGE. *A Social History of the Philadelphia Baptist Association, 1707–1940*. Philadelphia: Published by the Author, Eastern Baptist Theological Seminary, 1945. Printed by Westbrook Publishing Co. Pp. 247.

TOULMIN, HARRY. *The Western Country in 1793: Reports on Kentucky and Virginia*, ed. MARION TINGLING and GODFREY DAVIES. San Marino, Calif.: Henry E. Huntington Library & Art Gallery, 1948. Pp. xxiv + 141.

TROELTSCH, ERNST. *Protestantism and Progress: A Historical Study of the Relation of Protestantism to the Modern World*. Translated from the German by W. MONTGOMERY. London: Williams & Norgate; New York: G. P. Putnam's Sons, 1912. Pp. xii + 210.

————. *The Social Teaching of the Christian Churches*. 2 vols. Translated from the German under *Die Soziallehren der christlichen Kirchen und Gruppen*, 1911, by OLIVE WYON. With an Introductory Note by CHARLES GORE. "Halley Stewart Publication," I. New York: Macmillan Co., 1931. Pp. 445, 446–1019 (numbered consecutively).

TROLLOPE, FRANCES *Domestic Manners of the Americans*. With an Introduction by MICHAEL SADLEIR. Reprinted from the 5th ed. of 1839; 1st ed., 1832. "The English Library Series," ed. J. ISAACS. London: George Routledge & Sons, Ltd., 1927. Pp. xxx + 398.

TRYON, WARREN STENSON (ed.). *A Mirror for Americans: Life and Manners in the United States, 1790–1870, as Recorded by American Travelers*. Compiled and Edited by WARREN STENSON TRYON. 3 vols. Chicago: University of Chicago Press, 1952. Pp. xx + 230 + v, viii + 231–466 + v, viii + 467–793 + v.

TURNER, FREDERICK JACKSON. *The Frontier in American History*. New York: Henry Holt & Co., 1920. (1931 Printing). Pp. viii + 375.

————. *Rise of the New West, 1819–1829*. "The American Nation: A History Series," Vol. XIV, ed., ALBERT BUSHNELL HART. New York & London: Harper & Bros., 1906. Pp. xviii + 366.

————. *The Significance of Sections in American History*. With an Introduction by MAX FARRAND. New York: Henry Holt & Co., 1932. Pp. x + 347.

————. *The United States 1830–1850: The Nation and Its Sections*. With an Introduction by AVERY CRAVEN. New York: Henry Holt & Co., 1935. Pp. xiv + 602 + xi.

TYLER, ALICE FELT. *Freedom's Ferment. Phases of American Social History to 1860.* Minneapolis: University of Minnesota Press, 1944. Pp. x + 608.

UNIONUS, GUSTAF. *A Pioneer in Northwest America, 1841–1858: The Memoirs of Gustaf Unonius.* Translated from the Swedish by JONAS OSCAR BACKLUND; edited by NILS WILLIAM OLSSON; with an Introduction by GEORGE M. STEPHENSON. Vol. 1. Minneapolis: Published for the Swedish Pioneer Historical Society by the University of Minnesota Press, 1950. Pp. xii + 419.

VENABLE, W. H. *Beginnings of Literary Culture in the Ohio Valley. Historical and Biographical Sketches.* Micro-Offset Edition of the Original Edition of 1891. New York: Peter Smith, 1949. Pp. xv + 519.

WACH, JOACHIM. *Sociology of Religion.* Chicago: University of Chicago Press, 1944. Pp. xii + 412.

WALTON, R. G. "English Nonconformity and the Idea of Community," *Christianity and Society,* XII (Summer, 1947) 19–23.

WARD, JOHN WILLIAM. *Andrew Jackson: Symbol for an Age.* New York: Oxford University Press, 1955, Pp. xii + 274.

WATTERS, PHILLIP M. *Peter Cartwright.* New York: Eaton & Mains; Cincinnati: Jennings & Graham, 1910. Pp. 128.

WEBB, WALTER PRESCOTT. *The Great Frontier.* Boston: Houghton Mifflin Co., 1952. Pp. xiv + 434.

WEBER, MAX. *The Protestant Ethic and the Spirit of Capitalism.* Translated by TALCOTT PARSONS. Foreword by RICHARD HENRY TAWNEY. London: George Allen & Unwin, Ltd., 1930. Pp. xi + 292.

———. *The Sociology of Religion.* Translated by EPHRAIM FISCHOFF. With an Introduction by Talcott Parsons. Boston: Beacon Press, 1963, Pp. lxvii + 304.

———. *The Theory of Social and Economic Organization.* Translated from the German by A. M. HENDERSON and TALCOTT PARSONS. Edited with an Introduction by TALCOTT PARSONS. (Translation from Part I of MAX WEBER, *Wirtschaft und Gesellschaft*). New York: Oxford University Press, 1947. Pp. x + 436.

———. *From Max Weber: Essays in Sociology.* Under H. H. GERTH and C. WRIGHT MILLS, eds.

WEBSTER, HOMER J. *History of the Democratic Party Organization in the Northwest, 1824–1840.* Columbus, Ohio: F. J. Heer Printing Co., 1915. Pp. iv + 120.

WECTER, DIXON. *The Hero in America: A Chronicle of Hero-Worship.* New York: Charles Scribner's Sons, 1941. Pp. xiv + 530.

WENTZ, ABDEL ROSS. *The Lutheran Church in American History.* 2d rev. ed. Philadelphia: United Lutheran Publication House, 1933. Pp. 465.

WILDER, AMOS NIVEN. "Theology and Modern Literature." WILLIAM BELDEN NOBLE Lectures, Harvard University, Cambridge, 1956.

WILEY, ALLEN. "Methodism in Southeastern Indiana," *Indiana Magazine of History*, XXIII (March, 1927), 1–62; (June, 1927), 130–216; (September, 1927), 239–332; (December, 1927), 393–466. Reprinted from *Western Christian Advocate*, January–December, 1846.

WILSON, BRYAN R. "An Analysis of Sect Development," *American Sociological Review*, XXIV, No. 1 (February, 1959), 4–15.

WOOLMAN, JOHN. *The Journal of John Woolman*. With an Introduction by JOHN G. WHITTIER. Philadelphia: Friends' Book Store, 1914. Pp. viii + 315.

WRIGHT, LOUIS B. *Culture on the Moving Frontier*. Bloomington: Indiana University Press, 1955. Pp. 273.

YINGER, J. MILTON. *Religion, Society and the Individual: An Introduction to the Sociology of Religion*. New York: Macmillan Co., 1957. Pp. xvi + 655.

YOUNG, JACOB. *Autobiography of a Pioneer; Or, The Nativity, Experience, Travels, and Ministerial Labors of Rev. Jacob Young; with Incidents, Observations, and Reflections*. Cincinnati: Cranston & Curts; New York: Hunt & Eaton, 1857. Pp. 528.

Index

Index

Aaron, Daniel B., 8

Abolition; *see* individual denominations under antislavery movements.

Achievement emphasis of the frontier, 233

Adams, John Quincy, 204

Alexander, Dr., Presbyterian leader, 168

Allan, William T., 177

American Colonization Society, 67, 182, 189; criticized as obstacle to abolition, 67, 179

American pattern of organized religion, 5, 17, 213

Anabaptist heritage of Dissent, 242, 252 (n. 8)

Anglicans, in Virginia, 10–14 *passim*; and children, 164

Anti-intellectualism; *see* Dissent, individual denominations.

Anti-mission movements (Baptist); *see* Baptists

Architecture, frontier traditionalism in, 235

Arts, Dissenters suspicion of, 5–6, 14–15, 102, 104–5, 111–13, 114–15 117–18, 125, 133, 135, 138, 139, 141, 142, 144, 162, 163, 218, 219

Asbury, Francis, 16, 46–48, 52, 56, 90–91, 92, 106, 112, 124–25, 187, 217, 248 (n. 1); Journal, 46, 125

Associations (Baptist); *see* Baptists; individual associations

Atkins, Gaius G., 144

Aurora (Indiana) Baptist Church, 153

Aurora Missionary Society, Indiana (Baptists), 151

Axley, James, 56, 115

Baird, William D., 24, 26–27

Baltimore (Maryland) Yearly Meeting (Quaker), 62, 63; Indian missions of, 62, 63

Bangs, Nathan, 46–47, 108–9, 110–11, 114

Baptist Almanac, 88; ambivalence to literature and drama, 104–5

Baptist Home Mission Society, 153

Baptist Publication Society, 105–6

Baptists, as Dissenting denomination, 4, 5, 6, 7; early opposition to, 11–13, 15–16; and religious freedom, 11, 12, 15–16, 182–83; on separation of church and state, 12, 16; influence of, on Virginia society, 12, 14–15; ministry of, 33, 90; and disciplinary control over ministry, 33–34; and tradition of lay ministry, 34, 77, 82, 90, 147, 153, 154, 155; scarcity of competent ministers among, 34, 153; and founding of new churches, 35; articles of faith, covenant, and rules of decorum of, 35; interchurch assistance among, 35; and associations, 36, 42–43; dissension among, 36; church organization of, 36–37; and discipline of members and church courts, 37–41; transfer of membership among, 42; center of authority of, 42–43; church councils of, 43–44; democratic but disciplined life among, 44; emphasis of, on local church ordination, 90; opposition among, to ministerial education, 88–90; cultural outlook of, 103, 104–5; and controversy over education, 103–4, 134–

297

35, 152; and western opposition to
Sunday schools, 104, 152–53; and
sectarian rivalries, 126–29 *passim*;
literacy of, in Indiana, 134; ambivalence of, toward recreation,
139; pro-mission elements of, 145–
47 *passim*, 151–52; mission work
among Indians and its influence
on, 151–52; urban dependence of,
on missionaries, 153; and antislavery movements, 180–84; slavery as infringement on religious
freedom of, 182–83; and racism,
182–83
——Anti-missionism, 88–90, 145–
58 *passim*; causes of, 145, 146–
51 *passim*, 154–57; ignorance as
factor in, 146; lay ministry as
cause of, 147, 148; and prejudice
against Indians, 147; as Jacksonian sectionalism, 147; jealousy
against missionaries as element
of, 148; and alleged unscripturalness of missions, 149–50; predestinarianism as factor in, 149–50;
anti-creedal influence on, 150, latent function of, 154–57; as opposition to churchly trends, 154,
155–56; as preference for local fellowship and control, 154, 155; an-
ti-democratic aspects of, 157–58
Barrow, David, 180
Bascom, Flavel, 137–38
Bascom, Henry B., 50, 56, 186
Beecher, Lyman, 100, 168, 176, 177, 178
Bernhard, Karl, Duke of Saxe-Weimar
Eisenach, 138, 139
Bethel (Indiana) Baptist Church, 34
Bethel Missionary Baptist Association,
151
Biblical Institute (Methodist), 95
Birkbeck, Morris, 143
Blue River (Indiana) Missionary So-
ciety (Baptist), 151
Blythe, James, 31
Boehm, Henry, 53, 56, 248 (n. 1)
Books, Methodist distribution of; *see*
Methodist Book Concern
Boone, Richard G., 117, 132, 134
Boston University, School of Theolo-
gy; *see* Biblical Institute (Meth-
odist)

Bower, Jacob, 34
Bradley, James, 176
Bremer, Fredrika, 141–42, 144, 192
Brown, J. Newton, 18, 105
Brunson, Alfred, 199
Buck Run (Kentucky) Baptist Church,
Covenant, 35, 44; Articles of Faith
and Rules of Decorum, 35
Burke, William, 49, 126, 163

Cady, John F., 128
Calling, system of, 77–78, 82, 140–41,
164, 170, 200, 204, 215, 217–19;
effect of, on secular life, 78, 217–
19, 231–32
Calvin, John, 77, 80, 140, 161
Calvinism, historic basis of, 77; concepts of church and ministry of,
77; contrast of, to Dissent, 77; and
concepts of the "world" and state,
77–78, 79; early approach of, to
calling, 78–79; ideal of community of, 79; theocratic beliefs of,
79; aristocratic tradition and
democracy in, 79, 80; intellectual
and cultural interests of, 80, 103,
140; influence of, on Dissent, 81,
123, 140–41, 217–18
Campbell, Alexander, 89, 104, 150–51
Cantine Creek (Illinois) Baptist
Church, 182
Capers, William, 191, 223
Carroll, B. H., Jr., 154, 156; *The Genesis of American Anti-Missionism*,
154
Carter, Robert, 15
Cartwright, Peter, 50–51, 52–53, 56,
57, 91–97 *passim*, 114, 125, 126,
127, 164, 185–91 *passim*, 201, 223,
236
Chevalier, Michel, 228
Christian Advocate (Baptist), 150
Christian Advocate and Journal
(Methodist), 96, 111
Christian Baptist, The, 150
Church courts; *see* Discipline and also
individual denominations
Church, Troeltsch's definition of, 6,
83–84
Cincinnati, Ohio, opposition in, to
drama, arts, and scholarship, 102,
237; and maltreatment of Ne-

Methodist Book Concern, 110–11
Methodist Magazine, 111
Methodists, as frontier denomination, 4; contrast of, to Virginia Anglicans, 13; early attitudes toward, 13, 16; established as a new denomination, Christmas Conference of 1784, 45; organization and structure of, 45; officers of: bishops, presiding elders, circuit riders or itinerants, 45, 48–51; local preachers, class leaders, and lay leaders of, 45, 51, 53; and Asbury's leadership, 46–48; centralization of authority among, 48; and personal democracy of itinerants, 48–49; frontier circuits of, 49, 51; and low salaries of itinerants, 50; and rapid rise to prominence, 51–52; and enforcement of discipline, 52–56 *passim*; class as center of disciplinary control of, 53–54; church courts of, 57–58; and opposition to formal ministerial education, 90–96 *passim*; and reading programs for ministerial candidates, 91, 92–93; hostility of, to educated itinerants, 92; and failure of early efforts to maintain schools, 106; New England leadership of, in education, 106–7; and itinerants as teachers and principals, 107; and founding of colleges, 106, 107–8; and controversy over Indiana University, 108; growing interest of, in education, 108–9; and western ambivalence toward Sunday schools, 109–10; and itinerants as agents of Book Concern and periodicals, 110, 111; opposition of, to the arts, 111, 112–13, 115, 125; importance of hymnody for, 113–14; influence of revivalist songbooks on, 114–15; rules on personal habits of, 115; and antislavery movements, 184–92 *passim*; failure of antislavery rules of, 184; racism and separation of Negroes from, 186, 188, 189, 191; and double standard for slaveholders, 186; and acceptance of slavery, 187–88;

mission of, to slaves and its economic value, 190, 191; and individual opposition to slavery, 192; and mission to Indians, 192
Michigan Baptists, educational interests of, 104
Middle-class outlook of Dissent, 115, 208–9, 219
Miller, Samuel, 86–87, 101; *A Brief Retrospect of the Eighteenth Century*, 87
Ministerial education; *see* individual denominations
Ministerial travel (Quaker), 72–73
Mobility of frontier population, 129–30; denominational records on, 130
Moravians, 139–40
Music, as continental immigrant heritage, 103, 138–144 *passim*, 238

Negroes, discrimination against, 135, 174–75; barred from schools, 135. *See also* the individual denominations.
Nettleton, Asahel, 170
New Brunswick Presbytery, 159
New Lights (Presbyterian), 159, 160, 161
New School (Presbyterian), 179
Niebuhr, H. R., 174, 191
Nottingham, Elizabeth K., 127, 143
Novels, Methodist opposition to, 113; Quaker opposition to, 117; regarded as "lies," 135

Oberlin College, and Lane antislavery element, 178
O'Cull, Hugh, *see* Hugh Cull.
Ohio Yearly Meeting (Quaker), 62, 66, 250 (n. 2); work among Shawnee Indians, 63
Old School (Presbyterian), 179
Old Sides (Presbyterian), 160
Owen, Anning, 218
Owen, Isaac, 115–16

Parker, Daniel, 89, 149–50, 156
Paxson, Frederic L., 143
Peck, John Mason, 34, 36, 39, 42, 89–90, 145, 146, 148, 162, 182
Peer group control in Dissent, 201,